Hippies

from

A to Z

Their Sex, Drugs, Music
and Impact on Society
from the Sixties
to the Present.

by
Skip Stone

Hippies From A to Z

Their Sex, Drugs, Music and Impact on Society
from the Sixties to the Present.

Published by Hip, Inc.
PO Box 2993,
Silver City,
New Mexico 88062

To order this book online, view our catalogue
or purchase an electronic version visit our website at:
http://hippy.com

Written by Skip Stone

Cover Art by Skip Stone and David Vickers

Editing by Martin Trip and Sara Tonin

Page Layout and
Book Design by Martin Trip

ISBN Number:
1 -930258- 01-1

First Edition: January 2000

Printed in the United States of America

The publisher and/or the author is not responsible
for any errors, ommissions of facts or innaccuracies.

This book is for hippies and those studying hippies. It's underlying purpose is to resolve those misunderstandings about hippies and the Hippy Movement. Certain parts of this book contain frank discussions about sex and drugs that may offend some people. I suggest you avoid those sections if you don't have an open mind on these issues.

Table of Contents

Deadication

**This book is dedicated to those hippie saints
whose light brought us so much joy through the years
by opening our hearts and minds. May they**

Rest in Peace!

Our Inspiration:

**Gautama Buddha
Jesus Christ
Lao Tsu
Mahatma Gandhi
Henry David Thoreau
Bertrand Russell
Rev. Martin Luther King Jr.
Dr. Benjamin Spock
John F. Kennedy
Robert F. Kennedy**

Our Beat Brethren

**William S. Burroughs
Neal Cassady
John Coltrane
Miles Davis
Allen Ginsberg
Aldous Huxley
Jack Kerouac**

And of course...

**Carlos Castaneda
Mama Cass Elliot
Jerry Garcia
Jimi Hendrix
Abbie Hoffman
Janis Joplin
Timothy Leary
John Lennon
Jim Morrison
Jerry Rubin
Andy Warhol**

**And to the thousands of other Beautiful People
no longer with us who marched, sang, shouted, shared,
and lived their lives in testimony to Peace and Love.**

Preface

Beatniks and politics, nothing is new.
Strawberry Alarm Clock (Incense and Peppermints)

The term hippie is derived from "hip" or "hipster" used by the Beats to describe someone who was part of their scene. It literally means to know, so someone who's "hip" is "in the know", or wise. Hippies never adopted this term for themselves. They preferred to be called the "beautiful people." However the media played up "hippy" as the catch-all phrase to describe the masses of young people growing their hair long, listening to rock music, doing drugs, practicing free love, going to various gatherings and concerts, demonstrating and rejecting the popular culture of the early 60s.

The first recorded use of the word hippie was on Sept 5, 1965. San Francisco writer Michael Fallon used the term "hippie" while referring to the SF counterculture in an article about the Blue Unicorn coffeehouse where LEMAR (Legalize Marijuana) & the Sexual Freedom League met, and in reference to hippie houses.

During the Summer of Love, in 1967, the media played up the phenomenon in San Francisco, using the term "hippies" to describe the people who were flocking there. As the hippy scene progressed, and the media started reporting the negative side of hippy poverty, living in the streets, drug overdoses, teen pregnancies, and the antiwar movement that split the country, hippie came to mean something negative to a great many Americans.

...we condemned them, our children, for seeking a different future. We hated them for their flowers, for their love, and for their unmistakeable rejection of every hideous, mistaken compromise that we had made throughout our hollow, money-bitten, frightened, adult lives.
June Jordan

Today the term still generates anger, fear, hostility and resentment among many people. Unfortunately, this bigotry has been passed down to the younger generations. Yet many young hippies have adopted the term as theirs, and they are trying to give it a positive meaning again. After all what's so bad about Peace, Love and Freedom? Anyone who feels threatened by this really should take a look at their own life and find the source of their fears.

For my definition of hippy, please read the first chapter of this book, The Way of the Hippy. We all need to get beyond the stereotype and accept that there is a common belief system that defines hippies. In this book, I use the term hippies to describe those who participated in the counterculture of the '60s and early '70s as well as those who subscribe to the philosophy of that movement. This includes old hippies, young hippies and anyone else who has lived and espoused these values whenever or wherever that was.

The Hippy Movement started in the U.S. in the mid '60s and spread around the world. This book focuses on the events and personalities in the U.S. since this was where it all began. The movement has been relatively dormant through the '80s and '90s only to awaken again in time for the new millenium.

By the way, the three accepted spellings are "hippy", "hippie" and the plural, "hippies." The correct contraction for the 1960s is '60s. If any words in this book are unfamiliar please check the glossary for the definition.

Forward by Paul Williams

I wasn't yet a hippie when I started the first American rock music magazine (Crawdaddy!) in January 1966. One year later, when Jim Fouratt, Susan Hartnett, Claudio Badal and I started organizing the first New York Be-In, I was vaguely aware that this "hippie" creature the newspapers and TV were starting to talk about was me. I had scraggly, unwashed long hair, and I'd recently started smoking marijuana, and I believed rock and roll would change the world. And now...this guy Fouratt had called me up when he read about me and Crawdaddy! in the Village Voice's Scenes column and had invited me to a meeting at which Richard Alpert would describe the recent (1/1/67) San Francisco "Be-In," and representatives of the NYC Parks Dept and the rest of us (representatives of "the community") would discuss the possibility of doing something similar here.

Gosh, ME a member of the "hip" community?? I just moved here from Boston last month, and I'm only 18, and my magazine isn't even in the Underground Press Syndicate yet...

That's how it went in those days. Two years later, when I'd quit the rock magazine business and was living in a commune in the woods in Mendocino, California, I certainly was a hippie (my hair had gotten longer, and I believed in dropping out of civilization and its industrialized economic system altogether), and I knew it, and would probably have admitted it, even though I'd written an article in The Village Voice in October 1967 called "The Hippies Are Gone. Where Did They Go?" in which I complained about the label and told the following story about a popular TV program which had recently corralled Abbie Hoffman and me and a dozen other dubious-looking characters for a discussion of "The Hippies":

"Abbie Hoffman was on the David Susskind show a little while back, and about when it was beginning to get dull, at the start of the program, he let the duck out of the box. The duck had a little identifying plaque—HIPPIE—and it squawked and ran all over the place and finally vomited out in the audience. Susskind didn't want to run the segment. "But you said it was okay..."

"Yes, Abbie," said David, "but the duck freaked out. You let him get out of control."

"That's what you get for miscasting."

"The point is, it IS a hippie if it has the sign around its neck. That's what hippie is. It's a word for the people who read about hippies, and talk about hippies, and fret about hippies; it isn't anything real enough to hang a string of beads on."

I'm pleased to have been asked to write a Forward (even if it seems to be more looking Backward, so far) to Skip Stone's Hippy book, because on every page he puts his and our attention on the spirit of the hippy movement, rather than on the label. The label is a historical accident. But the spirit is as enduring and fresh as Abbie's playful and challenging laughter, whereas the label and its sociological history is as transient as Susskind's discomfort at the duck's vomit.

Skip asked me if I think the hippies succeeded in any of their goals. Well, we definitely did drop out and turn on. And I think we were rather successful at revealing America as the big fool and bully we saw it as. The more we taunted it and played pied piper to its children (ourselves), the less it was able to focus effectively on its Important Projects around the world. We represented alternative visions and values and we still do. The spirit lives on and continues to manifest itself in new and unexpected forms. May this book enable the natural friends of this ancient spirit to recognize it more readily and to continue to come up with new, ever more ridiculous, ways to express it. As Tim and Rosemary and John and Yoko and I sang in that hotel room recording in spring 1969, "All we are saying....is give peace a chance."

Paul Williams
October 1999

Introduction

People today are still living off the table scraps of the sixties. They are still being passed around - the music and the ideas.
Bob Dylan (1992)

Few authors or researchers have adequately explained the phenomenon of the hippie movement of the 1960s. The ongoing fascination and attraction many have for this period and the hippy lifestyle indicates that it has a special appeal to those who cherish personal freedom.

I believe there's a little hippie in all of us. It's a latent part of the human spirit that manifests when conditions are right. In this book, I will explore those conditions and the resulting manifestations and try to make some sense of it all.

There is no denying, that after more than thirty years we are still intrigued by hippies and the 1960s. Look at the '90s revival which included two Woodstocks, the Austin Powers movies, the rebirth of colorful hippy fashions, and the increasing use of psychedelic plants and chemicals.

Today we see a new movement of young hippies ready to take up where we left off. We have reached a turning point where we can look back at what happened, learn from our mistakes, reorganize ourselves, and with the help of this new, enthusiastic generation and modern technology re-ignite the movement.

Fortunately we are now able to get beyond the negative stereotype once foisted upon the "flower children" by the media and society. We must spread the word, because so much of the hippy philosophy is positive and loving, something sorely lacking in today's world. Many people find the hippie message of freedom, tolerance, love and peace a threat to the status quo. These individuals need to understand that we only want to improve the status quo for everyone. This book will show just how we did that back in the sixties.

Understanding the hippie phenomenon is the key to laying the groundwork for the new movement. As we examine various aspects of the hippy movement, keep in mind that the influence of these aspects is ongoing. Like a stone tossed into a pond, the big splash is followed by ripples that spread through society over time. It's my contention that the impact of the hippies was so great, that now, almost two generations later, we are still integrating it into our collective psyche.

The hippie meme[1] is so strong and deep that it is likely to continue manifesting its power for decades if not centuries. It's like Christianity, whose early adherents had to go underground after the reactionary forces tried to undermine and eradicate that movement, only to surface again and again, in distant lands where tolerance was more than a dream.

Like Christians, hippies will rise again and again, until the social structures that inhibit freedom crumble, and man learns to live in harmony with his fellow man and Mother Nature. These are the things we strive for and dedicate our lives and actions to achieve.

The first section of this book is an overview of the events, philosophy and lifestyles of the hippy movement. In the second section I've organized information about the hippies so it can be easily found. This book is meant to set the record straight about hippies, and to be a reference work for students and writers. But I hope it will also serve as a catalyst for others to explore further the influence of hippies upon society and help lay the foundation for the new hippy movements to come.

[1]A meme is a contagious concept (like a virus) that spreads quickly causing people to change their behavior.

Part I

The Way of the Hippie

...maybe it's the time of year. Yes, and maybe it's the time of man.
And I don't know who I am. But life is for learning.
Joni Mitchell/CS&N (Woodstock) 1970

What's a hippie? What's the difference between an old hippie and a new hippie? Once a hippie, always a hippie? These and similar questions are the source of much debate today. New subcategories like web-hippies, cyber-hippies, even zippies have become fashionable. But what is a hippie and are you one?

To answer this question, let's see what defines a hippie. Some say it's the way people dress, and behave, a lifestyle. Others classify drug users and rock and roll fans or those with certain radical political views as hippies. The dictionary defines a hippie as one who doesn't conform to society's standards and advocates a liberal attitude and lifestyle. Can all these definitions be right?

It seems to me that these definitions miss the point. By focusing on the most visible behavioral traits these limited descriptions fail to reveal what lies in the hippie heart that motivates such behavior. To understand The Way of the Hippy, we must look at those circumstances that preceded the birth of the hippy movement, the important events that changed our lives, our resulting frustration with society, and the philosophy that developed from our spiritual maturation. This book will examine these developments and put them in the context of humanity's ongoing social evolution.

Hippy is an establishment label for a profound, invisible, underground, evolutionary process. For every visible hippy, barefoot, beflowered, beaded, there are a thousand invisible members of the turned-on underground. Persons whose lives are tuned in to their inner vision, who are dropping out of the TV comedy of American Life.
Timothy Leary (The Politics of Ecstasy) 1967

My view is that being a hippie is a matter of accepting a universal belief system that transcends the social, political, and moral norms of any established structure, be it a class, church, or government. Each of these powerful institutions has it's own agenda for controlling, even enslaving people. Each has to defend itself when threatened by real or imagined enemies. So we see though history a parade of endless conflicts with country vs. country, religion vs. religion, class vs. class. After millennia of war and strife, in which uncounted millions have suffered, we have yet to rise above our petty differences.

The way of the hippie is antithetical to all repressive hierarchical power structures since these are adverse to the hippie goals of peace, love and freedom. This is why the "Establishment" feared and suppressed the hippie movement of the '60s, as it was a revolution against the established order. It is also the reason why the hippies were unable to unite and overthrow the system since they refused to build their own power base. Hippies don't impose their beliefs on others. Instead, hippies seek to change the world through reason and by living what they believe.

Imagine no possesions, I wonder if you can,
No need for greed or hunger, A brotherhood of man.
Imagine all the people sharing all the world.
John Lennon (Imagine)

To be a hippie you must believe in peace as the way to resolve differences among peoples, ideologies and religions. The way to peace is through love and tolerance. Loving means accepting others as they are, giving them freedom to express themselves and not judging them based on appearances. This is the core of the hippie philosophy.

...see the whole thing is a world full of rucksack wanderers, Dharma
Bums refusing to subscribe to the general demand that they consume
production and therefore have to work for the privilege of consuming,
all that crap they didn't really want anyway such as refrigerators, TV
sets, cars, ...all of them imprisoned in a system of work, produce,
consume, work, produce, consume, I see a vision of a great rucksack
revolution thousands or even millions of young Americans wandering
around with rucksacks, going up to mountains to pray, making children
laugh and old men glad, making young girls happy and old girls
happier, all of 'em Zen Lunatics who go about writing poems that
happen to appear in their heads for no reason and also by being kind
and also by strange unexpected acts keep giving visions of eternal
freedom to everybody and to all living creatures.
Jack Kerouac (The Dharma Bums) 1958

The hippy movement erected signposts for all to see. Some warn us of impending danger, others direct us towards richer, more fulfilling lives, but most show us the road to freedom. Freedom is the paramount virtue in this system. Freedom to do as one pleases, go where the flow takes you, and to be open to new experiences. This engenders an attitude that allows for maximum personal growth.

If you want to be free, be free, because there's a million things to be.
Cat Stevens (If You Want to Sing Out)

Our society only permits you one or two weeks a year of freedom to pursue your own agenda. The rest of the time we are slaves to the system. Hippies reject the 9 to 5 lifestyle and therefore are objects of ridicule by those whose lives run by the clock. Programmed people are jealous and resent the freedom we possess. The unmitigated freedom that hippies represent is the greatest threat to any system in which control equals power.

I like ideas about the breaking away or overthrowing of established
order. I am interested in anything about revolt, disorder, chaos,
especially activity that seems to have no meaning. It seems to me to be
the road towards freedom - external freedom is a way to bring about
internal freedom.
Jim Morrison

With all this freedom comes a lot of responsibility. The system does not make it easy for us to survive without sacrificing our values. Therefore we must discover alternative ways to make a living without being a drag on our planet's resources and our fellow humans. Hippies have pioneered numerous lifestyles and alternative businesses including communes, cooperatives, holistic medicine and health food. We focused everyone's concern on the environment to highlight our responsibilities to our planet and to future generations.

I've been smiling lately, dreaming about the world as one.
And I believe it could be, someday it's going to come.
Cat Stevens (Peace Train)

Other beliefs that spring from our core philosophy are: an earthy spirituality such as a belief in Gaia (the earth as an organism), the Greens movement (political activism), even shamanism and vegetarianism. These philosophical and political views reflect a respect for nature and the planet as a whole, something lacking in our capitalistic and materialistic societies. The world needs hippies to point out alternatives to the entrenched system and warn of the impending disasters that await us if we don't change our lifestyles. The goal is not to make everyone a hippie (what would we have to protest?). Rather we can try to influence others by example, through tolerance and love and teaching the virtues of the hippie way.

You create your own reality.
Seth (Seth Speaks)

So being a hippie is not a matter of dress, behavior, economic status, or social milieu. It is a philosophical approach to life that emphasizes freedom, peace, love and a respect for others and the earth. The way of the hippie never died. There have always been hippies from the first time society laid down rules, to Jesus, to Henry David Thoreau, to John Lennon, to you and me. I believe there's a little hippy in all of us. It's just been repressed by our socialization process. We need to find it and cultivate our hippie within. Only then can we reach our true potential.

I took the road less traveled by,
and that has made all the difference.
Robert Frost (The Road Not Taken)

As hippies age they come to terms with the same situations all humans must face. Wiser than before, let's help the younger hippies find a way to save the earth and achieve more freedom than exists in our wildest dreams. Let's find our common ground, build a worldwide community, and once again let our freak flags fly and become all we are destined to be.

Sex, Love & Hippies

Sex is full of lies. The body tries to tell the truth, but it's usually too battered with rules to be heard. We cripple ourselves with lies. Most people have no idea of what they're missing, our society places a supreme value on control, on hiding what you feel. It mocks primitive culture and prides itself on the suppression of natural instincts and impulses.
Jim Morrison

Many people accuse hippies of being promiscuous, having wild sex orgies, seducing innocent teenagers and every manner of sexual perversion. There's no denying that many hippies were involved in temporary sexual relationships and sexual experimentation unlike any generation in centuries. Yet this huge experiment with Free Love was an actual sexual revolution that liberated millions of Americans from the prevailing puritan sexual attitudes and hang-ups of the 1950's.

Instead of fulfilling the promise of infinite orgiastic bliss, sex in the America of the feminine mystique is becoming a strangely joyless national compulsion, if not a contemptuous mockery.
Betty Friedan (The Feminine Mystique) 1963

As kids growing up in America in the '50s and early '60s we were exposed to a variety of mixed signals regarding sex and love. Love was romanticized in the media as something that either just happened to you (love at first sight), or a thing that grew over time as a couple got to know each other better. Sex was something that was rarely discussed and when it was, our elders admonished us against such horrors as masturbation and premarital sex. This lack of communication between adults and children helped create the generation gap.

**First came love, then came marriage,
then came (you) in the baby carriage!**
Children's song

We were taught that proper sex was reserved for those who loved each other, got married, and had children. Thus sex, love, marriage and children were sold as a complete package that couldn't be separated. Any other type of sex was considered deviant and would lead to unfortunate consequences (bastard children, disease, perversion, and even death). These messages about sex never made it seem like fun, much less an intimate loving activity. The few interesting things we knew about sex we gleaned in whispers from our friends or from furtive glances at hidden copies of "Playboy" magazine.

Men and women are not free to love decently until they have analysed themselves completely and swept away every mystery from sex.
Aleister Crowley

Then in 1966 a book was published called "Human Sexual Response" by Masters and Johnson. An extremely thorough clinical study, it shed light on just what happens during sex. All of a sudden, sex became the hot topic in America. Another popular book, "Everything You've Always Wanted to Know About Sex (But Were Afraid to Ask)" answered some common questions about sex (not very well). Then came "The Joy of Sex" by Alex Comfort, which by its very title reflected America's changing attitude (in 1972) towards sex. At long last, the secret was out, sex can be fun.

We do not understand these Americans who, like adolescents, always speak of sex, and who, like adolescents, all of a sudden have discovered that sex is good not only for procreating children.
Oriana Fallaci (Italian author)

This rather sudden enlightenment concerning human sexuality didn't just happen due to a few books. America's willingness to discuss sex was a result of the profound Sexual Revolution already well underway. Sex was everywhere, and the media played it up. Sexually suggestive advertising took off once ad agencies discovered that sex sells. Foreign "blue" movies like "I Am Curious (Yellow)", and America's own "Deep Throat" challenged obscenity laws and paved the way for the porno industry.

The fashion industry took its cue and raised hemlines drastically, creating the mini-skirt and see-through blouses. Women expressed their newfound freedom by going one step further and freeing their breasts from the confinement of brassieres, much to the fashion industry's dismay and many a man's delight!

If it feels good, do it!
popular hippie saying

So what led to this sexual revolution in the '60s? How did we get from; "No sex before marriage" to "If it feels good do it?" The answer is simple. Hippies. The hippie movement had a profound influence on sexual freedom in the U.S. and elsewhere. This revolution in sexual attitudes was more than a reaction to the prudish mores of the '50s and early '60s. For hippies, true freedom meant a release from all social inhibitions.

You have to see the sex act comically, as a child.
W. H. Auden

Again the Beat generation must be credited with living and writing about sexual freedom. Allen Ginsberg, Jack Kerouac, William Burroughs and others lived unusually free, sexually expressive lives. Their writings influenced the hippies to open up when it came to sex, and to experiment without guilt or jealousy. Few others wrote about sex during the 50s.

All you need is love.
The Beatles (All You Need Is Love) 1967

Ginsberg was there at the first Human Be-In in San Francisco telling everyone to love one another. At Love-Ins, the hippies listened to, and experienced a different view of love and sex. We learned that sex is just another part of life like eating and sleeping. It's a completely natural way to express ourselves. We learned to overcome those fears programmed into us, and to share our bodies as easily as we share our food or our thoughts.

**If you can't be with the one you love,
love the one you're with...**
Steven Stills (Love the One You're With)

The concept of Free Love as expressed by hippies meant you were free to love whomever you pleased, whenever you pleased, however you pleased. This encouraged spontaneous sexual activity and experimentation. Group sex, public sex, sex with minors, homosexuality, all the taboos went out the window. This doesn't mean that straight sex, between two adults, or monogamy was unknown, quite the contrary. Nevertheless, the open relationship became an accepted part of the hippy lifestyle. This meant that you might have a primary relationship with one person, but if another attracted you, you could explore that relationship without rancor or jealousy.

**'Tis the most commonplace thing in the world, to love one man to
distraction and to fuck frenziedly with another; you don't give your
heart to him, just your body . . . .
There are two manners of loving a man:
morally and physically.**
Marquis de Sade

Free love made the whole love-marriage-sex-baby package obsolete. Love was no longer limited to one person, you could love anyone you chose. In fact love was something you shared with everyone, not just your sex partners. Love exists to be shared freely. We also discovered the more you share, the more you get! So why reserve your love for a select few? This profound truth was one of the great hippie revelations.

**Your daughter is old enough to do what she pleases . . . she likes to
fuck, loves to fuck . . . she was born to fuck, and . . . if you do not wish
to be fucked yourself, the best thing for you to do is to let her do what
she wants.**
Marquis de Sade

The feeling among hippies was that what two (or more) consenting adults (or teenagers) did in private was their business. It's likely that many a naïve youngster was seduced by an older more experienced hippy. Many of the young kids who ran away from home and joined the Hippie Movement were victims of child abuse (as are many runaways today). The hippie subculture thus rejected the prevailing moral code due to the manifest hypocrisy of adults. The tools of teenage rebellion were (and still are) sex, drugs and rock 'n' roll.

For hippies, sex was something spontaneous. If you met someone you were attracted to, and the circumstances were suitable, you had sex. It could happen in a crash pad, in a van, in the woods or at a festival. Free love was everywhere, but especially in places like communes, where sex was shared openly. Hippies didn't care what other people thought. I remember seeing TV news footage of hippies screwing in a city park, enjoying themselves with abandon, oblivious to camera crews and passersby.

It may be necessary to remind younger readers that all this occurred before AIDS became a concern. Nevertheless, venereal disease was a common problem among the sexually active. Teenage pregnancy became so prevalent that the social stigma faded somewhat. Fortunately, the sexual openness that created these problems was soon to be addressed in public, resulting in the opening of free clinics, sex education in schools, the liberalization of abortion laws, and sexual product advertising. These things are a direct result of the sexual promiscuity that the hippies unleashed upon society.

The puritanical inhibitions programmed by our parents, churches, peers and schools were suddenly irrelevant. But the biggest release of inhibitions came about through the use of drugs, particularly marijuana and the psychedelics. Marijuana is one of the best aphrodisiacs known to man. It enhances the senses, unlike alcohol, which dulls them. As any hippie can tell you, sex is a great high, but sex on pot is far fuckin' out!

The three inevitable goals of an LSD session are to discover and make love with God, to discover and make love with yourself, and to discover and make love with a woman.
Timothy Leary, "Playboy" interview, September, 1966.

More importantly, the use of psychedelic drugs, especially LSD, was directly responsible for liberating hippies from their sexual hang-ups. The LSD trip is an intimate soul wrenching experience that shatters the ego's defenses, leaving the tripper in a very poignant and sensitive state. At this point, a sexual encounter is quite possible if conditions are right. After an LSD trip, one is much more likely to explore one's own sexual nature without inhibitions.

All nature's creatures join to express nature's purpose. Somewhere in their mounting and mating, rutting and butting is the very secret of nature itself.
Graham Swift

The hippy reverence for nature and all things natural is part of the pagan belief system many adopted. Pagans see sex as a joyful expression of our animal nature and not as something to be repressed. Many hippie events resemble the pagan rituals of old (remember the maypole dance - Pagan!). Music, drink, dancing, and drugs are as much a prelude to sex as a celebration.

**Sex has been condemned so much,
you cannot enjoy it.**
Bhagwan Shree Rajneesh

Many hippies on the spiritual path found enlightenment through sex. The Kama Sutra, the Tantric sexual manual from ancient India, is a way to cosmic union through sex. Some gurus like Bhagwan Shree Rajneesh (Osho) formed cults that focused on liberation through the release of sexual inhibitions.

Coitus can scarcely be said to take place in a vacuum; although of itself it appears a biological and physical activity, it is set so deeply within the larger context of human affairs that it serves as a charged microcosm of the variety of attitudes and values to which culture subscribes. Among other things, it may serve as a model of sexual politics on an individual or personal plane.
Kate Millett (feminist)

This breaking down of society's sexual mores by hippies led directly to the Gay and Women's Liberation movements. Hippies brought sex out into the open, not as consciously as those two movements did, but automatically, because of their experimentation with free love. In fact the Gay and Women's Liberation movements are examples of what can be achieved through a more refined agenda and better organization. Hippies take note!

So hippies freed Americans from their puritanical sexual inhibitions through the practice of free love, experimentation with psychedelics, and rejection of the prevailing hypocritical morality. This resulted in the free flow of information about sex, an expansion of women's and gay rights, and society's keen interest in the health issues surrounding sex.

Hippies and Drugs

But I would not feel so all alone, everybody must get stoned.
Bob Dylan (Rainy Day Women nos. 12 & 35)

In the 1960s the hippies, en masse, undertook the largest uncontrolled experiment with drug use in the history of mankind. In those days it wasn't unusual to be handed a pill, and swallow it with the only instruction "You'll dig it, it's groovy." You trusted your fellow hippy and you wanted to get high and have a new experience. This was freedom. This was rebellion. This was cool. We discovered that Pandora's stash box was full of drugs!

**Purple Haze all in my brain, lately things don't seem the same. Actin'
funny but I don't know why. 'Scuse me while I kiss the sky.**
Jimi Hendrix (Purple Haze)

From laboratories in pharmaceutical companies, on college campuses and in bathrooms around the country came a plethora of new drugs with names like LSD25, DMT, purple haze, MDMA (Ecstasy), orange sunshine, synthetic mescaline, psilocybin, STP and many more. The purity and action of these drugs got more dubious as time went on, as unscrupulous dealers sought to capitalize on the drug craze. Along with methamphetamine, cocaine, marijuana, even heroin, hippies tried whatever they could get their hands on.

If you can remember the '60s, then you weren't there.
Unknown

Why did hippies use drugs so extensively without concern? Let's look at the history of drug use leading up to this situation. After World War II, the pharmaceutical industry exploded with research into new drugs. They produced drugs to prevent disease, to cure disease, to alleviate pain, to relieve upset stomachs, to keep you alert, to help you to sleep, to lessen worry, to reduce hyperactivity in children, to remove the symptoms of psychological disorders. Thanks to the industry's aggressive campaigns in the media and the doctor's office, every medicine cabinet filled up with drugs for every sort of ailment.

**One pill makes you larger, and one pill makes you small.
And the ones that mother gives you don't do anything at all.
Go ask Alice, when she's ten feet tall.**
Jefferson Airplane (White Rabbit)

I remember when I was a child of eight or so, having a headache or toothache, and my mother giving me an aspirin saying it would make it feel better. I, like many of my generation, was curious about drugs even at that age. I asked my mom "If it makes you feel better when you hurt, what does it do when you feel fine?" My thought was that it would make you feel really good! Yes, I had what it takes to be a drugstore cowboy even then.

Better living through chemistry
Dow Chemical advertisement

Drugs were portrayed as wonders of modern technology. We were led to believe that soon all diseases would be conquered by taking some drug. It was a time of unbridled optimism and the pharmaceutical propaganda worked well on us young children. After all, by the time I was eight, I'd downed thousands of vitamins, hundreds of aspirins, had vaccines on sugar cubes and in needles, drank colorful syrups for coughs, taken antibiotics to kill bad bugs inside me. And I was a very healthy child!

Life got you down? - Take a Pill!
Saturday Night Live

So in the early '60s, drugs were not seen as evil. Yes, heroin was that bad drug that junkies were addicted to. But all the rest were good and helped heal us, or at least made us feel better. It's taken a prolonged, decades long, anti-drug propaganda campaign to undo the pro-drug pharmaceutical company brainwash. Now kids are more confused than ever. Many eagerly spout the politically correct line "drugs are bad," while they wash down their Ritalin with caffeinated colas, then sneak a cigarette or a beer between classes.

Reality is a crutch for people who can't handle drugs.
Unknown

In the 1950's the Beats were fond of marijuana and wrote and sang about it, often in veiled terms. Illegal since the '30s, it was underground and occasionally someone famous would be busted with it. But the Beats were far fonder of alcohol as were most people. Alcohol was and is the true gateway drug, if any actually exists. We all have a drink before our first date with Mary Jane.

I saw the best minds of my generation destroyed by madness, starving hysterical naked, dragging themselves through the negro streets at dawn looking for an angry fix, angelheaded hipsters burning for the ancient heavenly connection to the starry dynamo in the machinery of night, who poverty and tatters and hollow-eyed and high sat up smoking in the supernatural darkness of cold-water flats floating across the tops of cities contemplating jazz.
Allen Ginsberg, Howl

The Beats were aware of the effects of marijuana: increased sensitivity and creativity. Artists, poets, writers, musicians, all felt inspired under its influence. It would usually surface at parties and along with alcohol (usually wine), helped lower inhibitions and get the party moving. It was in this group context where the uninitiated would usually encounter their first joint.

I get by with a little help from my friends,
get high with a little help from my friends.
The Beatles (With a Little Help From My Friends)

With the hippies, the group scene was just as important and influential. When you saw your friends all participating in an illegal act without negative consequence, and lots of positive ones, who could resist? It was peer pressure at its most effective. I smoked my first joint with my fellow cabin mates at a summer camp where I worked when I was 16. A few months later, I was at college smoking it every day, and had already taken my first LSD trip.

Feed your head!
Jefferson Airplane (White Rabbit)

It's interesting to speculate what might've been had LSD not become available to us. How much was it responsible for? More powerful than either mescaline or psilocybin, and far easier to mass produce, its impact cannot be underestimated. Many of today's technological wonders including the personal computer and the Internet are due to the inspiration and enlightenment of LSD (and marijuana). The famous author, Carl Sagan has admitted (posthumously) his use of marijuana to inspire his best-selling books Contact and Cosmos.

Avoid all needle drugs. The only dope worth shooting is Richard Nixon.
Abbie Hoffman

Colorful fashions, several art movements and of course the incredible outpouring of musical talent in the 1960s was directly due to the impact of psychedelic drugs. Having such open minds, hippies were the ones who experimented with and experienced the tremendous insights these drugs provide, thus unleashing a barrage of new ideas upon society.

LSD melts in your mind, not in your hand.
Unknown

What is it about LSD that makes it such an inspirational experience? I'm having a hard time coming up with an analogy for those who haven't had the LSD experience. But I'll try one. If using marijuana encourages thoughts about God (or whatever you conceive as the true nature of reality), and mescaline is like seeing or talking with God, then an LSD trip is experiencing the world as God. That is its mind-blowing potential.

The Shamans

The hippies were blessed to have among them some individuals who can be considered Psychedelic Shamans. These shamans led the way, first by experimenting themselves, then by reporting the results and promoting their realizations in various media. The following brief portraits are taken from Hippyland's Psychedelic Shamanism page. Please see the bibliography for recommended reading by these authors, or visit our online bookstore at http://hipplanet.com/bookstore/bookstore.htm

Aldous Huxley - It's widely known that Huxley experimented with psychedelics including mescaline and LSD. In fact as he lay dying, he asked for and received his last two doses of acid. His great works of fiction include 'Brave New World' about test-tube babies, consumerism and Soma, the drug of choice. I'm still longing to take a "Soma Holiday." Huxley's 'Doors of Perception of Heaven and Hell' is a classic of psychedelic literature. It's based on his experiences with mescaline and how it "opened the doors" of the mind. The Doors named their group after this book.

Timothy Leary - The high priest of LSD, Leary is clearly the King of Shamans. His role as professor at Harvard University soon took a back seat to his public persona once he discovered for himself the powerful insights available through psychedelics. Unable to restrain Leary's enthusiasm, Harvard dismissed him, allowing Leary to experiment with psychedelics on his own terms. Once freed from clinical restraints, Leary determined which factors enhanced and promoted "good trips." He was quick to realize that the LSD trip was a "religious experience" that transformed the tripper for life. He encouraged clergy, scientists, artists and many others to experiment with LSD and recorded their experiences. His legendary sessions in Millbrook, N.Y. yielded much data, but more importantly pioneered the personal and interpersonal psychedelic experience as never before.

Leary became the focus of public debate about the use of drugs, leading to the criminalization of LSD and other psychedelics. Leary himself became the target of governmental repression, with Richard Nixon calling him "the most dangerous man in America." Imprisoned, escaped, on-the-lam, returned from exile, Leary remained unfazed in his efforts to promote the psychedelic, shamanic experience. His numerous books exhort the reader to discover for himself the mind-expanding potential of psychedelics.

John Lennon - While John Lennon might have considered himself foremost an artist and musician, he nevertheless met the criteria of a shaman in today's society. His great influence among young people was due to his charisma and talent. Lennon's experiences with psychedelics, particularly LSD, changed his view of the world and the way he expressed himself through his music. Not only did he become more experimental and inventive, but his lyrics took on an otherworldly nature. His songs inspired countless thousands to open their minds and experiment with psychedelics. Some of his tunes were actually composed and recorded under the influence of LSD. John was a tireless promoter of the hippy/shamanic message of peace, love and understanding. His message reached the far corners of the planet.

Jim Morrison - Morrison, the songwriter and lead singer for the Doors, was an iconoclast who used his fame to get his message across. A poet and philosopher, Jim felt it necessary to push the envelope and society as far as one could to find freedom. He knew that drugs were just "Doors" to other worlds where few explorers ventured. His music, his lyrics and his passion took us to some dark places in our personal and collective psyches. Like any good shaman, Jim's real talent was taking us along on his journeys into these forbidden realms and opening our minds with his vivid perceptions.

Carlos Castaneda - Steeped in the shamanic tradition of the Nahuatl Indians of Mexico, Castaneda weaves a tale of initiation, revelation, power and transcendence in his series of books. The story of how Carlos meets and accepts his apprenticeship under the tutelage of brujo Don Juan is a masterpiece. The endless debate about whether it's a work of fact or fiction, notwithstanding, the teachings underlying the work have great merit. They give meaning to existence and provide a path, the warrior's, for those souls brave enough to confront their own weaknesses and transform themselves.

Terence McKenna - Terence McKenna is a man who, like Gordon Wasson, lived with the natives and learned their shamanic ways. Along with his brother, Dennis, they added much to our knowledge of ethnobotany, the native uses of psychedelic plants. McKenna's book, Food of the Gods, was a landmark in this field. Terence is well known for his work with Ayahuasca and DMT as well as his lectures on these and other subjects.

Alexander & Ann Shulgin - This husband and wife biochemist team has explored a huge range of psychedelic drugs including some that few, if any, have tried. They are known as the parents of Ecstasy. Their books Tihkal and Pihkal are filled with their psychedelic experiments and experiences as well as how-to make your own.

Ken Kesey - In contrast to Timothy Leary's experimental approach to psychedelics, Kesey explored the experiential. Along with his Merry Pranksters, Kesey felt that psychedelics were a new way to experience the world. Inviting diverse friends from Allen Ginsberg to the Hell's Angels to his place in La Honda he was able to transform groups of people via the communal "trip." After turning on hundreds of mind travelers, he decided to take his show on the road in a Day-Glo bus. Kesey and the Pranksters went on a psychedelic cross-country "trip" that inspired many including the Beatles (Magical Mystery Tour) to try to duplicate. The Pranksters' famous Acid-Test parties where LSD-laced Kool-Aid was dispensed accompanied by music (by such notables as the Grateful Dead) and light shows were modern day correlates to the shamanic rituals of old.

The War on Drugs

An unjust law is itself a species of violence.
Arrest for its breach is more so.
Mahatma Gandhi

In my opinion, the real reason for the War on Drugs, and the particular emphasis on marijuana, is that it is a way to control freethinking individuals. This works by either denying access to mind-liberating substances, or by imprisoning those who use them. Just as the FBI under J. Edgar Hoover maintained a list of subversive enemies of the state, today's enemy list includes anyone who uses (not necessarily abuses) drugs that are not beatified by our medical/industrial/ political machine.

If they can't control our minds, they must control our bodies, thus prisons multiply. They fear a loss of control over the workforce, the primary consumers, the taxpayers, and their political constituents. For if we stop obeying our masters, it's tantamount to a slave rebellion. That is all we are, slaves working for the next dollar. We are no longer individuals with freedom to delve beyond the system's programmed parameters.

This threat is real, since the system offers no alternatives. You're either on the bus or you're one of them. If you happen to be one of the 700,000 American Citizens who get arrested for a marijuana offense each year, you know which side you're on. Likewise, if you're one of the millions who live in fear that one day your illegal toke will get you busted or fired, paranoia is your constant companion.

This is an issue that no hippy or freedom loving American can ignore. It's symptomatic of a disease that has been growing within our system of government since Timothy Leary and Ken Kesey took LSD out of the lab and put it into the hands of the people. LSD would've been a great counter-espionage tool if the CIA could have controlled it. But it's precisely this lack of control, over the thoughts in peoples' minds, that the established order fears.

This is one issue hippies can unite on. Our brothers and sisters rot in jail while we debate whether we should legalize industrial hemp. AIDS and cancer patients live their last days in pain and nausea, some also in jail, while we hide our past and/or present illicit activities from families, friends and co-workers. Did your conscience and reason leave you somewhere back in the '70s? Does the word hypocrite ring any bells?

We must act on this issue, now! We must get beyond politically correct attitudes and realize our government has declared war on freethinking, freedom loving Americans. Only a sustained, well financed, organized, united effort can possibly change peoples' thinking about marijuana. Marijuana must be recognized for what it is: a medicinal herb, an effective pain reliever and anti-nausea agent for critically ill patients, a plant with 1001 industrial uses, a sacred sacrament for many religions, and a safe, alternative soft drug that can replace alcohol as a relaxing, non-aggressive recreational activity for millions of people.

In addition our government should finance research into the medical and cultural uses of other psychedelic chemicals. The shamanic and ritual use of plants for personal exploration has been an accepted part of many societies for thousands of years. To repress this use not only ignores an important element of human culture, but the lack of knowledge about these substances endangers the well-being of those who seek self-discovery.

Hippy Fashions & Lifestyles

The same costume will be ...amusing 30 years after its time.
James Laver

At the risk of seeming trite, we shall now delve into the superficial world of hippy fashions. Please bear with me as you will see it leads us to some very interesting places. Today, the fashion world has once again discovered the wonderful styles from the '60s. We've come full circle and clothes are not the only part of hippiedom to resurface for the new millennium. They're a symbol of the resurgence of hippie values in our culture.

In the '60s, without warning, hippies turned fashion upside down and inside out. They brought a tsunami of new styles and colors into fashion like never before. From Haight-Ashbury to London to Katmandu, the hippies took fashion on an eye-popping psychedelic journey.

The fashion rule in the '60s was that there were no rules. Anything went as long as it wasn't based on the drab, conservative styles of the early '60s. I doubt if fashion designers were able to keep up unless they dropped acid. This is because many of the hippie fashions were based on traditional designs from India, Nepal, Central America, Bali and Morocco. In addition to these foreign cultures, designers went back in time as far as the Renaissance for inspiration.

Many new fashions emanated from San Francisco, New York and London to some extent. The fashion leaders were the icons of our day. Rock 'n roll stars like Jimi Hendrix and The Beatles appeared in public and on record albums in all sorts of colorful costumes.

Of course your average hippie couldn't afford to shop like a rock star. Our stores were less like Harrod's and more like the Salvation Army. Nevertheless we were able to piece together something from bits of cloth. It was easy to take an old pair of blue jeans, holes and all, and just put some bright patches over the holes. If they didn't fit, you could open the seams and insert a triangle of something else, thus giving you flared bellbottoms. A cheap bandanna, an old vest, some beads and you were the height of fashion.

The elements that went into the hippy wardrobe were only limited by our psychedelic imaginations. Bellbottoms ruled the day, from striped, to blue jeans, to patchwork, to hip huggers; even leather pants were popular. Tops ran the gamut from Nehru shirts, to brightly colored African dashikis and Middle Eastern caftans, to halter tops, tie-dyes, and frilly, silky shirts for men! Women wore saris from India and sarongs from Bali and Java. Velvet, leather, batik, denim, Indian cotton and silk were all popular fabrics. Op art, paisleys and psychedelic designs appeared on clothes, occasionally making us dizzy! Footwear ranged from the basic sandal and Birkenstocks to zippered boots, platforms and bright patent leather shoes. Peasant dresses, long skirts and layering were also very popular.

Then there's that symbol of women's sexual freedom (or slavery), the mini-skirt! It was designed by Mary Quant in 1965, and was responsible for the huge surge in pantyhose sales. Along with see-through blouses and braless breasts, it's no wonder there was a sexual revolution.

Accessories included love beads, bandannas, leather vests and jackets with frills, and granny glasses. Jewelry, especially if made of silver from Mexico, India or Morocco was essential. Bangles, rings, earrings, nose rings, and ankle bracelets were worn, especially for parties or concerts. Necklaces were adorned with peace symbols, raised fists, yin-yang symbols, and other eastern esoterica. Hats ran the gamut from tall Jamiroquai numbers (John Phillips liked 'em) to small head-hugging Islamic numbers (Richie Havens). Fedora type hats were usually decorated with feathers, beads or other colorful objects (Hendrix & Dylan liked these).

It's amazing how many of these things have come back into fashion over the years. At the moment we are witnessing a complete resurgence thanks to so many movies like 'Austin Powers' and 'The '60s'.

Let's not forget how we let our Freak Flag fly! Men's long hair was symbolic of our disdain for convention. Most hippies just let it grow, perhaps trimming it once in a great while. Blacks, both male and female wore Afros, using Afro piks (combs) to tease their hair out to the max. Men grew long side burns, mustaches and beards. Women stopped shaving their legs and underarms (gasp!). Bras became a symbol of oppression and were considered too symptomatic of how the power structure sought to control women's sexuality for any liberated hippie gal to wear.

It must be added that no self-respecting hippie ever wore a logo of some corporation. This was heretical to the hippy movement. It's no wonder so many kids today, sick of having to conform to corporate ideals of fashion have instead sought out the Hippy Brand® of non-conformist, anti-establishment revolutionary, laid back sportswear! No logos, no commercials with sports figures, no multi-million dollar endorsements, no hype. Just cheap, comfortable, easily repaired, second-hand clothes to give you the look.

There was fashion for the nose as well. Scents filled the air wherever hippies gathered, and it wasn't just marijuana. Incense and perfume were standard accouterments of the day. The flower children had to smell like flowers, with lavender, rose, gardenia, and other floral scents. Patchouli was perhaps the most ubiquitous since it helped mask the smell of pot. Sandalwood and musk were popular scents for men.

At home, on college campuses, in crash pads, and on communes hippies decorated their living spaces with every sort of poster imaginable. These were large, cheap and colorful and would cover much of the wall space. Concert posters from the Fillmore, publicity posters or album covers were the most popular. But some posters also made a statements about the residents' political views. These included peace and love, antiwar, black power, and feminism posters that protested just about everything. A lot of the posters were just art from other periods; Aubrey

Beardsley and Maxfield Parrish were two very popular artists. Paintings from surrealists like Salvador Dali and M.C. Escher were great to contemplate while stoned. Tibetan mandalas and yantras were used for decoration as well as meditation.

Most furnishings were imported and hippies fueled the huge boom in imported goods. These included beaded curtains, large floor pillows, bean bag chairs, wicker tables and chairs, brass from India, statues of Indian gods (like Shiva, Ganesha, or Buddha), Moroccan carpets and kilims. Headshops and import stores like Pier One succeeded thanks to hippies.

Prior to the hippies, most homes had maybe one dusty plant in a corner. With the back to nature movement, hippies filled their homes with life. Sometimes there were more plants inside than outside, creating a sort of jungle, often with ferns, vines, and other lush foliage dominating rooms. Hippies loved to paint their rooms in bright colors and often added rainbows, stars, even murals on the walls.

An essential part of any hippy household was the stereo. Hippies bought the best sound systems they could afford. That is because the music of the era was so important to us. We got stoned to it, we danced, we partied, we meditated, we had sex, we even tripped to the music.

In the early sixties music went from monaural (mono) to stereo which in itself was a psychedelic effect that everyone could appreciate. Then there was quadrophonic (4 channel) sound. Things went as far as quintophonic (5 discrete channels) which was popular in movie theaters. I remember seeing the premiere of the rock opera 'Tommy' by the Who in a new theater that hyped it's state-of-the-art quintophonic sound system, a real mind blower. It's similar to today's Dolby and DBX systems.

The typical hippy vehicle was a VW bus or van or bug. Small campers and even schoolbuses were converted into living space for one to a dozen people. These were often painted (they usually needed a paint job badly) in bright colors and psychedelic patterns, which sometimes included flowers, peace signs, mystical symbols, even landscape paintings.

The act of putting into your mouth what the earth has grown is perhaps your most direct interaction with the earth.
Frances Moore Lappé

Food is an important part of every culture. Hippies developed their own cuisine, a mishmash of Indian, American, Middle Eastern, Mexican, Italian and Asian with an emphasis on vegetarian. Cheap meals are the rule with soups, fresh salads, a hearty main course (with lots of vegetables) and a dessert. Organic produce, especially from one's own garden is always preferred. Fresh fruit juices and smoothies (usually with yogurt and fresh fruit - similar to Indian Lassies, but improved upon by hippies) are great tasting, healthy treats.

Hippies helped popularize Indian food, especially curries and chapatis, dahl and basmati rice. Asian foods like tofu, soybeans, tamari, rice crackers, miso and tempeh are now part of many healthy American diets. We buy bulk foods like flour, grains, beans and nuts, sold by the pound, not prepackaged and left on supermarket shelves for years. Whole grain bakeries all over the country now offer a variety of multigrain breads which are far tastier and healthier than the traditional American white bread. Yogurt, kefir, goat milk, soy milk are all non-traditional dairy products popularized by hippies. You can thank us for all of these wonderful products being on the shelves.

Health food stores and cooperatives exist now in almost every town and city in the U.S. This is directly a result of the hippy fondness for health, quality and freshness. Hippies helped promulgate the laws that regulate organic produce found in many states (California & Oregon are good examples). Organic farming is now accepted as a regular practice across the country. Ironic isn't it, since we've had to educate the brainwashed farmers of America about the dangers of herbicides, pesticides and chemical fertilizers and teach them how to grow organically, the way it was done by their grandfathers. People think hippies are unhealthy, yet we were responsible for the health craze that swept the country in the '70s and '80s.

Holistic medicine, with origins in Asia, Africa, India, and native cultures around the world are studied, taught and practiced by hippies. Some of these include herbology, homeopathy, acupuncture, massage, reflexology, shiatsu, and ayurvedic medicine. Other things hippies do to stay healthy on their own include hiking, Tai Chi, Yoga, meditation, fasting, sweat lodges, hot springs and Sufi dancing.

Being naked approaches being revolutionary; going barefoot is mere populism.
John Updike

The Broadway musical "Hair!" was noted not only for it's wonderful music, but for the big nude scene. Going naked is one of the great freedoms that hippies discovered. Feeling the air and water on your exposed skin is both thrilling and invigorating. Puritan values and modesty be damned! Hippies weren't about to compromise. Nude beaches, nude sunbathing and swimming, nudist colonies, all proliferated thanks to hippies. Nudism puts us closer to nature. It erases our sexual hang-ups and fears, by dissolving the psychological link between nakedness and sex, thus letting us relax and enjoy the beauty of the human body.

I know in the shod state of mind I often feel paranoid, bitter, resentful and vengeful. The world seems like a dog eat dog kind of a place. By going barefoot the most profound change takes place. I find it impossible to hold the aforementioned negative emotions and instead become friendly, generous, humble, part of things - at peace with myself and generally glad to be who I am. I start to express myself instead of hiding away.
Jon, The Barefoot Pilgrim

Just the act of going barefoot is revolutionary for most people. Shoes confine more than just our feet. Walking barefoot puts you in direct touch with the world around you. You're more sensitive and aware. You're more vulnerable (watch out), but more open.

Hippies, ever concerned about ecology, were the first to promote biodegradable products and the use of natural ingredients in everything from fabrics to shampoo. We made sure that every product ingested by Americans had a label indicating all its ingredients. We boycotted those companies: whose products polluted the environment, used animals for testing, were prowar or very reactionary; or manufactured dangerous chemicals or weapons.

Fashion flourishes on surplus,
when someone buys more than he or she needs.
Stephen Bayley

It must be said that in general most hippies were anti-fashion. That is they rejected the corporate nature of the fashion industry as well as the power of individuals to dictate the way others should dress or conform to a set standard. The fashion industry was seen as part of the Capitalist propaganda machine that kept us slaving to consume the latest fashions. This is more true today than ever.

If it's not clothes, it's cars, toys, even our lifestyles that are marketed to us by demographics. And with Internet shopping they can track our every move. Many hail this as a great innovation, and the ultimate direct marketing tool. But isn't it just a more efficient way to keep us imprisoned in a consumer nightmare? Like gluttons, we are fed more and more tasty morsels until we are so fat with consumption that our lives serve no other purpose.

The hippies' rejection of prevailing fashion led us to explore other cultures and in doing so we learned and adopted many concepts and practices alien to Western society. Much of what we pioneered is now an important part of popular culture and thinking. Hippies influenced not only clothes but a wide range of ideas and attitudes thus changing society in the process.

Of course another part of hippy fashion is the language of the subculture. English exploded with many new words in the '60s. See the Glossary for a long list. And of course our music turned America and the world on its ear. See Part II for the exceptional music we enjoyed.

Hippy Activism

> **What really distinguishes this generation. . .**
> **is its determination to act, its joy in action,**
> **the assurance of being able to change things by one's own efforts.**
> Hannah Arendt (1972)

The popular stereotype of hippies describes them as lazy, unmotivated, even apathetic. At times we can be this way, especially when stoned. But if you look back at history, you'll find just how many causes we were actively involved with, and how many great things we accomplished. This chapter reviews the circumstances that led to the hippy movement, the major causes that hippies supported, the outcomes of our movement's activities, and those causes that still remain to be tackled.

> **Hippies started the ecology movement. They combated racism. They**
> **liberated sexual stereotypes, encouraged change, individual pride, and**
> **self-confidence. They questioned robot materialism. In four years they**
> **managed to stop the Vietnam War. They got marijuana decriminalized**
> **in fourteen states during the Carter Administration.**
> Timothy Leary (Chaos and Cyberculture)

Hippies were part of the first generation to face the real threat of nuclear annihilation as children. We were supposed to be reassured by the fallout shelters popping up everywhere and the drills we had in school where we hid under our desks. Nobody wanted to face the reality of nuclear war. We had to discover that reality ourselves, and bring it to the attention of our elders. Our parents' denial of the consequences turned to anger in our generation as we learned the truth.

> **Whenever you find yourself on the side of the majority,**
> **it's time to pause and reflect.**
> Mark Twain

This was the first of many startling discoveries we were to make as we matured into young adults. The legacy of WWII and the boom years that followed was a prevailing attitude that America could do no wrong. Victorious in war, we would lead the world in peace. Prosperity and optimism was taken for granted. Hell, we even figured we could walk on the moon!

> **Southern change gonna come at last!**
> **Now your crosses are burning fast, Southern Man.**
> Neil Young (Southern Man)

But all was not right in the land of plenty. At the start of the 1960s, civil rights was the issue of the day. Black people were demanding equality under the law. At that time blacks could vote in national elections, but in local elections, especially in the south, blacks were denied the franchise. This was only one of many rights denied black people. In theory, black people had equal rights, but in reality America was still practicing Apartheid. Segregation was the law in the south.

Think of all the hate there is in Red China,
then take a look around to Selma, Alabama.
Barry McGuire (The Eve of Destruction)

In 1960, black people were taking to the streets in organized protests. Sit-ins at segregated lunch counters in southern cities were inciting both blacks and whites to action. College students, many of them white, were getting involved in these actions and learned a few things about non-violent protest. This was risky in the south. Some protesters were beaten or murdered as a result of their activities.

If the button is pushed, there's no running away. There'll be no one to
save with the world in a grave.
P.F. Sloan/Barry McGuire (The Eve of Destruction)

The anti-nuclear movement started gaining ground in the early '60s as well. With more countries testing nuclear weapons, and production increasing dramatically, the concern was worldwide. President Kennedy urged Americans to build fallout shelters while Ban the Bomb demonstrations in America and Europe attracted tens of thousands of students and intellectuals such as Bertrand Russell who brought us the peace symbol.

We must learn to live together as brothers or perish together as fools.
Martin Luther King, Jr.

Civil rights and anti-nuclear protests often included marches, sit-ins, speeches and songs by famous people, signs with slogans, and chants. These protests were always marked by peaceful intent. If things got ugly it was usually due to police tactics or violent counter demonstrations (by such organizations as the KKK). The SDS, Students for a Democratic Society, got its feet wet in these early demonstrations. They would later organize anti-war campus protests around the country.

Why do we never get an answer, when we're knocking at the door?
With a thousand million questions, about hate and death and war.
'Cause when we stop and look around us, there is nothing that we need,
in a world of persecution, that is burning in its greed.
The Moody Blues (Question)

Young people began to get the idea that their government didn't really have the interests of the people as their main priority. Just as President Eisenhower had warned, the military/industrial complex was having undue influence on U.S policy making. There were big profits to be made in the arms race. And the legacy of the McCarthy witch-hunts of the '50s was back, haunting us as our paranoid government saw the threat of Communism everywhere.

Mankind must put an end to war, or war will put an end to mankind.
John Fitzgerald Kennedy

President Kennedy stood up to Premier Krushchev over Soviet nuclear missiles in Cuba, nearly causing WW III. But it was LBJ (President Lyndon Baines Johnson) who was to lead America into a full-scale war in Vietnam. Some believe Kennedy was about to withdraw from involvement in Vietnam when he was assassinated on November 22, 1963.

Ask not what your country can do for you,
but what you can do for your country.
John Fitzgerald Kennedy

People young and old saw the American dream buried along with Kennedy. We awoke quickly to face the nightmare of reality. It was only two days after President Kennedy died that LBJ escalated U.S. involvement in the Vietnam War.

Hey, hey, LBJ, how many kids did you kill today?
Anti-war chant

Eighteen months later, the U.S. Imperialists were getting even more involved in Vietnam. First they sent more advisors, then they started bombing North Vietnam and ramped up the draft. In March 1965, American foot soldiers first engaged the Vietcong on their home turf. Later that same month the SDS organized the first Teach-In about the Vietnam War at the University of Michigan. The following month, the SDS led the first anti-war march in Washington D.C.. Over 25,000 people showed up, including singers Phil Ochs, Joan Baez and Judy Collins.

Hell no, we won't go!
Anti-war chant

Student deferments and Conscientious Objector status became more difficult to obtain. Tens then hundreds of thousands of young people had to give up their dream of college to go fight a terrible war in a distant land. Some of them burned their draft cards, others fled to Canada to avoid the draft. As more and more of them returned in body bags or were termed MIA or "missing in action", it became clear we weren't winning in Vietnam.

You're old enough to kill, but not for votin'.
You don't believe in war, but what's that gun you're totin'?
P.F. Sloan/Barry McGuire (The Eve of Destruction)
- Topped the charts Sept 25, 1965

On October 16, 1965 a nationwide anti-war protest brought out 100,000 people in 80 cities around the U.S. By 1967, the opposition to the war was going full steam. On April 10th, a nationwide protest, Vietnam Week, started with draft card burnings (now illegal) and anti-draft demonstrations around the country. On April 15, a huge anti-war protest in New York City included 400,000 (equal to the number of soldiers in Vietnam at the time) who marched from Central Park to the United Nations. Speakers included Martin Luther King, Stokely Carmichael and Dr. Benjamin Spock.

Until the philosophy that holds one race superior, and another, inferior, is finally and permanently discredited and abandoned, everywhere is war.
Haille Sellassie/Bob Marley (War)

While the hippies celebrated their freedom with the Summer of Love in San Francisco, and Flower Power Day in New York, it was a Summer of Rioting in the ghettos of America. Blacks took to the streets in Chicago, Brooklyn, Cleveland, Baltimore, Newark and Detroit, where 43 died in some of the worst rioting in U.S. history. It was just the beginning of the "Long Hot Summer."

Burn, baby, burn!
Stokeley Carmichael

Why did blacks riot? Some saw a race war as the only way to freedom. Years of peaceful protests had not really changed much for black people. Despite the passage of various Civil Rights acts, there was still widespread discrimination, racism and economic inequality. The radicalized elements, especially the Black Panthers, were arming themselves and inciting others to confront the establishment, violently if necessary.

Our program is cultural revolution through a total assault on culture, which makes use of every tool, every energy and every media we can get our collective hands on... our culture, our art, our music, our books, our posters, our clothing, the way our hair grows long, the way we smoke dope and fuck and eat and sleep-it's all one message-the message is freedom.
John Sinclair (The White Panther Party Statement) 1969

The Black Panthers were the inspiration for other groups including the White Panthers and the Weathermen (a radical splinter group from the SDS) to use violence against the establishment. This took the form of bombings of symbols of the military/industrial/economic system like banks.

All we are saying is give peace a chance.
John Lennon (Give Peace a Chance)

The black and hippy protests going on during this period overlapped (time-wise), but most hippies were still intent on peaceful protest. On October 21 and 22, 1967, 35,000 anti-war protesters stormed the Pentagon. They were greeted with tear gas. Eventually all the demonstrators sat down in front of the Pentagon and the assembled troops (Military Police). The standoff continued while the protesters held teach-ins, sang songs, chanted and listened to speeches. Many demonstrators went up to the MPs and talked to them about peace and love. A famous photo shows a young man placing a flower in a guard's rifle muzzle. As day became night, some of the troops were won over. The protest was so peaceful at this point, no one felt threatened. People started fires to keep warm, and a community was forming.

Around midnight, paratroopers relieved the MPs and they started to clear out the demonstrators with force. 647 protesters were arrested, often after being severely beaten by the paratroopers and U.S. Marshals. In response, later that same week, draft deferments were eliminated for those who violated draft laws or interfered with recruitment, two common tactics of the protesters.

The draft is white people sending black people to fight yellow people to protect the country they stole from the red people.
The musical, "Hair"

In December a "Stop the Draft" movement was organized. It included 40 antiwar groups, and nationwide protests were coordinated. On Dec 5, 1967, 1000 antiwar protesters tried to close the New York City induction center, where draftees reported. 585 were arrested including Allen Ginsberg and Dr. Benjamin Spock.

There's battle lines being drawn. Nobody's right if everybody's wrong.
Young people speaking their minds
Getting so much resistance from behind.
Buffalo Springfield (For What it's Worth)

On December 31, 1967, Abbie Hoffman, Jerry Rubin, Paul Krassner, Dick Gregory, & friends pronounced themselves "Yippies." On January 16, 1968, they founded the activist Youth International Party which was to organize protest actions including the famous demonstrations during the Democratic Convention in Chicago.

The battle outside ragin' will soon shake your windows
and rattle your walls.
Bob Dylan (The Times they are a-changin')

For three days, 10,000 demonstrators were met by 12,000 Chicago police; 6,000 National Guard; 7,500 U.S. army troops; and 1,000 FBI, CIA & other services agents. These government agents then proceeded to riot, inflicting heavy damage upon the protesters. Outnumbered and outgunned, the only protection the protesters had was their voices. They shouted "the whole world is watching" while news cameras filmed some of the less violent events. Chicago Mayor Daly (and the U.S. government no doubt) wanted to teach the hippies and yippies a lesson.

Off the Pigs!
Huey Newton

Meanwhile the level of violence on the streets everywhere was rising dramatically. After the assassination of Martin Luther King Jr. on April 4, 1968, spontaneous riots erupted in 125 cities across the country. Oakland Police ambushed the Black Panthers. Eldridge Cleaver was arrested with a bullet-shattered leg and Bobby Hutton was shot and killed.

Make Love, Not War.
Unknown

Days later, hippies held a Love-in at Malibu Canyon, California and the Spring Mobilization against the Vietnam war began soon after. Students at Colombia and Boston Universities occupied administration buildings on college campuses to protest discriminatory academic and financial policies, and to add ethnic studies to the curriculum.

> **If we cannot now end our differences,**
> **at least we can help make the world safe for diversity.**
> John Fitzgerald Kennedy

Meanwhile, the Women's Liberation movement was gearing up. Women were deeply involved in the Anti-war movement from the start. They helped organize, contributed money, marched, sang songs and got arrested like everyone else. But women inspired by the civil rights movement had their own agenda. More women than ever were leaving the home and entering the work force.

> **Freedom is never voluntarily given by the oppressor;**
> **it must be demanded by the oppressed.**
> Martin Luther King, Jr.

Tired of being treated like second class citizens, exploited economically, sexually, and without equal rights, they decided to break from the other protest movements and get politically active. In 1966, NOW, the National Organization of Women was founded. By 1968 women groups had multiplied, demanding the right to abortion, childcare, and an end to economic, political, educational and sexual discrimination. Women had their work cut out for them trying to raise the consciousness of Americans taught to see them only as sex objects or mothers.

> **The ultimate measure of a man is not where he stands in moments of**
> **comfort, but where he stands at times of challenge and controversy.**
> Martin Luther King, Jr.

American society had never been attacked on so many fronts, so vociferously, as it did in the closing years of the '60s. The Women's movement was just one more log on the fire of discontent burning downing the conservative, white male dominated social structure.

> **When a nation is filled with strife, then do patriots flourish.**
> Lao-Tzu

During this time, a typical newscast would start with the latest violent clashes in the streets of some ghetto, followed by scenes of marches and speeches from some anti-war rally. Then a sobering set of statistics of dead soldiers in Vietnam, after which some conservative politician would be interviewed saying how we're winning the war, and if we would just re-elect him, it would be over in a jiffy.

> **One of the greatest casualties of the war in Vietnam is the Great**
> **Society ... shot down on the battlefield of Vietnam.**
> Martin Luther King, Jr.

As the troop level in Vietnam approached its all-time high of 543,000, the Vietnamese launched the surprise Tet Offensive, which marked the turn of the war in their favor. The My Lai massacre of a whole Vietnamese village including women and children by American soldiers was reported and the media had a field day. The war was leaving a bad taste in everyone's mouth by now. LBJ, deciding his Vietnam policy was a liability and a failure, decided not to run again for president (perhaps the fact that Robert Kennedy announced his candidacy had something to do with it), and ordered a partial bombing halt. Within two months, peace talks began in Paris.

**Those who make peaceful revolution impossible
will make violent revolution inevitable.**
John Fitzgerald Kennedy

As 1969 began, violence was everywhere. Students all over the country were taking over campus buildings and issuing demands. The U.S. launched the biggest ever bombing campaign against North Vietnam. In New York City, police raided a gay bar in Greenwich Village, which lead to the Stonewall Uprising where 2000 protesters battled 400 police, thus starting the Gay Liberation Movement. Cult leader Charles Manson and his followers murdered actress Sharon Tate and the LaBiancas.

You don't need a weatherman to know which way the wind blows.
Bob Dylan (Subterranean Homesick Blues)

As the Chicago Eight trial got underway, in which the Yippie leaders were charged with conspiracy and inciting a riot, the Weathermen began their "Days of Rage" with bomb attacks against establishment targets. On May 15, 1969, hippies camping out peacefully in People's Park in Berkeley were attacked and forcibly removed by police and the National Guard. On July 20, 1969, Man set foot on the moon. It seemed that we had to go that far just to find some peace. Then again...

**The important thing that you have proven to the world is that half a
million kids can get together and have fun and music and nothing but
fun and music, and I bless you for it!**
Max Yasgur, owner of the farm where Woodstock took place.

In the middle of all this mayhem, much to their eternal credit, over half a million hippies managed to have three days of peace, love, fun and music at the Woodstock Music Festival in August 1969. In a way this was one of the most political (or apolitical) statements ever made by hippies. At Woodstock, a huge, virtual city appeared without adequate planning for such a large group. The only agenda anyone brought with them was to have a good time, groove on the music and each other. Without leaders, without police, without government, without violence, they managed to feed, and care for themselves outdoors despite the heat, rain and mud. The Woodstock Nation had left its mark on the world.

**Darkness cannot drive out darkness; only light can do that.
Hate cannot drive out hate; only love can do that.**
Martin Luther King, Jr.

On October 15, 1969, another half million people took to the streets around the U.S. in peaceful protests during the first Vietnam Moratorium. One month later, 500,000 marched in Washington DC as part of the largest antiwar rally in U.S. history. Speakers included Eugene McCarthy, George McGovern, Coretta King, Dick Gregory, and Leonard Bernstein. Singing songs of peace were Arlo Guthrie, Pete Seeger, Peter, Paul, & Mary, John Denver, Mitch Miller and the touring cast of Hair.

What is the use of physicians like myself trying to help parents to bring up children healthy and happy, to have them killed in such numbers for a cause that is ignoble?
Dr. Benjamin Spock

By the end of the year over 100,000 soldiers had died or been injured in Vietnam, and a draft lottery had begun. A free concert given by the Jefferson Airplane and the Rolling Stones turned to tragedy at Altamont as the Hell's Angels killed a man waving a gun. It was a symbolic end to a violent year. Some say it marked the end of innocence for the Love Generation.

If it takes a bloodbath, let's get it over with.
Ronald Reagan, then Governor of California, on how to deal with student unrest.

1970 began in similar fashion with the student riots at University of California, Santa Barbara and the Weathermen bombing the Bank of America in Isla Vista and office buildings in five states. Three Weathermen were killed when a bomb they were working on exploded in a house in Greenwich Village, New York. On March 1, 1971 a bomb exploded in a Capitol restroom. The Weather Underground claimed responsibility saying it was in response to the U.S. involvement in Laos.

Turn the earth to sand and still commit no crime!
The Moody Blues (One More Time to Live)

The Vietnam War, wasn't the only topic that riled hippies. In 1969, a disastrous oil spill near Santa Barbara, California focused our attention (again) on the environment. Hippies were frustrated with the lack of government initiative towards cleaning up the environment and leniency with corporate polluters. So we organized, protested, and contributed to environmental groups and by 1970, the Ecology Movement was in full swing. The National Environmental Policy Act, or NEPA was signed into law and on April 22, the first Earth Day was declared. This landmark event, involving 20 million people, raised awareness about how humans were treating the planet and ways to mitigate the impending dangers to the environment. The Environmental Protection Agency (EPA) was established to monitor and clean up toxic wastes. The Nuclear Non-Proliferation Treaty also went into effect.

Soldiers are cutting us down!
Crosby, Stills & Nash (Ohio)

College protest had become so commonplace by 1970, that it was a horrible shock when the news reported thirteen unarmed student protesters being shot, and four killed by the National Guard at Kent State University, Ohio. Ten days later, police killed two students at Jackson State University during violent student demonstrations. The very same week, antiwar protesters in NYC were attacked by construction workers. It was clear that the ongoing protests were dividing the country and the violence was totally out of hand.

How many deaths will it take 'til he knows, that too many people have died?
Bob Dylan (Blowin' in the Wind)

Despite the peace talks (just how long DID they spend discussing the shape of the table?), the Vietnam War dragged on, taking more lives and further alienating us from our government. As more 'Nam veterans returned, they brought back horror stories about the war. Soon they were the focus of protests. Vets appeared at the forefront of the Peace Movement, and they were a powerful ally, since they had the respect of the warmongers.

Many people still think the protesters hated the soldiers who went to war. Far from it! All of us knew people who served in Vietnam and respected them. It wasn't their choice, they were drafted. At the start of the war many went with a spirit of "my country, right or wrong" and jeered the protesters. Once they got there, even the most devout, brainwashed soldier faced his own "apocalypse." When those lucky enough to survive returned, their attitudes were often similar to those who protested the war. Some hippies did resent the soldiers, since it was they and other men in uniform (acting as agents of the repressive government) who were involved in putting down some of the bigger demonstrations and beating the protesters.

I know vets who are so fucked up from their experience that they must take heavy prescription drugs for the rest of their lives otherwise they freak out. One vet, a distant relative of mine is denied contact with his family to this day. Why? Because they're afraid of him! I spent a few days with him just before they shipped him to 'Nam. I found him fun and full of life. When I saw him next he was close to being a vegetable, yet he was physically unharmed in the war!

The Vets' wounds mirror the wounds the country suffered. They still haven't healed. Most foreign policy debates now revolve around America's role as World Policeman. Fortunately it appears we have learned some lessons and now our government seems reluctant to put American soldiers on the front line, preferring to use our superior technology as the weapon of choice. Kill them from the air and Americans won't have to see the mangled, burned bodies of women and children below.

But the selective service system still exists to register young men who turn 18 so they can be drafted should the need arise. America can find it all too easy to justify intervention when "ethnic cleansing" (Bosnia, Kosovo, East Timor) is involved, or when its so called "strategic interests" are at risk (the Gulf War). The attitude is shoot first, ask questions later. One should never feel we are at peace when we still have the nuclear capacity to wipe out (almost) all life on the planet.

On the environmental front, hippies established and

> There is a Creator.
> Look in the mirror and laugh.
> Look in the heart and smile.
> Look at the Creation and cry.
>
> We are the caretaker of the Creation.
> We have forgotten who we are.
> We have forgotten why we are here.
>
> The trees speak of the Creator.
> The birds sing of the Creator.
> The Creation speaks to us.
> Are we listening or are we too busy?
> Skinwalker

supported such organizations as Greenpeace, Earth First!, Friends of the Earth, etc. They lobbied Congress and took direct action against those whose only motivation was economic gain regardless of the impact on the planet's ecology. Some of their efforts are as legendary as they are dangerous. One day we'll all look back on these brave activists who risked their lives and freedom and hail them as heroes. You, too, can be a hero by supporting such organizations that put the common good above selfish short-term interests. Earth is the mother of us all, and we must treat her with respect.

I have a dream, that my four little children will one day live in a nation where they will not be judged by the color of their skin but by the content of their character.
Martin Luther King, Jr.

Although much has been achieved in the area of Civil Rights, racism, discrimination and economic inequality still plague minorities in America. Until we end the cycle of bigotry and fear that one generation passes on to another, this problem will continue to haunt us. Hippies practice Love and Tolerance for all beings, and this is an important message to share with everyone. Remember, actions speak louder than words and hugs are warmer than handshakes.

Think Globally, Act Locally.
bumper sticker

Nuclear, biological and chemical threats still hang over our heads. Perhaps more than we realize. The technology has filtered down to where maniacal despots without inhibitions can get their hands on weapons of mass destruction. We face a challenging moral dilemma dealing with such people. Our lack of resolve on this issue will come back to haunt us one day.

The Marijuana Issue

Just say NO to INTOLERANCE!
Hippyland

It does seem that hippies as well as many other groups have a reluctance to get involved in an issue unless something personal is at stake. One issue that is getting hot now certainly affects hippies personally. The issue is marijuana. Everyone has an opinion whether it be to legalize, decriminalize, medicalize or industrialize. Until we all get together on this issue, THEY will have the upper hand. It has been politically unfeasible to discuss this issue with the anti-drug hysteria that has swept the U.S. for three decades. Now things are changing. This is one issue that can unite us again.

Marijuana has been used for millennia to heal, inspire, clothe, and warm humanity. It can even feed us as it's one of the best protein sources known. Yet we have vilified this magical herb to where even innocent children suffer when their parents are given 20 year jail terms, often on a first offense. At one point we decriminalized it in many states. Now it's classified by the U.S. government as more dangerous than heroin. Thousands of people are in need of its medicinal properties and are denied such comfort by law.

One who breaks an unjust law that conscience tells him is unjust, and who willingly accepts the penalty of imprisonment in order to arouse the conscience of the community over its injustice, is in reality expressing the highest respect for law.
Martin Luther King, Jr.

Today, we have a War on Drugs which is really a War on Americans. Our government even takes women and children prisoners every day this war continues. We justify such actions as a deterrent, yet handing out 20-30 year sentences to (some) first time offenders, is far worse than how we punish many murderers. PLEASE END THE WAR! PLEASE FREE THE PRISONERS!

With our thoughts we make the world.
The Buddha

YOU can make a difference! As this issue heats up, get involved with your statewide and national organizations. NORML (National Organization for the Reform of Marijuana Laws) is a good place to start. Remember, all drugs are NOT created equal. Your mind and your body are yours. No one has a right to tell you how to use them or how to heal them. FREE YOUR MIND.

Big Brother is Here

The purpose of this program is to expose, disrupt, and otherwise neutralize the activities of the various new left organizations, their leadership, and their adherents.... We must frustrate every effort of these groups and individuals to consolidate their forces or to recruit new or youthful adherents. In every instance, consideration should be given to disrupting organized activity of these groups and no opportunity should be missed to capitalize on organizational or personal conflicts of their leadership.... The organizations and activists who spout revolution and unlawfully challenge society to obtain their demands must not only be contained, but must be neutralized.
FBI director J. Edgar Hoover in "Disruption of the New Left" counterintelligence memo dated May 14, 1968

It's clear that there has been a coordinated effort on the part of the federal government, local agencies, even the media to disrupt, discredit and undermine the legitimate right to protest in the United States. The extent of this conspiracy has yet to be determined because so many documents relating to this period are still classified. To justify their invasive actions, they accused hippies of being communists the same way McCarthy condemned liberals in the '50s. In other words, hippies were the enemy!

Big Brother is Watching You!
George Orwell (1984)

Agents infiltrated every student group, every left-leaning political group, and every minority organization, to carry out J. EDGAR's dictum. They used every counterespionage tactic available at the time, including tailing people, informants, tapping phones, keeping confidential records on individual members' activities including drug use, sexual liaisons, and other information that had nothing to do with their political activities. Is it any wonder these groups lost their leadership, their focus, their energy? With agents everywhere, who could be trusted?

The truth is that U.S. leaders cannot tolerate dissent from within if it threatens the established order. As a result the great tradition of protest has come to a grinding halt in the U.S. There is now an underlying feeling that if you voice your "politically incorrect" opinions in a coordinated fashion you'll get into trouble.

We have miles and miles of pretty files of your forefather's fruit. And now to suit our great computer, you're magnetic ink.
The Moody Blues (Threshold of a Dream)

Thanks to the Internet, our government has new methods to pry into our personal lives. They now can and do intercept any communication transmitted over the Web that they choose. They scan websites for pornography, drugs and other things they disapprove of. They have agents monitoring chatrooms and postings. They look for keywords. Once they've found a suspect they read his/her incoming and outgoing e-mail. Then they do the same to those people that person has contact with, and so on. And they cry that this isn't enough! They want more power over what is said and done on the Internet. Our government thinks they should be controlling everything, everywhere.

It riles them to believe that you perceive the web they weave, so keep on thinking free!
The Moody Blues (Threshold of a Dream)

Big Brother is here, friends. He is watching, listening, taking notes, making lists of names. The danger of this is that we will each eventually have a file. Whether it gets used against us depends upon what we do. It is another means of controlling us. If a person were to decide to get vocal about his/her opposition to government policies, they could just simply access their file, and haul him/her in on some trumped up charge (perhaps statements made out of context, or an agent-provocateur can lead the person into some illegal activity). I'm sure writing this book will put me on an enemy list in some government agency (if I don't have a huge file already!). What I wonder is, will anybody care when I'm hauled away for speaking my mind.

The Astrology of the Hippy Movement

This is the dawning of the Age of Aquarius.
"Aquarius" from the play "Hair" *

The Hippy Movement was less of a movement and more of an unseen force that permeated the minds and hearts of hippies around the world. In cities, on college campuses, in communes hippies everywhere were part of a collective consciousness that appeared rather suddenly in the 1960s. We shared a growing awareness of ourselves, our humanity, and our environment. As we interacted with each other we taught and learned about life, love, sex, drugs, peace, activism, freedom, cooperation, beauty, art, and music. What is so amazing about this font of knowledge is its source. Virtually none of it came from our parents (unless they happened to be very aware themselves). None of it came from our schools, government, or churches (unless you happened to be Buddhist or Hindu or Taoist already).

So where did all this knowledge and awareness come from? Astrologers point to the stars and the positions of the outermost planets, Uranus, Neptune and Pluto. Beginning in October, 1965 we witnessed a rare, powerful conjunction of Uranus and Pluto (it happens about once every 200 years or so). Uranus represents the urge to be free. It brings sudden changes usually by destroying the old to make room for the new. It replaces outdated attitudes with new, more constructive ones.

Pluto forces us to transform and regenerate. It takes that which is sick, no longer of value and either destroys it or transmutes it via healing and cleansing into something useful and positive. When the two planets are conjunct (aligned together) their energy intensifies and focuses. Since the aspect occurred in the sign of Virgo, this means the focus was analytical, and critical with an emphasis on communication and service to others. The whole astrological scenario was extremely conducive to revolutionary ideas and activities, if not outright revolution.

A time for love, a time for hate, a time for peace,
I swear it's not too late.
The Byrds (Turn! Turn! Turn!)

Indeed revolution was on the agenda, and might've happened, if not for another very profound astrological event that occurred in September 1966. This was a sextile (60°) of Uranus (again) and Neptune. This is another positive aspect that represented an unusual combination of powerful energies at work during the period. Again we have the need for freedom combined with sudden destruction of the old ways (Uranus), but this time creating new opportunities (sextile) for spiritual growth, artistic creativity, and idealism (Neptune).

Neptune is symbolic of the higher form of love. With Neptune in Scorpio, the sign of powerful emotions, enormous latent energy, and strong sense of purpose, it's no wonder there was an explosion of creativity and new ideas in the Arts and Music, as well as spiritual, sexual and chemical experimentation. This aspect, following after the previous one, probably helped people refocus their energies towards transforming themselves, and creating new forms of expression. There's no doubt that this aspect set the stage for the Summer of Love. Indeed in July 1967, this aspect occurred again (Neptune Retrograde), with Neptune going direct in August, emphasizing the lesson further!

The planet Uranus is key to the Movement's revolutionary ideas, originality, experimentation, and quest for freedom. Pluto made us toss out the old ways that were useless, transmute that which was worth saving, heal ourselves and our environment, and integrate those new transformative ideas into our collective consciousness.

C'mon people now, smile on your brother,
ev'ry-body get together, try to love one another right now.
Chet Powers/Youngbloods (Get Together)

Neptune, the intuitive, idealistic, artistic, inspirational planet was directly responsible for the new forms of music and art that developed. But more importantly, as the higher vibration of Venus, the planet of Love, it helped us see and understand the true nature of universal Love. Love of all things, our fellow man, nature, the planet, the universe, even God, the very source of Love. It's no coincidence we called our awakening to this knowledge, the Summer of Love.

Neptune also represents escapism, drug use and abuse. This was certainly an important part of the Hippy culture. Besides all the wonderful, creative, inspirational tendencies these astrological events portray, there was a definite downside. Many kids dropped out of school, ran away, got addicted to certain hard drugs, overdosed and some even died. While Hippies relished their freedom, many refused to take responsibility for their actions. Fortunately, the Neptune aspects (conjunction and sextile) were very positive and the long-term effects were likewise very good.

These astrological events, because they involve the outer planets, occur over a long period of time, affect a large number of people, influence social structures and can bring about great changes that take many years to manifest. They also affect generations in different ways since our natal (birth) astrology differs (particularly the outer planets). Whereas one generation may be open to the changes, another might be highly reactionary, as was the case in the 1960s. Even though young people in the '60s had virtually no power (the voting age was still 21), our in-your-face, extremely vocal radicalism and the violent conservative backlash only served to underline the hypocrisies, outdated attitudes and serious failings of the system.

The deeper, more subtle, changes that the Hippy Movement generated are still being integrated into our social and political structures as well as our collective psyche. It appears that the confluence of planetary influences, combined with a rebellious open-minded generation, a range of innovative ideas, new powerful psychedelic chemicals, and increasing social pressures to conform, succeed, and fight an unwinnable war served to spark individually and collectively a far reaching transformation, unlike any seen before.

When people ask, "What happened to the Hippies?" they are wondering why the Summer of Love ended. Astrologically, planets and people change their positions over time. What motivated and inspired us astrologically no longer exists. Other forces dominate our lives at the present. However it serves no purpose to forget and bury the past. Let the past inspire us to improve our lives and those conditions surrounding us so that new generations may benefit from our wisdom and enlightenment.

The moral, social, ethical, and environmental dilemmas we face now are but a taste of things to come for our children and grandchildren. It's time we reexamine our lives, put the past in proper context, learn some important new lessons, and relearn some old ones. I believe that we all have within us this incredible store of knowledge and wisdom. Certain conditions bring it out, be they astrological, social, chemical, or spiritual. We must re-ignite the spiritual lamp so we can light the way for the generations to follow.

* By the way, the words to the song Aquarius (quoted above) weren't written by an astrologer and make very little sense since the moon goes into everyone's second house once a month, and Jupiter aligns with Mars almost once a year. Therefore they don't indicate anything like the "dawning of an age." (I suppose they could've been referring to the U.S. natal chart progressed into the 1960s, but I doubt it). However, the sign Aquarius is ruled by the planet Uranus which as you can see was the big influence during the Hippy Movement. I guess the "Age of Uranus" didn't quite have the same ring....

Hippy Philosophy & the Hippy Dream

We are stardust, we are golden,
and we've got to get ourselves back to the garden.
Joni Mitchell/CS&N (Woodstock)

So what do hippies want anyway? What is their utopian fantasy? It's easy to criticize the existing system, but just what do hippies have to replace it? Many accuse the hippies of being dreamers (one of the more benign accusations!). But I like to think that hippies are bringing a message to humanity. An urgent message. We need to change. Now!

We all want to change the world.
The Beatles (Revolution)

How? How about rethinking our whole relationship to the planet. Once upon a time people thought about the future in terms of decades and generations. They were concerned about the legacy they would leave their children and grandchildren. Today that seems so far from our thoughts. Our primary concern is; "What can I get now?"

It seems as though there's some kind of "land grab" going on, except it's not just land that people are grabbing, it's resources and power. It's like a party where no one got enough to eat, and the last few morsels are left, and everyone's eyeing them covetously, ready to fight for that last bite.

It's a problem of too many people, diminishing resources, human greed, rampant consumerism, and massive development of the few remaining untouched places like the rainforests. Our utopian fantasy doesn't necessarily require something to be done, but rather so many things for us to refrain from doing. That's the first step. Let's preserve what we have before greedy individuals and corporations gobble it up.

I'm just beginning to see...
The trees are drawing me near, I've got to find out why.
The Moody Blues (Tuesday Afternoon)

Then on an individual basis, hippies maintain that we must get back in touch with that part of ourselves that we lost. That innocence about the world, that hope for a future full of wonders. We want to reclaim our right to a healthy life and a healthy planet. We are all infected to some degree with a disease that requires us to consume way more than we need to survive. If all this greed had some noble purpose, perhaps it could be justified, but unfortunately it has become an end unto itself.

Like a true Nature's child, we were born, born to be wild.
Steppenwolf (Born to be Wild)

Many hippies consider themselves pagan. Paganism is the belief that nature in itself has the answers to life's most important questions. Paganism is a way of showing respect for the natural paradise we have on earth. It puts us in touch with that animal essence which we all repress, but is the key to our health and survival. The idea that Mother Nature knows best is the basis for the Ecology movement. To second-guess nature, to manipulate her for personal gain is likely to have unexpected consequences which will backfire in the long term.

That organism, that creature of which we are each a part, is the biosphere, the living surface of this planet Earth. That stirring we all feel, that move towards group-consciousness, is the biosphere of Earth becoming aware of its existence. It is being born. We are waking up.
Paul Williams (Das Energi)

Gaian philosophy is an outgrowth of paganism. Paganism sees everything living as imbued with spirit. Gaianism goes one step further and sees the entire planet as one evolving entity, of which we are an integral part. Thus to clear cut rainforests, to pollute the seas, the land and the air is not just showing disrespect it's raping our loving host that provides us with everything we need. In our endless greed we take and take, throwing the system out of balance. Many believe that Gaia will attempt compensate and restore the balance, probably by unleashing some plague upon mankind to reduce our numbers, if she doesn't kill us off completely.

Our responsibility as individual cells of a living organism, is to perform our individual functions as well as possible. Our orders come from within...we are free to be ourselves... Our lives will grow richer and richer as the health of the total organism improves.
Our destiny is unimaginably high.
Paul Williams (Das Energi)

Man's shortsightedness is blinding him to the true nature of the world. Our interconnectedness and dependence upon the ecological balance of the planet as a whole has been lost ever since Western science and religion split long ago. Hippies seek to regain this awareness so we can act in accordance with the needs of the greater system, rather than be a severe burden upon it. It's our Dharma.

Without stirring abroad, One can know the whole world;
Without looking out of the window One can see the way of heaven.
The further one goes The less one knows.
Lao Tzu

This awareness, once attained, requires us to reassess our role as human beings on the planet Earth. The questions; "Why are we here?" and "What is the meaning of life?" are the most important questions we can ask ourselves. As I said before Paganism provides those answers. We are here to serve the planet in the highest capacity we are capable of realizing. Truly, our needs are few. Those needs manufactured by our society are just tools used to keep us slaving for our rich masters while they destroy our common wealth.

One thing I can tell you is you've got to be FREE!
John Lennon (Come Together)

Freedom is shedding those false needs and finding one's true place in the greater scheme. Understanding the interdependence of life is seeing beyond the material illusion (Maya) and witnessing the dance of energy that is the true nature of the universe. This is called enlightenment. Hippies seek enlightenment in various ways. Drugs can provide but a fleeting glimpse of the true nature of reality. We know that before you can change the world, you must change yourself and find peace within. Yoga and meditation bring us this inner peace and help us to act in balance with our surroundings. Eastern mysticism from Ashtanga Yoga to Zen Buddhism provide us with various paths to enlightenment.

Hippies are the most open-minded folks when it comes to religion. We study many of the world's religions and take what makes sense and enhances personal freedom and reject the dogma. So our philosophy is a mélange of the teachings of Christ, Buddha, Lao Tzu, Krishna, Gandhi, even some latter-day saints like Lennon, Leary and Morrison. Some hippies choose a particular religion or guru to follow, while others blaze their own path, following the Tao wherever it takes them like a true Dharma bum.

If you meet Buddha on the road, kill him.
Book title by Sheldon Kopp

Of course we know that a perfect planet is unrealistic. A lot of hippies believe people come to this planet to work out their Karma. Human beings must live and learn by their mistakes. But we need to see examples of how to live in peace and harmony before we can change ourselves. Christ and Buddha were two such examples, and look at how many lives they influenced. Imagine what a whole nation of Bodhisattvas could do! This is our dream. To live in harmony with each other and our planet. How close we come to achieving it depends upon each person's willingness to change themselves. May we all see the light.

The Old Hippies

**Old hippies don't die, they just lie low until the laughter stops
and their time comes round again.**
Joseph Gallivan

Whatever happened to all the old hippies? The millions who protested, rallied
marched, sat-in and boycotted? Are they now just rebels without a cause? O
have they turned into apathetic yuppies? We must ask these questions, because
now is the time for them to come forth and accept the powerful role for which
they are destined.

When we were young, our ideals motivated us to challenge the system. W
wanted to change everything, to correct the wrongs, to reveal the hypocrisies, to
bring freedom and equality to everyone, everywhere. Now we are older and
presumably wiser, but are we still motivated by such high ideals?

The most important kind of freedom is to be what you really are.
Jim Morrison

We were the essence of freedom. By rejecting the social program, its values, it
prejudices and its fears, we discovered something beautiful inside ourselve
yearning to be free. We were free to think, to do and to be whatever we wanted
Once we stopped seeking and experiencing this freedom, an important part of us
stopped growing.

This is what happened to most of the old hippies. As they got older they married
had kids, got jobs, took on much more responsibility. They became part of the
system. I wouldn't describe it as "selling out", it's more like adjusting priorities
Now it's up to them to rediscover their lost ideals and use the power they now
possess to act according to those once highly regarded principles.

Your children are not YOUR children.
Kahlil Gibran

A common problem with the old hippies is that they want to prevent "their"
children from making the same mistakes they did in their youth. This is the
instinctual parental prerogative. However, the problem lies in thinking that one's
youthful activities (considered 'indiscretions' in politically correct terms) were a
mistake! I hear this over and over again. I tell you one and all: What you did in
the '60s was very important! You were Free in a way as you haven't been since
Whether you smoked a joint, dropped acid, had uninhibited sex, smelled like a
buffalo, wore clothes you wouldn't get caught dead in now, whatever, it was the
most perfect thing you could do!

Your sons and your daughters are beyond your command.
Bob Dylan (The Times they are a-changin')

Decrying your mind-expanding experiences as innocent mistakes, belittles
yourself, and does you more harm than good. Then to inflict this attitude upon

our children is to commit a great hypocrisy. Politicians in the public eye won't come out and admit their questionable youthful activities and so set a bad example. Why is the "common wisdom" to lie to your children about your past? Do you believe that sets a good example? Do you think kids won't see through your hypocrisy? You will lose your children just as your parents lost you when you did your hippie thing.

> **I'm frightened for your children,**
> **that the life that we are living is in vain.**
> The Moody Blues (The Story in Your Eyes)

Old hippies everywhere, this is a call to arms! You are needed! The children of today are our last, best hope to fulfill those beautiful dreams we had. There are young hippies everywhere asking the same questions we did. Only they're not finding the answers! Everywhere they are faced with politically correct brainwashed propaganda instead of truth! Get over your lingering doubts about the past. It's our future you need to be concerned about.

> **The sage does not hoard. Having bestowed all he has on others,**
> **he has yet more; Having given all he has to others, he is richer still.**
> Lao Tzu

What are YOU doing to make this world a better place? Investing in mutual funds? Buying that new SUV? Joining a country club? It's time to GET REAL again! It's time to wake up! If you're not part of the solution, you're part of the problem!!! Have you forgotten who you are? What you are? Why you're here?

> **We are here to make a better world. No amount of rationalization or**
> **blaming can preempt the moment of choice each of us brings to our**
> **situation here on this planet. The lesson of the '60s is that people who**
> **cared enough to do right could change history. We didn't end racism**
> **but we ended legal segregation. We ended the idea that you could send**
> **half-a-million soldiers around the world to fight a war that people do**
> **not support. We ended the idea that women are second-class citizens.**
> **We made the environment an issue that couldn't be avoided. The big**
> **battles that we won cannot be reversed. We were young, self-righteous,**
> **reckless, hypocritical, brave, silly, headstrong and scared half to death.**
> **And we were right.**
> Abbie Hoffman

Want to remember that feeling you had before, when you felt you could change the world? Maybe it's time for you to reassess your life, your goals, your programming. What really matters? Not just to you and yours, but to us and ours. Your responsibility doesn't end with your family. That's the cop-out that transformed the hippies into yuppies. It's taken quite a bit of maturity for these yuppies, especially the very successful ones to realize that success is hollow if you haven't really done something for the common good.

> **Expose yourself to your deepest fear; after that, fear has no power,**
> **and the fear of freedom shrinks and vanishes. You are free.**
> Jim Morrison

Cue Hippy Commercial: Are you tied down by job, kids, mortgage, and credit card debt? Remember when you were FREE? What did that freedom taste like? Do you think you'll ever experience it again in your lifetime? Will your children ever get a chance to be free like you once were? Or have they already sacrificed their souls to please you by accepting the values of this materialistic society?

> **We can change the world, rearrange the world.**
> **It's dying - if you believe in justice.**
> **It's dying - if you believe in freedom.**
> **It's dying - let a man live his own life.**
> **It's dying - rules and regulations, who needs them!**
> **Open up the door.**
> Crosby, Stills & Nash (Chicago)

It's way too easy to sit back in our comfortable homes, build our little nest eggs and pretend that those scenes of violence, hunger, war, and ethnic cleansing on CNN have nothing to do with us. You think we were naïve when we thought we could change the world. Well guess what? WE DID!

You can point to the wonders of modern technology (we created them) and think that it will solve our problems. Sorry, but that's being naïve! Look at what's being done to solve these problems and think: What more can be done? What hasn't been tried? What can I do?

> **Feed them on your dreams.**
> Crosby, Stills & Nash (Teach Your Children)

Travel to foreign lands and see what industrialization is doing to them. Just so we can have cheap goods from plastic toys to computers, other countries are having to turn their agrarian societies into industrial wastelands, where there are no pollution controls, and the air, land and water is poisoned. Where once there were fields of rice, now there are skyscrapers in choking haze.

Look around and see how things have changed since you were a kid. You think our emphasis on materialism, conformity and success is healthy? For you, your kids or the planet as a whole?

Have you noticed the anger seething below the surface of many young people today? The violence, the intolerance, the invasions of privacy and the repressive conformity they face everyday? Is it really surprising that this anger suddenly bursts forth with deadly results? Violence, it seems, is the only way nowadays to express outrage at the system that succeeds in getting attention. Once upon a time, we had peaceful ways of venting our frustrations.

> **If you're not part of the solution,**
> **you're part of the problem.**
> Eldridge Cleaver, Black Panther (Soul on Ice)

Why wait until these problems appear on your doorstep, or perhaps your child's school? Our hypocrisy and apathy will come back to haunt us. You CAN still make a difference. Get involved. Readjust your priorities. Spend time with your kids. Be honest with them! Please! That's all they ask. Share your youthful experiences, your lost ideals, your beautiful dreams for them and the world. Listen and learn!

That's what real love amounts to- letting a person be what he really is. Most people love you for who you pretend to be. To keep their love, you keep pretending- performing. You get to love your pretense. It's true, we're locked in an image, an act- and the sad thing is, people get so used to their image, they grow attached to their masks. They love their chains. They forget all about who they really are. And if you try to remind them, they hate you for it, they feel like you're trying to steal their most precious possession.

Jim Morrison

Tell your children about hippies. Hippies were real! We didn't pretend and put on airs. We didn't fake anything. We weren't selfish. We shared what little we had. We were honest about our feelings and acted accordingly. Yes, we were young, naïve, but somehow wiser than generations before or after. We were concerned about the important things that now seem forgotten. In our subsequent striving for success we have trampled upon those values we once cherished.

Meet the new boss, same as the old boss.
The Who (Won't Get Fooled Again)

What hasn't changed, over the years, is the power structure that caters to the rich and powerful. The government, industry, international trade, laws, and political system are all biased towards those with influence. Money buys influence and put those without it at a great disadvantage, and thus nothing has changed.

To be a revolutionary you have to be a human being.
You have to care about people who have no power.
Jane Fonda

This is what the Antiwar, Civil Rights, Black Power, Environmental, Women's and Gay Liberation movements were about. Getting our due portion of power and influence. Those who are oppressed, discriminated against, disadvantaged all need a way to influence society to their benefit. Those elements of our world that can't buy influence need aware individuals to represent their interests. These elements include the poor, the sick, children, animals, ecosystems, and natural resources.

It's a fool who plays it cool by making this world a little colder.
Beatles (Hey Jude)

Ideals are nice to visit once in awhile. Don't be afraid. The only thing that will change is you, for the better. If you know something's not right, why don't you try to fix it? Just give it the attention it deserves and you'll have an influence.

The punishment which the wise suffer who refuse to take part in the government, is to live under the government of worse men.
Plato

So old hippies, ex-hippies, and those who regret never getting involved, what are you going to do with the rest of your lives? What legacy are you going to leave your children?

You must be the change you wish to see in the world.
Mahatma Ghandi

We need to find our voice again. Once more we must point out the system's hypocrisies and lies and say enough is enough. We must not let them rule us with fear. We must stand together. United we stand, divided we fall victim to the system. That's how it's been for over 30 years now. How many more years will it take, before we're allowed to be free? The answer, my friend lies with you and me.

The Ballad of "It"
by Tibby Deaux

The Man schemed and planned to rid this land
of the hippies he wanted to smite.
He holstered his gun, 'cause he thought he'd won,
when the hippies just dropped out of sight.
Thus, began a brand-new plan:
He'd give the country to the right.
With some help from God and a big heavy rod
he'd make sure we all saw the light.
"Get it in your head: The hippies are dead!"
That's what he told us to make us contrite.
He told us to be wise and learn from their demise;
that nobody can standup to his might.
The Man continued to thrive, spouting his jive,
as his people just trembled with fright.
With the hippies no more
and no one minding the store,
his strangle-hold grew ever so tight.
He said,
"Don't act too tough. I'll take all your stuff,
if you even think about putting up a fight!
I'm meaner than mean and I'm running this scene.
I'm your pilot and this is MY flight!"
So, we flew and we flew and nobody knew
how deep we would fly into the night.
Then, we went online in 1999;
that's when the hippies learned how to byte.
The Net became a tool for reaching the cool:
Their spirits we hoped to excite.
It was a sight to behold,
when the young joined the old,
and the hippies decided to unite.

The Young Hippies

There's a whole generation with a new explanation.
John Phillips/Scott McKenzie (San Francisco)

I was very surprised to find when I started Hippyland that it wasn't just attracting old hippies like myself. There seems to be a large contingent of young people who consider themselves hippies. If Hippyland is any indication, they are legion. In fact, 85% of Hippyland's huge audience is under 30. What does this mean? To me it means the time is right for the second coming....of hippies. From what I can see, this new group from another generation has what it takes.

The torch has been passed to a new generation of Americans.
John F. Kennedy

This new cohort of hippies is facing the same trials and tribulations we did, excluding Vietnam. Our mail indicates that these young people view Hippyland as an island refuge in a sea of intolerance, apathy, hypocrisy, and violence. On Hippyland they can express themselves, communicate with like-minded souls, learn more about hippies, form communities and evolve.

Get up, stand up! Stand up for your right! Don't give up the fight!
Bob Marley (Get Up, Stand Up!)

From the rants on the Protest Page and in Hippyland's forums, it appears that intolerance is rampant especially among young people. Young hippies feel discrimination, rejection, even humiliation from their peers. It's as politically incorrect to be a hippy these days as it ever was. In fact non-conformity leads to alienation which can lead to worse things, like violence. Take Columbine High School as a good example.

Cannot believe what I see. All I have wished for will be.
All our race proud and free.
Donovan (Wear Your Love Like Heaven)

Yet these young hippies continue to go out among their cohorts spreading the simple message of love and peace. Unfortunately, many feel alone. In small towns they often stand out like a Peter Max poster in a funeral home. They long for acceptance. Once they discover other hippies their age that they can talk to (often on the Internet), they find the courage to face the intolerance of their home towns.

When others demand that we become the people they want us to be,
they force us to destroy the person we really are. It's a subtle kind of
murder. The most loving parents and relatives commit this murder with
smiles on their faces.
Jim Morrison

Like the hippies before them, they long for community, and are willing to uproot themselves from home and family to find it. Many are seeking out communes, forming drum circles, starting websites, traveling around the country and the world, seeking freedom and fellowship.

Question Authority!

hippie button

Some of these very young hippies, amazingly are anti-drug. A few of them have really good reasons, but for many it's still an indication of the indoctrination from the anti-drug programs at school. These individuals lump all drugs in the same category, and can't distinguish among soft, hard, prescription, and those accepted by society like alcohol and tobacco. They see all illegal drugs as "dangerous or deadly." Many grow out of this prejudice and open their minds. It's not necessary to do drugs to be a hippy, but tolerance and understanding about drugs is essential.

So who are these young hippies? From what I can determine, they're a very diverse group who arrived on the hippy scene via different paths. There are ravers, wiccans, punks, pagans, and a lot of Christians. Most are American but there are many Canadians, English, Dutch, German, Swedish, Russians, Czech, Brazilians, even Japanese. In fact just about every westernized country has hippies (source: Hippyland's logs).

What are these young folk into? Let's examine two groups, the ravers and punks, and their lifestyles. The rave scene is highly developed in Europe. Indoor and outdoor venues cater to a mostly young crowd who come to experience the electronic music, their friends, and certain psychedelic drugs. The music varies from light trance to heavy hardcore with 160 beats per minute. The bass registers in your gut and you can't help but move to it, while the rhythm and synthetic sounds put you in a hypnotic state. The feeling of dancing to the heavy house beat with hundreds or thousands of others is an energizing, uplifting high in itself. Under the influence of Ecstacy, Mushrooms, or LSD it's like merging into a group mind.

The ravers are a natural progression from the hippies and represent the Kesey school of experiencing the world (albeit an artificial one) under the influence of psychedelics. Like the '60s acid tests, the group experience is what's important here. Fortunately ravers don't drink a lot of alcohol since it doesn't mesh well with other drugs, so you don't get the aggression of a Woodstock '99 mosh pit.

The rave scene is segmented not just by the variety of music and drugs but by attitude. There's an interesting offshoot called Candy Ravers. They like their "candy" (drugs), but they also subscribe to a philosophy that goes by the acronym PLUR, which stands for Peace, Love, Understanding and Respect. They've formed a tight, loving community. These young ravers have the hippy spirit and are eager to learn more and join forces with other hippies.

Many punks follow the hippy philosophy, with their own radical twists. They reject the existing system and authority. Many adopt alternative lifestyles, some even eschewing drugs and alcohol (straight edge punks). They are dissatisfied with the social program and the limited opportunities available since most restrict their freedom. Their attitude and extreme dress (not to mention things like piercings) make them stand out as easy targets for scorn and ridicule (like hippies). Their loud music is full of important messages that need to be heard. Unfortunately, even us old hippies have trouble listening to it, just like our parents and our music.

I think many of these punks whose philosophy is non-violent, but seek change and freedom are certainly welcome among hippies. They may dress weird, listen to different music, and have unusual lifestyles, but as long as their attitude is one of cooperation and respect they can be a part of the movement. In fact they might be the ones to challenge our tolerance, our values, and our agenda, forcing us to re-evaluate our own philosophy. This is healthy and should be encouraged.

**You begin saving the world by saving one man at a time;
all else is grandiose romanticism or politics.**

Charles Bukowski

If you subscribe to Lawrence Kohlberg's Theory of Moral Development, which says that moral development is conditional upon being exposed to role models that exhibit different levels of morality, then you might have some hope for humanity. Then we can assume that young people, if exposed to higher levels of morality, will adopt that morality. There is no limit to how far we can go, so long as we have appropriate models to learn from.

Keep the Faith!

Unknown

The crisis in morality that we are facing today is due to the lack of good role models for young people. Let's see... We have a president who lies to the public and to his family. We have the richest man in the world whose idea of success is to crush his rivals, dominate an industry, and has so much money that he hasn't a clue what to do with it (although he is now coming around). We have minority sports figures who hawk clothes and get paid more just for the use of their name and face than all the people in third world countries making those clothes. We have another man running for President who refuses to acknowledge his own drug use, yet passes more stringent drug laws that would've put him in prison. In ghettos, we have drug dealers as the most successful role models.

So what do we get? We get a government that lies to its people to control them. We get industry that pursues short-term profits regardless of long-term damage to world ecology. We get children killing each other in school because of social ostracism for non-conformity. We get jails full of people doing time for victimless drug crimes.

The solution? A revolution in education is required. Every child should have a number of options available for education. Self-education must be encouraged so each child can pursue his or her interests apart from the majority. Self-pacing is essential so each student can absorb knowledge as quickly or slowly as necessary without waiting for others or "failing" to keep up. Communication between student and teachers (one student might have a number of teachers in one subject) will become more direct, more frequent and more effective. Thanks to the technology available now (computers and the Internet), this is not only possible but the most efficient system for education. These changes will minimize the typical brainwashing we've been putting our children through. We are about to witness the most significant change in education, EVER! (Pluto in Sagittarius for the next 20 odd years will make it so).

It's going to take a revolution in education, (one that includes morality and ethics as well as appropriate role models like hippies), coordination and communication, and unification of hippies young and old (via sites like Hippyland) to create a vibrant atmosphere for another movement. So let's join forces with these Young Hippies and set a new agenda for the millennium.

A Message to Young Hippies

Now is the time for all young hippies to come to the aid of their planet. Yes, I mean that. We need you now! I know you're young, inexperienced and unsure of yourselves. Our society has a plan for each of you. You can conform and be a part of the system, or you can discover who you really are, and express your unique individuality. The system has little tolerance for self-expression if it veers beyond the acceptable conformity. You've probably already experienced the alienation this engenders.

We, the old, tired hippies offer you a pact. We offer you our wisdom, our resources (yes, some of us have money), our considerable skills, our time and attention. In return you provide us your enthusiasm, your energy, your voices, your concerns. We can teach you our ways, you can teach us yours. Together we must discuss, organize, prioritize, coordinate, motivate, and activate our brethren.

We must develop an agenda for the new millennium. We must save our planet. We must demand tolerance. We must fight injustice. We must change the system. We must take only what we need. We must be examples to others. We must show them how futile and wasteful their programmed lives are. We must promote PLUR, Peace, Love, Understanding and Respect.

**A friend is someone who lets you have
total freedom to be yourself.**
Jim Morrison

We tired old hippies embrace you, surround you with LOVE, welcome you into our community, and initiate you into the tribe. You have a peer group without peer. We are your true family. Two (or three) generations together can do far more than one generation could possibly dream. We have a great deal of unfinished business that needs tending. Time is running out for those who want to make a difference. Join us, and together we will change the world for the better.

Hippyland is just one place where we can meet and make our plans. Hippies of all ages are welcome. Online communities are forming now. It's your life, your planet, your future.

Conclusion

Love is but a song we sing and fear's the way we die.
You can make the mountains ring or make the angels cry.
Chet Powers/Youngbloods (Get Together)

The Hippy movement was called the counterculture because it rejected the prevailing social norms. It succeeded as a cultural revolution, but not as a political one. We failed to overturn the power structure (this was not everyone's goal). When we tried to field a presidential candidate, George McGovern, we learned the futility of working within the system and playing by their rules.

Culturally we swept away the social mores of the previous generations. We experimented with alternative lifestyles, using our own inner guideposts of Love, Peace and Understanding to light the way. Anything that conflicted with these dearly held beliefs was rejected.

We liberated both sex and love from conventional stereotypes and found their deeper meaning, as the way to connect with the universal energy. We focused everyone's attention on the environment, showing how centuries of human abuse had taken their toll. We redefined the meaning of peace on an individual and collective basis. How peace within and peace without are tied together. We discovered that what's in your heart influences the state of affairs around you.

We learned activism and organized and demonstrated against the Vietnam War, and the inequities and hypocrisies of our system. We stood up to abuse, whether verbal, physical or emotional to get our points across. Many of us put our futures in jeopardy to prevent others from having to go to war.

We highlighted the abuses of government, corporate greed and problems inherent in the system, which led to many regulations now in effect to protect individual and environmental rights. We started the health craze by examining our lifestyles and our unhealthy consumption patterns. We pioneered healthy alternatives and living with nature rather than destroying it.

There can't be any large-scale revolution until there's a personal
revolution, on an individual level.
Jim Morrison

We expanded our minds and in doing so we cast off the shackles of social conformity. We, each and every hippy, by our vivid existence, stood as examples of freedom which threatened and still threatens the conservative social fabric of America.

Our art, music and literature stand above the garbage produced by the more recent mass consumer culture. Those achievements stand as a testament to the exceptional creativity, and innovative thinking that flows from free minds.

Being a hippie is much more difficult and demanding than conforming to society's dictates. A hippie accepts a higher level of social, ecological, ethical and moral responsibility than most people are willing to accept. Unfortunately, this often puts us at odds with the system. Our consciences won't allow us to follow along like sheep. If we must, we will rebel again and again.

We haven't all overdosed or sold out to the system. We exist on the edge of society, awaiting the call of a new generation to lead the charge. Many of us are in the system, dormant agents ready to awaken and do what is required. New parts of this system (The Internet is one) are our creation. We are already using them to our advantage.

We are ready, willing and able to lead other generations in the good fight to transform our society into one more understanding, more active, more balanced with nature, and more respectful of individual rights and freedom. Once again we stand at a threshold where we can either descend into an ever more totalitarian system, or free ourselves to become one harmonious species, with unlimited potential.

Power to the People!

Part II
Landmark Hippy Events

This chapter reviews some of the major events of the hippie movement. These events defined the nature, objectives and results of our counter-cultural assault on the establishment. Anyone who participated in these events shared at least some of the hippy beliefs, and should consider themselves a part of history.

Antiwar Protests

War does not determine who is right - only who is left.
Bertrand Russell

The strength and power of the Peace movement was nowhere more evident than during the numerous antiwar protests staged around the country. Students, teachers, women, children, veterans, writers, singers, activists, pacifists, radicals, even parents and grandparents took part in the effort to end the war in Vietnam. Although many of these protesters would never be considered hippies at home or work, the leaders of this country, and the conservative elements all chose to derisively label the participants "hippies." Indeed if desiring an end to war and speaking your mind made you a hippy, so be it. This labeling only served to further divide the country. If hippies are looked down upon, then by labeling all the protesters thus, politicians could safely assume that they didn't represent the REAL America, and ignore their opinions.

They could also justify using heavy handed, sometimes brutal tactics to break up peaceful

Hippy Timeline

Here are some of the more important events of the 1960s-1970s. They include the antecedents and descendants of the hippy movement, the Civil Rights, Antiwar, Black Power, Ecology, and Sexual, Women's, Gay Liberation movements. The psychedelic and the protest movements were greatly enhanced by the revolution in music, so we've included some influential music milestones. The information here has come from various sources. I've tried to verify as many as I could, but there's always a chance something is wrong. Please let us know if you see any inaccuracies or have anything to add. E-mail:

timeline@hippy.com

1960

January - Bob Dylan, age 19 plays at the Wha in Greenwich Village and visits Woody Guthrie in the Hospital.

Jan - Civil rights demonstrations in Atlanta.

Feb 1 - Four black students stage a sit-in at a segregated Greensboro lunch counter in North Carolina, after being denied service due to racial discrimination.

Feb 13 - France becomes the fourth nuclear power.

Feb 17 - Martin Luther King arrested due to Alabama bus boycott.

Feb 20 - Jimi Hendrix and the Rocking Kings, play their first gig in Washington.

Feb 23 - Whites join Negro students in sit-ins at Winston-Salem, North Carolina Woolworth store.

Mar 15 - Lunch-counter sit-ins spread to 15 cities in 5 southern states.

April 15 - Students protest racial segregation and use of nerve gas at the White House.

April 18 - The Beatles first public performance.

May - Payola scandal. Radio and TV personalities accused of accepting bribes from record companies to play certain artists.

May 6 - Civil Rights Act of 1960 signed by Eisenhower.

June - June Baez & Seeger perform at Newport Folk Festival

July - Sidney Cohen's survey of 5,000 individuals who had taken LSD 25,000 times concludes it is safe.

July 6 - The Subterranean – a movie based on Jack Kerouac's novels about the Beat Generation premieres in New York.

Aug 9 - Timothy Leary, 39, tries psilocybin mushrooms in Cuernavaca.

Aug 10 - Antarctic Treaty creates peaceful scientific preserve.

Oct 25 - Martin Luther King, Jr. is sentenced in Atlanta to 4 months in jail hard labor for sit-in which violated his probation.

Nov 8 - John F. Kennedy defeats Richard Nixon, becomes 35th U.S. president.

Nov 9 - Brian Epstein first sees the Beatles.

Nov 14 - Federal marshals escort four Negro girls into two desegregated white schools in New Orleans, Louisiana.

Nov 15 - The first U.S. submarine armed with thermonuclear missiles, sails on its first patrol.

Nov 17 - Anti-integration riots in New Orleans.

Nov 30 - Seven black college students arrested in Little Rock, Arkansas after 2 days of "sit-in" demonstrations.

Dec 5 - Supreme Court prohibits segregation in waiting rooms and restaurants serving interstate bus passengers

Dec 20 - Birth control pills go on sale in the US.

1961

Jan 17 - Eisenhower warns of increasing power of "military-industrial complex."

Feb 1 - Four black students arrested at "whites only" lunch counter in Greens-

demonstrations by denying the required permits to march or assemble, thereby turning the right to protest into an illegal act. Many thousands of young people were arrested, and now have criminal records, and many of those have lifetime scars and injuries as a result of the beatings they received at the end of a policeman's baton or a guardman's rifle butt.

Millions of mind guerrillas...
Raising the spirit of peace and love,
not war.
John Lennon (Mind Games)

Students spearheaded the antiwar movement, since they were the ones who were being drafted and dying in Vietnam. The SDS, Students for a Democratic Society, helped organize and coordinate protest activities in cities around the country. They held teach-ins on university campuses informing students about what was really happening with the war, and how to protest effectively.

It ain't me, it ain't me,
I ain't no military son.
Creedence Clearwater Revival
(Fortunate Son)

Students seeking to avoid the military draft and service in Vietnam had few options. Student Deferments were cut back drastically. It was next to impossible to get Conscientious Objector status. Some students burned their draft cards in protests, then evaded the draft by running to Canada. As veterans came back from 'Nam, either because their tour was up, or due to injury, they began to take part in the anti-war movement, and many threw their medals over the Capitol's fence.

A thousand people in the street.
Singing songs and carrying signs...
Buffalo Springfield (For What it's Worth)

Almost all the protests were relatively peaceful. Many arrests were due to the sit-ins taking place on government or private property. Since Peace was the highly sought goal, peace was the way to achieve it. More radical elements did try to stir up trouble. This was partly due to desperation, but also because some radicals had revolutionary ideologies, which required an armed struggle to succeed. The Black Panthers and the Weathermen struck fear in the hearts of many with their violent tactics. Most hippies did not support their dubious methods.

How successful was the anti-war movement? It certainly raised awareness among all Americans, especially the media. Unfortunately our government didn't know how to end it and still save face. So it continued to drag on, while the peace talks went nowhere.

It was amazing just how many years and casualties it took before the U.S. government finally stopped the war and withdrew from Vietnam (1973). Our country was unable to accept defeat, and still refuses to admit just how big a mistake was made in Vietnam.

This brings up the question, what does it take for the people of a democratic country to legally protest government policy and be heard and acknowledged by our elected officials, and not be oppressed and silenced? Since the voters never get to set policy, how can we change it if we feel it is wrong? Don't suggest we elect someone different. When was the last time a candidate lived up to his/her campaign promises (what few they bother to make anymore)?

Why do those who protest and those who organize protests automatically come under government scrutiny, have their private lives invaded, have a classified file listing their every move, and likely have their personal correspondence monitored?

These actions serve two purposes. To limit free speech and persecute those who practice it. This hasn't changed since the war days. Yes, now we have the Freedom of

boro, South Carolina.

Feb 18 - Bertrand Russell, 89, leads march of 20,000 & sit-down of 5,000 anti-nuke outside U.K. Defense Ministry and is jailed for 7 days.

Mar - Richard Alpert (Ram Dass) takes psilocybin as part of the Harvard Project.

Mar 1 - John Kennedy initiates $17 dollar nuclear missile program, increases military aid to Indochina & announces creation of the Peace Corps.

Apr 11 - Bob Dylan's first billed performance at Gerde's Folk City.

Apr 12 - Yuri Gagarin of the USSR is the first man in space.

Apr 25 - Bay of Pigs, Cuba. U.S. planned invasion is defeated by Castro.

May 4 - Freedom Riders leave DC for a southern tour to test integration in bus stations.

May 28 - Amnesty International founded.

July - Ban The Bomb Demonstrations start worldwide.

July 19 - First Telstar Satellite Live TV Transmission across the Atlantic.

Aug 13 - East German border guards begin construction of Berlin Wall.

Sept 15 - U.S. starts underground nuclear testing.

Sept 17 - 1,140 arrested in London Atom Bomb protest that included march and sit-in.

Oct 6 - President Kennedy advises Americans to build fallout shelters.

Dec 11 - First two U.S. Army helicopter units land in South Vietnam.

1962

Feb 16 - Boston SANE & fledgling SDS (Students for a Democratic Society) hold first anti-nuclear march on Washington with 4000-8000 protesters.

Apr 25 - U.S. resumes atmospheric nuclear testing after 3 year moratorium.

Aug - Ban the Bomb demonstrations at the UN, and in London, Helsinki, Tokyo, Hiroshima

Sept - Timothy Leary founds International Foundation for Internal Freedom (IFIF) to promote LSD research & publish The Psychedelic Review.

Oct 22 - Cuban Missile Crisis - Soviet missile bases in Cuba, Kennedy orders naval blockade.

1963

Jan - Alabama Gov. Wallace's "Segregation Forever" speech at inauguration.

Apr 3 - SCLC & volunteers stage sit-in in Birmingham, Alabama.

Apr 12 - Martin Luther King & Ralph Abernathy go to jail in Birmingham.

Jun 11 - JFK Proposes the Civil Rights Bill.

Jun 12 - Civil rights leader Medgar Evers assassinated.

July - Timothy Leary hosts Freedom House groups in Zihuatanejo, Mexico, Dominica & then Antigua.

July - Newport Folk Festival July 26-28, includes Bob Dylan, Joan Baez, Phil Ochs and Pete Seeger.

Aug 5 - First Nuclear Test Ban Treaty signed.

Aug 28 - Martin Luther King's "I Have a Dream" speech, Wash DC Civil Rights March, 200,000 attend.

Aug 30 - U.S. -Soviet Hotline installed.

Sept - Timothy Leary, Richard Alpert, and other Harvard alumni LSD researchers move to the Hitchcock's estate in Millbrook, New York.

Sept 24 - Nuclear Test Ban Treaty ratified by Senate.

Oct 10 - Nuclear Test Ban Treaty takes effect.

Oct 13 - Beatles on TV at London Palladium. 15 million get to see them perform "She Loves You" and "Twist and Shout."

Nov 2 - Military junta overthrows Vietnam leadership on orders from Washington.

Nov 22 - JFK Assassinated in Dallas, Texas; LBJ sworn in.

Nov 22 - Aldous Huxley dying, decides to take LSD one last time, dies tripping.

Nov 24 - LBJ escalates the Vietnam War.

Nov 29 - Beatles "I Want to Hold Your Hand" Released.

1964

Jan 8 - LBJ declares "War on Poverty" in State of the Union address.

Jan 11 - U.S. Surgeon General declares cigarettes cause lung disease.

Jan 30 - New military junta takes over in South Vietnam.

Information act, but that hasn't stopped the federal and local governments from spying on individuals simply because they speak their minds, and protest the activities of the government. There are hundreds if not thousands of government employees who do nothing but monitor and sift through the personal lives of American citizens and foreigners alike.

Why does the government feel so threatened? Well, there ARE terrorists, conspirators, and drug dealers who break laws. But I'm discussing activists who protest government policies. Nowadays if something is illegal, and you choose to protest that fact, it is assumed that you are engaged in or promoting an illegal activity, and therefore warrant closer scrutiny. Just the act of opposition to government policy is now being looked upon as illegal activity in itself. That puts us one big step closer to dictatorship, and Big Brother.

We set policy and govern based on numbers, money, and statistics without regard to the needs and feelings of the people behind the stats. This is a great failing of our emerging technocratic system. Once upon a time our justice system actually examined the person who committed a crime and looked at the circumstances, the person's contributions to society, testimonies of friends, etc. before sentencing. Very often people would be let off with a warning. Now we have mandatory minimum sentences, which treat people like a statistic, not human beings, thus making a mockery of justice.

We must reform this system before it gets further out of hand. Government has too much power over individuals. Agencies are given mandates that conflict with civil rights and the right to privacy. Our leaders seek to protect their own interests and positions at whatever cost to individual freedom. This is not how our system is supposed to work. We have it within our power to change this. The safeguards built into our system by the Bill of Rights and the legal system must be used to protect our common interests. We must exercise the power we have been granted. We must become a self-governing nation, or lose our freedoms to a Police State.

Ken Kesey, the Hell's Angels and the Acid Tests

You're either on the bus or off the bus.
Ken Kesey

Ken Kesey, the bestselling author of "One Flew Over the Cookoo's Nest" and "Sometimes A Great Notion", was at the forefront of the Psychedelic Movement. He participated in some early LSD experiments at Stanford University, and managed to abscond with some of the drug, which he used to turn-on everyone he met. At his place in La Honda, California, Kesey hosted a ongoing party of friends who called themselves the Merry Pranksters.

In 1964, Kesey gathered together his Pranksters and loaded them into a bus (now an icon of the Hippy Movement) with the destination sign reading "Furthur." They took off on an LSD fueled psychedelic cross-country journey that spanned not just a continent but two social movements, the Beats and the Hippies. This bringing together of such personalities as Neal Cassady, Allen Ginsberg, and Jack Kerouac with Kesey, Timothy Leary and Richard Alpert (Ram Dass) was a symbolic passing of the torch from one movement to the other.

Then, one day in August 1965, Hunter S. Thompson (author, "Fear and Loathing in Las Vegas"), rolled in, escorted by a gang of Hell's Angels. Kesey welcomed and treated the Hell's Angels as individuals, not representing some kind of threat. As usual he turned them on to LSD (the first time for them). Also at Kesey's place that fateful day were Allen Ginsberg and Richard Alpert

Feb 7 - Beatles arrive in New York to 10,000 screaming fans.
Feb 9 - Beatles first appear on Ed Sullivan Show, 74 million people watch, then the largest audience in the history of television.
Mar 16 - President Johnson requests $1 billion for the "War on Poverty."
Apr 23 - Beatles at the Hollywood Bowl.
May - Bob Dylan's first visit to England, meets The Beatles & Rolling Stones; turns The Beatles on to marijuana.
July - Millbrook LSD sessions with Timothy Leary.
July - Ken Kesey's First Magic Bus Trip to NY.
July 2 - LBJ signs US Civil Rights Act: public facilities opened to all.
July 18 - Race riot in Harlem, NY.
July 23 - Senate passes $947 million antipoverty bill.
July 30 - House of Representatives passes Wilderness Act, 373-1. The bill establishes 9.1 million acres of federally protected wilderness in national forests, and mandates more.
Aug - Ken Kesey & his Merry Pranksters visit Timothy Leary & Richard Alpert at Millbrook.
Aug - Beatles first U.S. tour: 25 North American cities.
Aug 4 - Three missing civil rights workers found dead in Mississippi.
Aug 11 - Beatles' A Hard Day's Night movie released.
Aug 20 - LBJ signs anti-poverty program.
Aug 23 - Beatles Hollywood Bowl concert.
Aug 28 - Race riots in Philadelphia.
Aug 31 - LBJ signs food stamp bill.
Sept 3 - LBJ signs Wilderness Act into law.
Oct 14 - Martin Luther King, Jr. wins Nobel Peace Prize.
Oct 16 - China explodes first atomic bomb, becoming fifth nuclear power.
Nov 3 - Lyndon Johnson and Hubert Humphrey elected in a landslide victory over Senator Barry Goldwater.
Dec 2 - Sit-in at Sproul Hall, University of California, Berkeley, 800 arrested. Start of Free Speech Movement. Joan Baez sings on Sproul Hall steps.
Dec 10 - Martin Luther King, Jr. awarded Nobel Peace Prize.

Time Magazine calls young people "generation of conformists."

Jan 4 - President Johnson outlines "Great Society."

Feb - Martin Luther King, Jr. and 770 other protesters arrested in Selma, Alabama for picketing county courthouse to end discriminatory voting rights.

Feb 8 - U.S. starts bombing North Vietnam.

Feb 18 - Secretary of Defense Robert McNamara calls for nationwide network of bomb shelters.

Feb 21 - Malcolm X shot and killed.

Mar 3 - Owsley starts LSD factory, making large quantities of acid available for the first time.

Mar 6 - First American soldier officially sets foot on Vietnam battlefields.

Mar 7 - Alabama State troopers attack 525 civil rights workers as they prepare to march.

Mar 8 - 3,500 Marines land to protect Da Nang air base.

Mar 16 - Quaker Alice Herz, 82, immolates self in Detroit in protest of the Vietnam War.

Mar 16 - Police break up demonstration of 600 in Montgomery, Alabama.

Mar 17 - 1,600 people demonstrate at Montgomery, Alabama courthouse.

Mar 21 - Martin Luther King Jr. leads march from Selma to Montgomery, Alabama joined by 25,000 marchers.

Mar 24 - SDS organizes first Vietnam War teach-in at University of Michigan 3000 attend.

Mar 25 - Civil rights worker shot and killed by KKK in Alabama.

Mar 28 - Martin Luther King calls for boycott of Alabama on TV.

Apr - 25,000 U.S. troops stationed in Vietnam.

Apr 2 - Ken Kesey busted for marijuana first time.

Apr 17 - SDS leads first anti-Vietnam War march in Washington. 25,000 attend including Phil Ochs, Joan Baez and Judy Collins.

Jun 11 - Beatles awarded the MBE by the Queen.

(Ram Dass), two of the more gentle philosophers of the beat/hippy/psychedelic movement. You'd expect some kind of fireworks with such a mix of energies and ideas.

Incredibly, the Angels fell under Kesey's spell (like everyone else), and thus began a long relationship (4 1/2 years) between the Hell's Angels and the Hippy Movement. It was defined by Hell's Angels providing security and bodyguards for many hippy events, rock stars and concerts in those years. There is little doubt the Hell's Angels were heavily involved in distributing the drugs that many hippies consumed during that period. The relationship soured after the disastrous 1969 Altamont concert where they provided security for the Jefferson Airplane and the Rolling Stones. A man waving a gun was killed right in front of the stage, by the Angels, who were absolved of responsibility. The film Gimme Shelter was used in evidence and it's clear the Angels were just doing their job in a very difficult situation. The incident was just one of many violent episodes that year.

Kesey along with his Merry Pranksters inspired and coordinated the Acid Tests (see below). Kesey had several brushes with the law, went on-the-lam in Mexico, and returned to face the music. Kesey and the remaining Pranksters now take his famous bus on an annual tour around the US and England. They are followed by an ever growing entourage of hippies.

The Acid Tests

The famous Acid Tests were put on by Ken Kesey and the Merry Pranksters in the mid-'60s in California. These psychedelic happenings evolved into the San Francisco scene leading up to the Summer of Love. What Kesey did was mix together music, acid, and light shows into a potent brew of mind-expanding phantasmagoria. Many attending these acid parties took LSD for the first time. Word got out and the acid tests drew more and more people.

Kesey promoted the LSD trip as a new way of experiencing everything. His psychedelic bus, the parties at his house, and the Acid Tests were all experiments with mind expanding anarchy. Those who participated in these events were true adventurers, explorers of the unknown. It's hard to measure the impact of these events, but we were soon to see some of the results surfacing in San Francisco (see below). Kesey eventually held a graduation ceremony for the core Acid Test participants. They were given a certificate verifying they had survived.

The Acid Tests inspired Stewart Brand, who produced the Trips Festival party in San Francisco in January, 1966. It was a three-day festival of music at Longshoreman's Hall with dancing and a light show that would simulate "an LSD experience without LSD." Kesey and the Merry Pranksters showed up, (along with the Grateful Dead, and lots of real acid) as this was the most public of the acid tests. The success of this event inspired Bill Graham to start holding these parties on a regular basis at the Fillmore Auditorium.

Be-In, San Francisco 1967

It was billed as a Gathering of the Tribes, the First Human Be-In. On January 14, 1967, 50,000 beautiful people gathered at the Polo Grounds to listen to Timothy Leary, Allen Ginsberg, Richard Alpert (Ram Dass), Dick Gregory, Jerry Rubin, Lawrence Ferlinghetti, Gary Snyder talk about life, love, enlightenment and peace. San Francisco rock bands The Grateful Dead, The Jefferson Airplane and Quicksilver Messenger Service entertained the crowd. The diggers were there handing out free food, some of which may have been laced with LSD.

This was a highly charged, symbolic event that brought together the political, spiritual,

July 8 - Chicago school integration protests.

July 8 - U.S. forces, previously in Vietnam only as military advisers, authorized for combat for the first time.

July 10 - Rolling Stones' "I Can't Get No Satisfaction" hits #1.

July 24 - Bob Dylan's "Like A Rolling Stone" enters charts.

July 25 - Dylan goes electric at Newport Folk Festival.

July 28 - President Johnson sends 50,000 more troops to Vietnam.

July 30 - LBJ signs Medicare bill.

Aug - Ken Kesey meets Hunter Thompson who introduces the Hells Angels to the Merry Pranksters; Allen Ginsberg & Richard Alpert are at the party.

Aug 11 - Major race riot (6 days) in Watts, California leaves 35 dead.

Aug 13 - National Guard enters Watts riots in Los Angeles.

Aug 14 - Sonny and Cher release "I Got You Babe."

Aug 23 - Premiere of Beatles' movie "Help!"

Aug 31 - Burning draft cards becomes illegal.

Sept 5 - San Francisco writer Michael Fallon applies the term "hippie" to the SF counterculture in an article about the Blue Unicorn coffeehouse where LEMAR (Legalize Marijuana) & the Sexual Freedom League meet, & hippie houses.

Sept 25 - "Eve of Destruction," sang by Barry McGuire top of the charts.

Oct 1 - Anti-pollution bill sets emission standards for cars.

Oct 16 - 100,000 anti-war protesters nationwide in 80 cities.

Nov - "Unsafe at Any Speed" about the automobile industry's disregard for safety, published by Ralph Nader.

Nov 2 - Quaker Norman Morrison self-immolates in front of Secretary of Defense McNamara's office. McNamara pukes.

Nov 22 - Bob Dylan marries Sarah Lowndes & moves to Woodstock, N.Y.

Dec 25 - Timothy Leary busted for pot at the Mexican border.

1966

Jan 3 - The Psychedelic Shop (head shop) opens on Haight Street, San Francisco.

Jan 14 - March on Atlanta to protest ouster of Julian Bond.

Jan 17 - B52 collides, drops 4 10-megaton H-bombs on Spain, none explode, cover-up follows.

Jan 20 - Ken Kesey busted again for marijuana with Mountain Girl.

Jan 21 - First light show, Grateful Dead, 10,000 people in S.F.

Feb 19 - Jefferson Airplane and Big Brother and the Holding Company with Janis Joplin perform at the Fillmore.

Mar 3 - GI Bill grants veterans rights to education, housing, health and jobs.

Mar 11 - Timothy Leary sentenced in Texas to 30 years for trying to cross into Mexico with a small amount of marijuana.

Mar 25 - Anti-Vietnam war protests in NY bring out 25,000 on 5th Ave. Other protests in 7 US cities and 7 foreign cities.

Apr - FBI releases file on LSD, drug gets bad press due to unvalidated propaganda (Hoover plot).

Apr - 30 Mississippi blacks build tent city under President Johnson's window to protest housing conditions in their state.

Apr - Discotheques are the rage in NY and LA. Andy Warhol puts on light shows.

Apr 7 - Sandoz stops supplying LSD to researchers due to controversy.

Apr 12 - NY Stock Exchange hit with anti-war leaflets.

Apr 16 - Timothy Leary busted at Millbrook by G. Gordon Liddy & FBI for possession of marijuana.

May 15 - Antiwar demonstration in Washington D.C., 10,000 attend.

July 29 - Bob Dylan's motorcycle accident.

Aug 5 - Lennon says Beatles more popular than Jesus.

Aug 18 - Red Guard begins to wipe out western influence in China.

Sept - George Harrison goes to India for 6 weeks to study sitar with Ravi Shankar.

---

literary, musical and shamanic leaders of a generation. At the time it seemed like a good thing to do. Just get together and experience the vibes. Looking back we can see that it was a chance for us to view our numbers, to feel our power, to communicate our love, and to outline the agenda for a movement. That was the subtext. Allen Ginsberg said we should use our "flower power" peacefully. Timothy Leary said we should "turn-on, tune-in and drop-out" of the social program. Jerry Rubin encouraged us to get active on the political stage. Ram Dass urged us to "Be Here Now" and find enlightenment in the moment. The musicians made us dance and reminded us that life should be joyful.

Many who participated in this seminal event look back and remember a special light that surrounded them during the Be-In. Inside this collective experience in the light there was a tremendous feeling of community, togetherness and oneness. But then the light faded and they found themselves back in the park, listening to music, separate once again. But that feeling was to linger as winter led to spring....

Monterey Pop Festival: June 16-18, 1967

Billed as "Music, Love, and Flowers", the Monterey Pop Festival was that and so much more. Festival attendees were urged to "Dress as wild as you choose." This was the first big rock festival, a showcase for the West Coast music scene. 200,000 showed up for the three-day non-profit event in California at the Monterey County Fairgrounds, the site of the annual Monterey Jazz Festival.

Organized by Lou Adler and John Phillips of the Mamas and Papas, with the help of rock impresario Bill Graham and others, Monterey attracted the cream of musical acts. It was Paul McCartney who suggested both Jimi Hendrix and The Who (in their first American concert). Other performers included Eric Burdon & The Animals, Simon & Garfunkel, Canned Heat, Big Brother & The Holding Company with Janis Joplin, The Steve Miller Band, The Byrds, The Jefferson Airplane, Ravi Shankar, Buffalo Springfield, The Grateful Dead, Scott McKenzie, and of course The Mamas & The Papas.

The event turned out to be the biggest rock concert of its day. It was a prelude to the larger rock festivals to come later. The crowd was treated well, the event was highly organized and ran pretty smooth. Hawaiian orchids were handed out at the gate, ushers showed people to their seats, and a special batch of purple Owsley acid was available. A typical San Francisco light show added to the psychedelic feel of the festival.

For three days the fans were treated to some of the best music by young creative talents at their peak. Jimi Hendrix and Janis Joplin made rock history as they both blew the crowd away with music that touched our souls. Before Monterey, they were almost totally unknown in the U.S. But Janis Joplin was the first to steal the audience's heart with her rendition of Big Mama Thorton's blues tune, "Ball and Chain." No woman singer before or since has been able to pierce your heart with emotion like Janis.

Pete Townsend and Jimi Hendrix got in a fight over who would follow whom. Pete lost the coin toss, so his band went on first, smashing their guitars, their instruments and the stage for their patented climax. Jimi needed no such stunts. He wooed the audience with his mastery, his control over every sound possible from a guitar. His soulful, yet gut wrenching sound tore through virgin ears and immediately everyone knew, that music would never be the same. But just to top Townsend, Jimi set his guitar on fire after making love to it.

Ravi Shankar played a mesmerizing three-hour set that saw the audience respond with a very long standing ovation. His

Sept - Timothy Leary holds press conference at NY Advertising Club announcing formation of a psychedelic religion - League for Spiritual Discovery ("Turn on, tune in, drop out") & starts nightly presentations at the Village Theater.

October 6 - LSD becomes illegal. Love Pageant Rally in the Panhandle of Golden Gate Park, San Francisco, in protest as participants eat blotter acid.

Oct 29 - The National Organization for Women founded in Washington D.C. Activist, feminist organization seeks economic equality, abortion, sexual and reproductive rights for women.

Oct 31 - Acid Test Graduation for Kesey and the Merry Pranksters.

Nov 5 - Walk for Love and Peace and Freedom: 10,000 + in New York City.

Dec - Cream's first album: "Fresh Cream" released. Eric Clapton, Jack Bruce, and Ginger Baker.

1967

Jan 14 - Gathering of the Tribes, First Human Be-In, 20,000-50,000 attend in Golden Gate Park, San Francisco, California.

Jan 27 - US, USSR, UK sign treaty banning nuclear weapons in space.

Feb - 25,000 US troops sent to Cambodian border.

Feb - Beatles release "Strawberry Fields Forever," "Penny Lane," "Michelle," "Yesterday."

Mar - Scientist reports LSD causes chromosome damage (never validated).

Mar 3 - The Berkeley Barb starts the smokable banana rumor (based upon Donovan's song "Mellow Yellow").

Mar 3 - Alice B. Toklas dies.

Mar 13 - Senator Eugene McCarthy introduces the Equal Rights Amendment (ERA) in the Senate. He had 37 co-sponsors.

Mar 18 - First U.S. supertanker wreck. Torrey Canyon spills 90,000 tons of oil onto English shores.

Mar 26 - Be-In at Central Park in NY. 10,000 attend.

Apr 5 - Grayline tour bus company starts hippie tours of Haight-Ashbury.

Apr 10 - Vietnam Week starts. Draft card

burnings and anti-draft demonstrations.

Apr 15 - Anti-Vietnam War protest. 400,000 march from Central Park to UN. Speeches by Martin Luther King, Stokely Carmichael and Dr. Benjamin Spock.

May - Paul McCartney announces that all the Beatles have "dropped acid."

May 9-12 - Boston to Pentagon Walk for Peace and sit-in inside Pentagon.

May 19 - First U.S. air strike on Hanoi.

May 20 - Flower Power Day in NYC.

May 26 - The Food and Drug Administration reports that there are no known psychedelics in banana peels.

June 2 - "Sgt. Pepper's Lonely Hearts Club Band" album by the Beatles released.

June 9 - Haight-Ashbury Free Medical Clinic opened.

June 16 - Monterey Pop Festival, Jimi Hendrix, Janis Joplin, Grateful Dead, Mamas & the Papas, Ravi Shankar, and many others perform.

June 21 - Summer Solstice Party in Golden Gate Park.

June 25 - Beatle Song, "All You Need Is Love" debuts on T.V., 100,000 flower children now in the Haight-Ashbury area.

June 30 - 448,400 US troops now in Vietnam.

July - The Summer of Love in San Francisco.

July - Summer of Rioting in the US. Blacks take to the streets in Chicago, Brooklyn, Cleveland and Baltimore.

July 1 - "Sgt. Pepper" hits #1.

July 7 - Time magazine cover: The Hippies, The Philosophy of a subculture.

July 11 - Newark riots start long hot summer.

July 24 - 43 Die in Detroit rioting, worst in U.S. history.

July 26 - H. Rap Brown arrested for inciting a riot in Maryland.

July 29 - "Door's Light My Fire" and "Procol Harem's Whiter Shade of Pale" vie for #1.

Aug 7 - George Harrison pays a visit to Haight-Ashbury.

Aug 26 - Jimi Hendrix's "Are You Experienced?" hits the charts.

performance instantly made him an icon of Indian music. Some bands like the Byrds and the Mamas and the Papas were about to break up, and their performances reflected the discontent.

Monterey Pop was made into a movie which had limited success on its first release. Now it's considered a classic documentary of the period thanks to the premiere performances of Janis & Jimi. The Festival also inspired other promoters to book multiple acts at large outdoor venues, as the psychedelic rock scene swept the country. It succeeded due to the professionalism of the organizers. As the precursor to Woodstock, it showed that there was a big market for outdoor concerts. And it was just the beginning of a summer to remember....

The Summer of Love: San Francisco: 1967

If you're going to San Francisco, be sure to wear a flower in your hair.
John Phillips/Scott McKenzie (If You're Going to San Francisco)

San Francisco has always had a different attitude marked by tolerance. During the late 1950s and early '60s, it was a bohemian hangout. Jack Kerouac, Allen Ginsberg and other writers, artists and musicians lived and partied hard in places like North Beach and across the bay in Berkeley. In 1964, the University of California in Berkeley was home to the Free Speech Movement. So it was the perfect setting for a revolution in style, attitude, and consciousness.

Things really started to develop when Ken Kesey and the Merry Pranksters held Acid Tests in the area in 1965. These parties where Electric Kool-Aid (spiked with LSD), psychedelic music by the likes of the Grateful Dead, and the first light shows appeared, were the sparks that lit a thousand candles. Those candles lit many more at events like The 1966

Trips Festival which added guerrilla theater, mime performance, and body paint to the psychedelic ritual.

By 1967, things were really coming together; the music, the drugs, and of course thousands of beautiful people. That year started with the "Gathering of the Tribes, the first Human Be-In." Businessmen in the Haight began to realize that there was something going on in the city that was attracting thousands of young people. They decided to actively promote the upcoming summer as "The Summer of Love" to give business a push.

Made up my mind to make a new start. Going to California with an aching in my heart. Someone told me there's a girl out there. With love in her eyes and flowers in her hair.
Led Zeppelin (Goin' to California)

San Francisco is one of the most magnificent cities in the world. Golden Gate Park is the cultural heart and gathering place. Just off the park's Panhandle lies the Haight district. What a scene it was in 1967, with fabulous psychedelic music, light shows, free flowing drugs, new fashions, and young people everywhere. Haight-Ashbury tried to accommodate the influx and developed according to the needs of these cultural pioneers. Many of these hippies were runaways, and usually broke. Free clinics, free food (thanks to the Diggers), free clothes and crash pads all helped what was an overwhelming situation. Since the vibe was loving and sharing, you can add free sex and drugs into the mix.

But the hype went too far. They started doing Greyhound tours of the Haight. Small town straights looked out of the bus windows upon something so alien, it was like visiting a colorful, cosmic zoo, complete with running commentary. The media played it up, and the kids came in droves to be a part of the scene.

Aug 27 - Beatles in India with Maharishi informed of Brian Epstein's death, overdose.

Sept - Richard Alpert meets Bhagwan Dass at the Blue Tibetan in Katmandu, stays in India & follows him until he meets his guru.

Sept 15 - Donovan performs at the Hollywood Bowl.

Oct 3 - Folk singer Woody Guthrie dies.

Oct 8 - Che Guevarra killed in Bolivia by US-trained troops.

Oct 12 - Big Brother and the Holding Company's "Cheap Thrills" with Janis Joplin at top of LP charts.

Oct 20 - Seven KKK members convicted of conspiracy in 1964 murders of three civil rights workers.

Oct 21-22 - Anti-war protesters storm the Pentagon.

Oct 21 - "Diggers" exorcise the Pentagon. 35,000 Demonstrate, 647 arrested.

Oct 26 - Draft deferments eliminated for those who violate draft laws or interfere with recruitment.

Nov 14 - Air Quality Act provides $428 million to fight air pollution.

Nov 20 - National Commission on Product Safety established.

Dec - Beatles release "Magical Mystery Tour."

Dec - 486,000 American troops in Vietnam, of the 15,000 killed to date, 60% died in 1967.

Dec - "Stop the Draft" movement organized by 40 antiwar groups, nationwide protests ensue.

Dec 5 - 1000 antiwar protesters try to close NYC induction center. 585 arrested including Allen Ginsberg and Dr. Benjamin Spock.

Dec 5 - Beatles open Apple Shop in London.

Dec 8 - Otis Redding records "Dock of the Bay."

Dec 10 - Otis Redding dies in plane crash.

Dec 22 - Owsley busted, stops making acid.

Nov 30 - Senator Eugene McCarthy enters the presidential race running on an antiwar platform.

Dec 31 - Abbie Hoffman, Jerry Rubin, Paul Krassner, Dick Gregory, & friends pronounce themselves "Yippies."

1968

Jan 1 - The United Nations inaugurates the International Year of Human Rights.

Jan 15 - The Jeanette Rankin Brigade, a coalition of women's peace groups, demonstrates against the Vietnam war at the opening of Congress. 5000 women attend.

Jan 16 - Youth International Party (Yippies) founded.

Jan 18 - Eartha Kitt visiting LBJ at White House speaks out against the war.

Jan 21 - Battle of Khe Sanh begins; 5,000 Marines isolated and under attack by 20,000 North Vietnamese troops.

Jan 22 - B-52 carrying H-bomb crashes in Greenland.

Jan 23 - USS Pueblo seized by Korea.

Jan 31 - Viet Cong launch Tet Offensive a massive 25-day assault throughout South Vietnam, surprising the US forces by its size and scope. Antiwar sentiment in US increases.

Feb - Timothy Leary evicted from Millbrook house.

Feb - Beatles go to India to visit Maharishi Mahesh Yogi at Rishikesh on the Ganges river. Mia Farrow, Donovan follow.

Feb 4 - Neal Cassady, beatnik, Dharma Bum, Merry Prankster, found dead in Mexico.

Feb 8 - George Wallace announces candidacy for President on law and order platform. Senator Robert Kennedy says the US cannot win the Vietnam War.

Feb 13 - US sends 10,500 more combat troops to Vietnam.

Feb 16 - President Johnson ends draft deferments for graduate students.

Mar 6 - Walter Cronkite, breaking a code of neutrality among major newscasters, opposes the Vietnam War in a national television broadcast.

Mar 9 - General William Westmoreland requests 206,000 more troops for Vietnam.

Mar 12 - Eugene McCarthy wins 42% of New Hampshire vote in presidential primary.

On June 16, the Monterey Pop Festival drew national attention by showcasing the San Francisco sound with groups like the Grateful Dead, Big Brother and the Holding Company with Janis Joplin, Jimi Hendrix and the Jefferson Airplane. Both Janis & Jimi were relatively unknown until their legendary performances at Monterey. On June 21 the hippies held a Summer Solstice party in Golden Gate Park. By June 25, the day the Beatles debuted the song, "All You Need Is Love" on T.V., 100,000 flower children were gathered in the Haight-Ashbury area living it. On July 1, the Beatles' LSD inspired Sgt. Pepper album hit # 1. On July 7, Time Magazine's cover story was "The Hippies: The Philosophy of a Subculture." On August 7th, George Harrison paid the Haight a visit with his wife, Patti. On August 26, Jimi Hendrix's "Are You Experienced?" hit the charts.

Surely something cosmic was happening. (Please read the chapter "The Astrology of the Hippy Movement" for a possible explanation of the forces at work during the summer of 1967). The Haight at its peak was the center of an LSD-fueled revolution in consciousness, music, art, fashion and lifestyle. The novel experiments that were tried during these years were not failures. They opened doors through which we discovered our true selves and our common humanity. Sure there were bad trips, rip-offs, diseases, run-ins with authority, but these were isolated incidents and a small price to pay for being part of a revolution.

Within a few years, the media attention moved away, and so did many of the hippies. Some went back home, some moved to communes around the state, some traveled to other hippy havens. There was a gradual decline in the Haight-Ashbury area, but today it's come back somewhat and now it's a nostalgic tourist attraction, but not much of a hippy scene.

The Democratic Convention, Chicago: 1968

Our demonstrations shall be entirely peaceful. We are not seeking a confrontation.

David Dellinger, leader of National Mobilization to End the War in Vietnam and the planned protests in Chicago.

It was to be a peaceful demonstration against the continuing War in Vietnam and the fact that the Convention was a farce, since the outcome had been predetermined (Humphrey to be nominated). Earlier that year, Martin Luther King, Jr. and Robert Kennedy had been assassinated. With our popular, peace loving leaders gone, the nomination of Hubert Humphrey, and rejection of the peace platform would be another serious blow to activists.

Each night, America watched as the airwaves broadcast the events from Chicago. The whole Democratic Convention and the nomination of Humphrey/Muskie took a back seat to the events unfolding on the streets outside. Yippie leader, Abbie Hoffman had called for 500,000 protesters to demonstrate in Chicago. In response, Mayor Daly had 12,000 policemen stationed around the Convention center. He got another 6,000 National Guard; 7,500 U.S. army troops; and 1,000 FBI, CIA & other services agents to deal with only 10,000 unarmed peaceful protesters who showed up.

Jerry Rubin and Abbie Hoffman's Yippies did threaten to "roar like wild bands" through Chicago and spike the city's water supply with LSD. But these were just the usual media grabbing pranks they used. Tom Hayden, Rennie Davis (leaders of the SDS) and David Dellinger were the organizers of the larger protest. All these men were later part of the Chicago Seven conspiracy trial.

Mar 16 - My Lai massacre 200 - 500 Vietnamese villagers killed. LBJ decides to send 35,000 to 50,000 more combat troops to Vietnam. Robert F. Kennedy announces candidacy for President.

Mar 31 - LBJ announces decision not to run again and offers partial Vietnam bombing halt. Gallup Poll shows only 26 percent approve of Johnson's handling of the war.

Apr 4 - Martin Luther King shot and killed in Memphis, Tennessee.

Apr 5-12 - The week following Martin Luther King Jr.'s murder sees black uprisings in 125 cities across the U.S.

Apr 6 - Oakland Police ambush Black Panthers. Eldridge Cleaver arrested with a bullet-shattered leg. Bobby Hutton shot and killed.

Apr 8 - Bureau of Narcotics and Dangerous Drugs established (DEA).

Apr 11 - LBJ signs civil rights bill banning housing discrimination. Major call-up of reserves for duty in Vietnam. Love-in at Malibu Canyon, California.

Apr 15 - Start of Spring Mobilization against the Vietnam war. Chicago Mayor Daley tries to get his city under control during riots; orders "shoot-to-kill" in cases of arson, looting, or rioting.

Apr 23 - SDS leads students, takes over 5 buildings at Colombia University for a week. 700 arrested.

Apr 24 - 300 Black students occupy administration building at Boston Univ. demanding black studies and financial aid.

Apr 25 - Paul Horn, flautist, records in the Taj Mahal.

Apr 26 - Two hundred thousand students boycott classes to protest war.

Apr 29 - The rock musical "HAIR!" opened on Broadway at the Biltmore Theater.

May 6-30 - Student demonstrations in France result in a general strike. Ten million workers strike as 10,000 battle police in Paris.

May 10 - Vietnam peace talks begin in Paris.

May 29 - Poor People's Campaign protesters storm Supreme Court building.

June 3 - Andy Warhol shot by Valerie

Solanis, author of S.C.U.M. manifesto.

June 5 - Bobby Kennedy assassinated by Sirhan Sirhan moments after winning California primary.

June 10 - General Westmoreland sees no military victory in Vietnam due to political restraints.

June 14 - Dr. Benjamin Spock and three others convicted of conspiracy to abet draft evasion.

June 24 - National Guard ordered out in Washington D.C. as looting breaks out in black section of city.

July 1 - Nuclear nonproliferation treaty signed by 61 nations.

July 20 - LBJ tells South Vietnamese President Thieu the US will continue Vietnam War at current pace.

July 25 - Cleveland Mayor Carl Stokes calls National Guard back to slum areas.

Aug 1 - 541,000 U.S. Troops in Vietnam.

Aug 8 - Nixon and Agnew nominated during Miami riots.

Aug 10 - Eight GIs killed by friendly fire in Vietnam. Senator George McGovern announces candidacy for President.

Aug 21 - Soviets invade Czechoslovakia to crush the "Prague Spring" reform movement.

August 25-29 - Democratic Convention in Chicago. Demonstrations & police riot 10,000 demonstrators vs. 12,000 Chicago police; 6,000 National Guard; 7,500 U.S. army troops; and 1,000 FBI, CIA & other services agents

Aug 28 - Humphrey and Muskie nominated (on platform supporting the war) amid violent antiwar protests in Chicago. Bystanders and press also beaten by police.

Oct 18 - John & Yoko busted for drugs. Two black Olympians raise fists in black power salute when receiving medals at Olympics.

Nov - First "Whole Earth Catalog" published by Stewart Brand.

Nov 5 - Nixon elected President, Spiro T. Agnew, VP. Defeated Humphrey by only half a million votes.

Nov 6 - Student Strike at SF State.

Nov 28 - More than 200 women from 37 states and Canada convene in Chicago for the first national Women's Liberation Conference. Jimi Hendrix performs

The Whole World is Watching!

Chant on the streets of Chicago during the 1968 Democratic Convention, as the police were beating the demonstrators, passersby, and the media, who broadcast it all.

Apparently, there was a planned conspiracy to teach the demonstrators a lesson. On the one hand the protesters were ordered out o the park where they gathered. On the other hand all the streets leading away were blocked by bayonets and machine guns. It's clear the strategy was to surround and beat the shi out of the demonstrators. Firsthand report: indicate the unflinching brutality that wa: meted out not only to the young protesters but also to reporters, cameramen, an passersby. Priests, ministers, and even Allen Ginsberg had come to ensure that the protest were peaceful. But the anger rose as the polic tactics and violence took their toll. Mor demonstrators turned out each day, but eac day they were met by more police an National Guardsmen. It was a police riot tha appeared on TV and was witnessed b millions.

Humphrey lost his presidential bid, n thanks to the way the events in Chicago wer handled. Mayor Daly also faced a lot o fallout, and lost some power. The Yippie an SDS leaders went on trial for conspiracy an inciting riots. The trial became a stage wher Abbie Hoffman and Jerry Rubin satirized th whole hypocrisy. The conspiracy charge were dropped, and the "inciting a riot" convictions were overturned on appeal. Th heavy-handed tactics by law enforcement i Chicago convinced many militant faction that we were at war. They soon adopted mor violent ways, using bombs to get thei message across.

It seems that violence begets violence, an our society is one of the most violent on th planet. Hippies use non-violent means t protest. However it has been shown that whe the use of force is applied to break-up peacefu rotest, the cycle of violence increases on both ides. Apparently the powers that be have earned this lesson to some degree. Thanks o the preponderance of recording devices, nd events like the beating of Rodney King, t's become somewhat easier to see that the erpetrators of violence are brought to justice, egardless of what kind of uniform they wear nd that the victims are compensated.

Woodstock Music and Arts Festival: 1969

The New York State Freeway's closed, man. Far out!
Arlo Guthrie at Woodstock

Possibly the most defining moment of the Hippy Movement was the Woodstock Music Festival, held on Max Yasgur's farm in Bethel, New York on Aug 16, 17 & 18, 1969. Despite organizational problems and major hassles, it lived up to its billing of "Three Days of Peace and Music."

This event marked the peak of the flower power/hippie movement. Prior to Woodstock, here had never been a concert with 70,000 people, much less 500,000. Originally planned to accommodate about 100,000 people, organizers did their best to deal with he growing horde.

Good morning! What we have in mind is breakfast in bed for 400,000.
Wavy Gravy of the Hog Farm

But it was the horde itself, along with a few groups like the Hog Farm and the Merry Pranksters who kept things under control. There were few if any policemen on the site, and surprisingly, they weren't needed! There was no violence either at the festival or in the surrounding communities. No burglaries either. The worse crime seemed to be trespassing, which most people did to get to and from the site.

at New York Philharmonic Hall.
Dec 13 - Vietnam death toll now 30,057 Americans since January 1, 1961.

1969

Jan - Sex education in schools attacked by the John Birch Society, called "communist."

Jan 28 - Santa Barbara, Ca. oil well blowout.

Feb - Massive strike at University of California Berkeley for ethnic studies.

Feb - "The Bitch Manifesto" published by the radical feminist group Redstockings. They sought to raise the consciousness of women.

Feb 11 - 200 students smash computers with axes & set computer center on fire during sit-in protesting professor's racism at St. George Williams College, Montreal.

Feb 13 - 33 students arrested at administration building sit-in at University of Mass.

Feb 18 - Students seize building and boycott started at Howard University.

Feb 24 - Students occupy Administration building at Penn State.

Feb 27 - Police charge student picket lines, club and arrest two Chicano leaders at U.C. Berkeley.

Feb 27 - Thousands rampage through nine buildings at U of Wisconsin, Madison over black enrollments.

Mar 12 - Paul McCartney marries Linda Eastman.

Mar 20 - John & Yoko fly to Gibraltar, get married then fly to Amsterdam for one week "lie-in" for peace.

Mar 20 - James Earl Ray sentenced to 99 years for murder of Martin L. King, Jr.

Apr - 543,000 US troops now in Vietnam.

Apr 4 - Smothers Brothers TV show canceled because it is too controversial.

Apr 9 - 300 Harvard students led by SDS seize University Hall and evict eight deans.

Apr 10 - Police called into Harvard, 37 injured, 200 arrested.

Apr 11 - Start of 3 day student strike at Harvard.

Apr 22 - Harvard faculty votes to create black studies program & give students vote in selection of its faculty.
Apr 22 - City College of NY closed after black & Puerto Rican students lock selves inside asking higher minority enrollment.
Apr 23 - Sirhan Sirhan sentenced to death for murder of Bobby Kennedy.
Apr 24 - U.S. B-52s launch biggest attack on North Vietnam. Protests in 40 cities.
May 15 - Hippies in People's Park in Berkeley attacked by police and National Guard.
July - Stephen Gaskin starts The Farm commune in Tennessee.
July 3 - Brian Jones of Rolling Stones dies.
July 14 - "Easy Rider" movie premieres.
July 20 - Men walk on the Moon. "That's one small step for man, one giant leap for mankind."
July 27 - Police raid on gay bar in Greenwich Village, NYC. Results in Stonewall Uprising. 2000 protesters battle 400 police, start of Gay Liberation Movement.
Aug - Blind Faith forms, with Eric Clapton, Ginger Baker from Cream and Steve Winwood from Traffic.
Aug 9 - Sharon Tate & LaBiancas found murdered by Charles Manson & The Family.
August 15 - 17 Woodstock Music Festival draws 500,000 people gathered for three days of peace and music.
Aug 24 - Movie "Alice's Restaurant" released with Arlo Guthrie.
Aug 26 - FBI reports 98% increase in marijuana arrests from 1966 - 1968.
Sept 3 - Ho Chi Min, leader of North Vietnam, dies.
Sept 24 - Chicago Eight trial begins. Tom Hayden, Abbie Hoffman, Jerry Rubin et. al charged with conspiracy to incite riots.
Oct - Is Paul dead? Beatles controversy.
Oct 8-11 - The Weathermen's "Days of Rage" bombings of corporations.
Oct 21 - Jack Kerouac, beat author of "On the Road" dies.
Oct 30 - Supreme Court orders desegregation nationwide.
Nov 15 - Peace Day, the first Vietnam Moratorium. 500,000 + march in Wash.

We all sang the songs of peace.
Melanie (Lay Down)

The big attraction of course, was an outstanding music event. On the bill were Jimi Hendrix, The Who, Janis Joplin, The Jefferson Airplane, Crosby Stills & Nash (in their second public performance), The Grateful Dead, Santana, Joe Cocker, Ravi Shankar, Richie Havens, Creedence Clearwater Revival and many more popular musicians of the day.

We must be in Heaven!
Wavy Gravy

The flower children didn't let the heat, rain and mud dampen their enthusiasm. Like the organizers, they too were unprepared. Some had to walk 20 miles to get to the site since the N.Y. Thruway was closed. Many didn't bring enough food or drink for three days, and it was nearly impossible for trucks to get to the site to resupply the vendors. To get through, they shared everything, their food, their drink, their drugs, their shelters, even their clothes. They stuck it out, got off on drugs and each other, grooved to some of the best music ever, got lost in space, and found themselves part of a magical moment in the history of a movement.

The people of this country should be proud of these kids
Bethel Chief of Police

Woodstock, like the sixties themselves, can never be repeated again. Attempts to capture the spirit and feeling fall short, leaving us to wonder just what it was about this event and the people involved that made it so special.

Tragedy at Altamont
On December 9, 1969, the Rolling Stones put on a free concert to mark the end of their highly successful American Tour. At the last

minute, the location was changed to Altamont Speedway, a drag strip 40 miles east of San Francisco. The program included Santana, The Jefferson Airplane, Crosby, Stills, Nash and Young, the Flying Burrito Brothers, The Grateful Dead (who decided not to play), and The Rolling Stones.

The poor planning of this event led to some major problems. First, a raceway is not the best venue. Second, the stage was built quickly, and it was low and close to the audience. Last, the Hell's Angels were chosen to provide security and were paid with $500 in beer. When 300,000 people showed for the event, it was very crowded.

The film "Gimme Shelter" documents some critical events at concert. It's clear that the crowd was in an unusual frame of mind for a concert. The happy, smiling beautiful people seemed to be outnumbered (at least near the stage) by zombie like space cadets. The scene was tense as the Angels had their hands full trying to keep people from rushing the stage. Marty Balin of the Jefferson Airplane got in the middle of things and was knocked out by an Angel. The overall vibe wasn't improved when the Rolling Stones took the stage. Their selection of music included violent songs like "Street Fighting Man" and "Sympathy for the Devil."

**And as I watched him on the stage,
My hands were clenched in fists of rage.
No angel born in Hell,
Could break that Satan's spell.
And as the flames climbed high into the night,
To light the sacrificial rite,
I saw Satan laughing with delight,
The day the music died.**
Don McLean (American Pie)

During the Stones' performance, a man started towards the stage waving a gun. The Angels showed no mercy and the man was

DC for peace. Largest antiwar rally in U.S. history. Speakers: McCarthy, McGovern, Coretta King, Dick Gregory, Leonard Bernstein. Singers: Arlo Guthrie, Pete Seeger, Peter, Paul, & Mary, John Denver, Mitch Miller, touring cast of "Hair!." 200,000 protest in San Francisco.

Nov 17 - First round of SALT talks in Helsinki.

Nov 20 - 78 American Indians seize Alcatraz Island and demand its return.

Nov 20 - DDT use banned in residential areas.

Nov 24 - Lt. William Calley charged with murdering 102 So. Vietnamese civilians at My Lai.

Nov 25 - President Nixon orders all US germ warfare stockpiles destroyed.

Dec 1 - First draft lottery since W.W.II held in NYC.

Dec 8 - Raid on Black Panther headquarters in LA - four hour shoot-out.

Dec 24 - Rolling Stones "Altamont" concert erupts in violence, one spectator killed.

1970

January 1 - Nixon signs National Environmental Policy Act (NEPA).

Feb - Timothy Leary sentenced to 10 years for Texas/Mexico border marijuana bust.

Feb 4 - Riot in Isla Vista, Calif. protesting Chicago verdicts.

Feb 4 - President Nixon proposes environmental cleanup and Environmental Protection Agency.

Feb 18 - Chicago Seven acquitted of conspiracy charges.

Feb 19 - Chicago Seven Trial verdict: Dellinger, Davis, Hayden, Hoffman, & Rubin found guilty of crossing state lines to incite riot.

Feb 19 - Explosions in 3 office buildings in NY; and in Calif; Wash; Maryland; Mich; possibly done by the Weathermen.

Feb 25 - Isla Vista, California Bank of America bombed.

Feb 26 - U.S. Army discontinues surveillance of civilian demonstrations and files of demonstrators.

Mar 6 - Three Weathermen blow themselves up by accident in Greenwich

Village, NY.

Apr 1 - Cigarette advertising banned on radio and TV.

Apr 7 - Referring to student unrest, Ronald Reagan, Governor of California says; "If it takes a bloodbath, let's get it over with."

Apr 10 - Paul McCartney announces breakup of Beatles.

Apr 22 - First Earth Day. Millions participate.

Apr 30 - Nixon sends troops into Cambodia.

May 4 - Four college students killed by National Guard at Kent State University, Ohio.

May 5 - Nuclear nonproliferation treaty takes effect.

May 8 - Construction workers attack antiwar demonstrators, Wall St., NY.

May 9 - 100,000 attend antiwar rally, Wash. D.C.

May 14 - Police kill two at Jackson State during violent student demonstrations.

Jun 15 - Supreme Court OKs conscientious objector status on moral grounds.

June 11 - Daniel Berrigan arrested by FBI for kidnapping/bombing conspiracy.

Aug 10 - The Equal Rights Amendment was passed by the U.S. House of Representatives by a vote of 350-15.

Aug 26 - The "Women's Strike for Equality" organized by NOW celebrates the 50th anniversary of the 19th Amendment giving women the right to vote. 50,000 women march on Fifth Avenue in New York and across the country more than 100,000 women were involved in demonstrations and rallies in more than 90 major cities and towns.

Sept 12 - Timothy Leary escapes prison (San Luis Obispo) with help from the Weather Underground, joins Eldridge Cleaver in Algiers.

Sept 18 - Jimi Hendrix dead at age 27.

Oct 4 - Janis Joplin dies.

Oct 13 - Angela Davis arrested on kidnapping, murder and conspiracy charges.

Dec - Paul McCartney sues to dissolve Beatles.

Dec 2 - Environmental Protection Agency (EPA) activated.

killed. Fearing a riot, the Stones continued their set, but left quickly afterwards. Charges against the Angels were dropped, as it was justifiable homicide. The Angels were just doing their job.

The tragedy at Altamont might've been avoided with better planning. Did the fact that it was a "free concert" contribute to events? Were there some "bad" drugs that added to the overall negative vibe? Did the location at a motor speedway make the situation worse. Was it too crowded? Did Altamont mark the end of the innocence for the Love Generation? These questions remain unanswered.

There is no doubt that all the publicity surrounding the concert contributed to the decline in festival type events. Certainly the relationship between the Hell's Angels and the hippies soured.

Kent State Massacre: 1970

Tin soldiers and Nixon coming, we're finally on our own.
Crosby, Stills, Nash & Young (Ohio)

On April 30, 1970, President Nixon announced that he would expand the war by invading Cambodia. This set off campus protests nationwide.

Being the good student activist, I attended one at my school. I remember students getting very angry. I know I felt more emotion than I'd experienced in a long time. Instead of winding down the war, it seemed like we were getting deeper. We had been told for years, that unless we win this war, the evil communist system would spread throughout Southeast Asia. Now it appeared the domino theory was right, but it was the U.S. doing the invading.

What made students mad was the fact that if the war expanded, our chances of getting drafted increased. Also it seemed all our protests for years had been in vain. Nixon and the military machine were going to do whatever they wanted, regardless of how millions of Americans felt.

All protesters should be put into concentration camps.
Ohio Attorney-General Paul Brown

The situation on college campuses was getting serious. But at Kent State University, in Ohio, a series of events led to the calling in of the National Guard. Kent State was actually more conservative than other campuses in Ohio, but the invasion into Cambodia alarmed students everywhere. On May 2 the ROTC building at Kent State was torched. Firemen attempting to control the blaze were stoned, and their hoses slashed. The Guard arrived hours later.

The authorities assumed it was outsiders, particularly the SDS, that were stirring up trouble. There were anonymous threats to the town's water supply and to businesses. Curfews were set and when crowds of students assembled, the Guardsmen were used to break them up. The governor said he would "use any force necessary" to quell the disturbances.

When trouble-makers have long hair, use bad language and go barefoot and even destroy property, they have to be stopped.
Resident of Kent, Ohio after massacre

The students quickly resented the tactics being used against them. They resisted by having sit-ins, yelling obscenities and a few threw rocks at the Guardsmen. Students were roughed up and some were bayoneted. On that fateful May 4, Guardsmen opened fire for 13 seconds killing 4 students and injuring 9 more with 61 bullets. The bloody news was on every newspaper's front page and TV news broadcast, accompanied by the image of a young woman, kneeling over a student

1971

Jan 7 - DDT use outlawed by U.S. Court of Appeals.

Jan 12 - Rev. Philip Berrigan and 5 others indicted for conspiracy to kidnap Henry Kissinger and bomb federal buildings.

Jan 12 - Ralph Nader forms Earth Act group.

Jan 25 - Charles Manson and followers found guilty of murder.

Jan 25 - Supreme Court makes first decision against sexual discrimination in hiring.

Mar 1 - Bomb explodes in Capitol men's room. Weather Underground claims responsibility "in retaliation for the Laos decision."

Mar 1 - U.S. stops licensing commercial whale hunters.

Mar 8 - Supreme Court rules that objection to a particular war is not sufficient grounds for conscientious objection.

Mar 23 - Congress votes to lower voting age to 18.

Mar 29 - Lt. Calley convicted for My Lai massacre.

Mar 29 - Charles Manson, et al sentenced to death after longest trial in Calif. history.

Apr 19 - Over 1000 Veterans demonstrate against the Vietnam war in Wash D.C., throwing their medals over the Capitol fence.

Apr 20 - School busing upheld to end segregation by Supreme Court.

Apr 23 - Vietnam veterans return medals and ribbons in antiwar protest.

Apr 24 - Over 350,000 Veterans march in Wash D.C. and SF to protest war in Vietnam.

Apr 26 - 50,000 demonstrators in Washington D.C., set up "Algonquin Peace City."

May 3-5 - May Day antiwar protest, protesters attempt to shut down Washington D.C. Over 13,000 arrested.

May 11 - Indian occupation of Alcatraz ends after 19 months.

Jun 13 - Pentagon Papers appear in NY Times.

June 30 - The 26th Amendment to the

Constitution ratified, giving 18-year-olds the right to vote as well as kill (Vietnam).

July 3 - Jim Morrison of The Doors dies in Paris.

Nov - Nixon starts withdrawing troops from Vietnam.

Nov 20 - Women's March on Washington D.C. demanding the repeal of abortion and contraception laws and an end to forced sterilization. 2500 show up (25% men).

Dec. - Greenpeace founded in Vancouver, Canada.

1972

Jan 25 - Shirley Chisholm first black woman to run for President.

Feb - Life Magazine states: "Today's high school generation is interested security, stability, & comfort."

Feb 24 - After 16 months in prison, Angela Davis is released.

Feb 28 - President Nixon arrives in China, the first president to ever visit.

Mar 22 - National Commission on Marijuana & Drug Abuse recommends legalization of marijuana.

Mar 22 - Equal Rights Amendment prohibiting sex discrimination passes Senate.

Mar 30 - North Vietnamese launch massive attack. Troops go south through the DMZ into South Vietnam, U.S. resumes bombing.

Apr 10 - Biological Warfare Treaty signed by U.S. and 120 nations.

Apr 15 - President Nixon & Canada P.M. Pierre Trudeau sign pact to clean up Great Lakes.

May 2 - FBI director J. Edgar Hoover dies.

May 9 - President Nixon orders mining of N. Vietnam's ports.

May 15 - Gov. George Wallace shot during primary campaign in Maryland.

May 18 - Margaret Kuhn starts Gray Panthers to protest discrimination against elderly.

May 22 - Nixon makes first U.S. presidential trip to Moscow.

May 26 - U.S. and USSR freeze nuclear weapons at current level.

June 4 - Black activist Angela Davis

bleeding to death, crying. Her anguished faced echoed the feelings of a whole generation pleading and questioning... Why?

More should have been killed.
Resident of Kent, Ohio after massacre

The reaction of students was nationwide. One third of U.S. campuses were involved in America's first student strike. One hundred thousand students marched in Washington D.C. to protest the Kent State shootings and the Vietnam War. On Wall St. in New York construction workers (hardhats) attacked antiwar demonstrators. And 10 days after the Kent State massacre, police at Jackson State killed two students during violent demonstrations.

The four victims did nothing that justified their death. They threw no rocks nor were they politically radical.
Investigation into the Kent State incident

There were many investigations into the shooting, each reaching different conclusions. There were claims by the National Guard that there was a sniper, that they were surrounded, that they were out of tear gas. An FBI investigation found all these claims were baseless (thousands of pages of this report are still classified, and unavailable for public view). A county grand jury whitewashed the event placing all the blame on the students and University administration, and commending the National Guard's actions. Ohio's Governor refused to testify as to his role, though many held him responsible for the tragedy.

Some believe the whole event was a criminal conspiracy that involved many people going way up the federal chain of command. The Nixon Administration's reluctance to investigate, the subsequent conviction of Attorney General John Mitchell for obstructing justice, and Nixon's own

Watergate scandal further support the contention that this was just one more "dirty trick." Some contend that Yale University was originally the target of the lesson, but a refusal by the Chief of Police there to cooperate made them choose Kent State.

An open wound on the American Conscience.
The Christian Science Monitor

The fallout from the massacre deepened the huge divide between generations. The War in Vietnam had found its way into America's heartland. This single event and the judicial, political, and social response highlighted just those very things that students were protesting. The insensitivity towards civil rights, the suppression of legal protest, the resorting to violence on the part of the government, the politicizing of the judicial process, the misuse of power, the cover-ups and conspiracies of corrupt leaders all typified the hypocrisy and lack of ethics in our system.

Eventually a settlement was reached in a civil suit brought against the guardsmen, the Governor and others by the surviving victims and parents of the deceased. An apology was issued. A gymnasium was built on the massacre site despite protests by students and parents of the victims. New rules now define how law enforcement behaves on college campuses and in confrontations with protesters. But really, just how much has changed? Has the system improved, or has it just gotten better at hiding abuses of power?

First Earth Day: 1970

There are no passengers on spaceship earth. We are all crew.
Marshall McLuhan

In 1969, the Santa Barbara oil spill shocked the nation as images of dead seagulls and fish covered in oil splashed across our TV screens and newspapers. In those days no one was

found not guilty of murder, kidnapping and conspiracy charges.
Jun 14 - EPA bans DDT in the USA.
Jun 17 - Watergate Break-In.
Jun 29 - Supreme Court rules state death penalties unconstitutional - cruel and unusual punishment.
July - First Rainbow Gathering in Colorado.
July 1 - Gloria Steinem launches feminist magazine, "Ms."
July 10 - Democratic Convention nominates George McGovern for president of the United States.
Aug 11 - Last U.S. military unit in Vietnam withdrawn.
Aug 18 - Water Pollution Control Act passed by Congress over Nixon's veto.
Aug 21 - Republican National Convention nominates Nixon and Agnew again.
Aug 23 - 1100 antiwar protesters arrested outside Republican National Convention.
Aug 28 - Consumer Product Safety Commission established.
Sept 5 - Arabs kill Israeli athletes at Munich Olympics.
Nov 8 - Nixon re-elected in a landslide. McGovern's complaints about the Watergate break-in ignored.
Nov 13 - U.S. and 90 countries sign International Oceanic Pollution pact.
Dec 18 - Full scale bombing of N. Vietnam resumes.

1973

Jan 27 - Vietnam ceasefire agreement signed after 58,000 U.S. casualties, U.S. military draft ends.
Jan 30 - McCord and Liddy found guilty of Watergate burglary & wiretap attempt.
Feb 28 - 250 American Indians (AIM) occupy Wounded Knee, South Dakota.
Mar 29 - Last American troops withdrawn from Vietnam.
Apr 16 - US bombs Laos.
Apr 30 - Nixon accepts resignation of H.R. Haldeman & John Ehrlichman & fires John Dean. Nixon denies knowledge of break-in or cover-up.
July 20 - Senate subpoenas Watergate tapes.
Oct 10 - Spiro Agnew resigns.
Oct 16 - Kissinger awarded Nobel Peace

Prize.

Oct 23 - Nixon Impeachment begins (note Aug 8!).

Nov - Congress passes "Freedom of Information" act.

Nov 7 - War Powers Act passed over Nixon's veto - requires congressional approval for military actions over 60 days.

Nov 9 - Six Watergate defendants sentenced.

1974

Feb 4 - Patty Hearst, 19, kidnapped by the SLA (Symbionese Liberation Army).

Feb 12 - SLA demands that Randolph Hearst begin food distribution to poor.

Apr 1 - Jane Fonda arrives in Vietnam on second visit.

Apr 15 - Patricia Hearst participates in bank robbery with SLA members.

May 17 - SLA shoot-out in LA.

July 30 - Two articles of impeachment voted against President Nixon.

Aug 8 - Nixon Resigns amid Watergate scandal.

Sept 4 - Nixon pardoned by President Ford.

Sept 7 - CIA operation against Chile's Marxist govt. disclosed.

Sept 16 - President Ford announces conditional pardon for draft evaders and deserters.

Nov 21 - Freedom of Information Act passed over President Ford's veto.

Dec 21 - NY Times reports on CIA illegal domestic activities during Vietnam War.

1975

Apr 17 - Khmer Rouge takes over Cambodia.

Apr 30 - Fall of Saigon. North Vietnamese troops enter Saigon.

Sept 18 - Patty Hearst captured in San Francisco.

Nov 20 - CIA and FBI charged with illegal surveillance of US Citizens and plotting to assassinate foreign leaders.

1976

Feb 12 - Production of Red Dye No. 2 banned.

prepared for oil spills. There was no special equipment to contain the oil, mop it up, clean the beaches, or save the animals. We could only guess at the long-term consequences of such spills. New wells were popping up along the California coast. Suddenly, everyone realized the threat to wildlife, fisheries, and beaches that such development entailed. It was another unfortunate event that focused America's attention on the environment.

Students were already organized to protest the Vietnam War and the draft. So they were the ones to mobilize for a new cause (it really wasn't new, it's just the timing was right). Wisconsin Senator Gaylord Nelson got the idea to organize students and hold environmental teach-ins at schools across the country. Denis Hayes, a Harvard law student was named national coordinator. The first Earth Day took place on April 22, 1970. Twenty million people participated, making it the largest organized demonstration in history.

Look at mother nature on the run in the 1970's.
Neil Young (After the Gold Rush)

I remember in New York City, students were let out of classes early to participate in the many events planned all over the city. They closed Fifth Avenue to cars for the events. 100,000 people showed up for an ecology fair in Union Square. There were demonstrations against polluting companies. Pollution of the land, air and water were primary on the agenda. Some people organized neighborhood clean-ups and planted trees. Congress shut down and folk singer Pete Seeger sang at the Washington Monument. Public speeches, parades, marches, rallies on college campuses, and teach-ins raised awareness of our imperiled ecosystems.

Earth Day got the ecology ball rolling, and by the end of the year the Environmental Protection Agency was established and the Clean Air and Clean Water Acts were passed into law. The momentum continued as new environmental organizations like Greenpeace and Earth First! were created while membership in established conservation groups like the Sierra Club mushroomed.

It is not for him to pride himself who loveth his own country, but rather for him who loveth the whole world. The earth is but one country and mankind its citizens.
Baha'u'llah

In later years we became aware that the problems of the environment are global in scale. Overpopulation, ozone depletion, global warming, deforestation, and species extinction are serious problems we all share. In response Earth Day went international, and on the 20th anniversary in 1990, 200 million people in more than 140 countries participated in events that focused on saving the rainforests, eliminating hazardous wastes, recycling and acid rain.

President Clinton has bestowed the Presidential Medal of Freedom to Gaylord Nelson for his concern and involvement in environmental issues.

1977

May 2 - 2000 members of Clamshell alliance occupy site of nuclear reactor in Seabrook, NH, 1400 arrested.
Jun 6 - Washington Post reports U.S. developing neutron bomb.

1978

Jun 15 - Tellico Dam project in Tennessee halted by snail darter per Endangered Species Act.
July 18 - American Indian Movement (AIM) leads march from Alcatraz to Wash D.C. to protest legislation depriving Indian land rights.

1979

Feb 1 - Patty Hearst released from jail.
Mar 28 - Three Mile Island Radiation Accident.
Sept 23 - 200,000 in NYC for nuclear weapons protest.

1980

Dec 8 - John Lennon murdered outside his apartment entrance in NYC.

1981

May 11 - Bob Marley dies from brain cancer.

1986

Apr 26 - Chernobyl Nuclear accident in Soviet Union.

1995

Aug 9 - Jerry Garcia, RIP, dies at age 53.

1996

May 31 - Timothy Leary's dead or so it seems...

1997

Apr 5 - Allen Ginsberg dies.

1998

Jan 5 - Sonny Bono dies in ski accident.

Hippie Music:
Songs With A Message

Do you believe in rock 'n roll?
Can music save your mortal soul?
Don McLean (American Pie)

Hippies use music to express themselves emotionally, spiritually, and politically. Music can make a statement, give voice to a movement, even unite us. As hippies explore their inner worlds, music guides them along in their quest for meaning. Without drugs it can get you high. With drugs, well, let's just say, music can be a religious experience.

To explain the impact of music as a social phenomenon, we need to go back before the hippies to the Civil Rights Movement. The protesters would sing a song called "We Shall Overcome." The Rev. Wyatt Tee Walker, an associate of Dr. Martin Luther King, Jr., said:

"One cannot describe the vitality and emotion this hymn evokes across the Southland. I have heard it sung in great mass meetings with a thousand voices singing as one. I've heard a half dozen sing it softly behind the bars of the Hinds County Prison in Mississippi. I have heard old women singing it on the way to work in Albany, Ga. I've heard the students singing it as they were being dragged away to jail. It generates power that is indescribable. It manifests a rich legacy of musical literature that serves to keep body and soul together for that better day which is not far off."

So the early sixties saw music becoming more than just entertainment. It was now music with a message. And the messages our poets sang helped us identify with important issues and events that concerned us all. They spurred us to action. These songs had an impact on the consciousness of not just hippies but all society. Some of these songs also broke new ground musically. One way or another they hit us deeply, made us think, made us dream, made us feel as one people.

The musicians listed below were the inspiration for much of the music that has been made since. This includes Heavy Metal, Punk, Disco, Rap, Hip Hop, and Techno. Some of the artists in this list, many of the greatest, devoted the last years of their lives to sharing their music with the world. They touched millions of us, each in a unique way.

Also visit:

Hippyland's Music Page - Links to other great music sites.

Famous Hippy Quotes - Our page of great quotes from the Beats and hippies in music and literature.

Hipplanet's Music Store to buy the music on this page or other great music!

The Musicians & Their Music

 = Recommended CD

 = Hit Song

The Allman Brothers

Greg and Duane Allman, and Dicky Betts could really jam. Their live concerts are the stuff of legend. Their southern rock sound conquered the north as well. Duane's death in a motorcycle accident was a shock, but the band carried on and has scored many hits since.

 Eat a Peach - This recording includes "Melissa," "Blue Sky," and the 33+ minute "Mountain Jam."

 Another great choice is **Live at Fillmore East** with "Whipping Post." This band could really put on a show.

America

America's laid back, easy listening sound won many fans. Their soft acoustic melodies and crisp harmonies put America on the Pop map with tunes like "Horse With No Name," "Ventura Highway" and "Sandman."

Their first album, **America**, was very timely with an American Indian flavored cover, and ran up the charts. Their latest release is called Human Nature (1998).

 History: America's Greatest Hits (1975) has most of their best songs.

The Animals

The Animals were part of the original British Invasion that included the Beatles, The Rolling Stones, Herman's Hermits and the Dave Clark Five. Eric Burdon, the lead singer, is a legend among blues rockers. "House of the Rising Sun" and "We've Gotta Get Out of This Place" are two of their big hits.

 The Best of the Animals - Remastered from mono! - remember that?

The Association

This pop group specialized in upbeat love songs. Their great melodies, tight harmonies, and lively rhythms made them very popular. "Cherish" and "Never My Love" are classic love songs.

 Greatest Hits - This release includes "Cherish," "Windy," "Never My Love," and "Along Comes Mary."

We're more popular than Jesus now;
I don't know which will go first- rock and roll or Christianity.
John Lennon

The Beatles

When the Beatles came to America in 1964 it really was an invasion of new music, style and attitude. They not only turned the music world upside down with their electric guitars, their happy harmonies, long hair and mod fashions, but suddenly music was fun like it hadn't been since Elvis. We boomers couldn't get enough of them, as Beatlemania swept the country.

With fame and fortune theirs, they realized they could do anything, and decided to experiment with new sounds, new electronic techniques, and new drugs. What followed was the most innovative music the world had ever seen. The Beatles got serious about their music and the messages it conveyed. After all they were the biggest band ever and their influence was worldwide.

Credit John Lennon with much of the creative new work and deeper messages. George Harrison took the Beatles on a turn to the East with Ravi Shankar inspired sitar work and philosophical lyrics. Paul McCartney added a much-needed light cheery touch to their music. There's no way we can measure the profound impact of the Beatles on other artists and the course of human history. I don't know a single hippy who didn't love them. As a group the Beatles had their ups and downs, and when they called it quits, no one wanted to believe it. Fortunately their legacy lives on in some of the best music to ever slip through our ears and grace our minds.

She Loves You - (1964) Their first hit single in the U.S., this record is so full of joy, you couldn't help but be happy listening to it. The Beatles' infectious harmonies, their haircuts, their appeal to teenage girls made their first trip to the U.S. to be on the Ed Sullivan show one of the high points of Rock and Roll. Beatlemania was here to stay.

Yesterday - (1966) **Yesterday and Today** The best song Paul McCartney ever wrote (according to John). A melancholy ballad lamenting a lost love, it affected just about everybody.

I Am the Walrus - (1967) **Magical Mystery Tour** Beatles fans debated the meaning of the lyrics in this John Lennon tune. The Beatles were in their most experimental phase in the studio and many of the special sound effects that were to become a Beatle trademark can be heard here. And just what DID the chorus sing at the end of the record?

With A Little Help From My Friends - (1967) **Sgt. Pepper's Lonely Hearts Club Band** Not a drug song! Yeah, and Yoko's the best thing to ever happen to the Beatles. Not! Ringo's singing was fortunately overshadowed by the lyrics and its placement on Sgt. Pepper's Lonely Hearts Club Band. The best version ever done was by Joe Cocker, live at Woodstock!

🎼 **Lucy in the Sky with Diamonds** - (1967) **Sgt. Pepper's Lonely Hearts Club Band** Gee, they couldn't even fool ol' pussy footin' Spiro Agnew into believing it was just about a girl (with Kaleidoscope eyes!). Now we knew just what inspired the Beatles latest creative spurt.

🎼 **Let It Be** - (1970) **Let It Be** Another McCartney hit, supposedly a tribute to his mother, Mary, not a drug song, yeah, right.

💿 **Sgt. Pepper's Lonely Hearts Club Band** - (1967) This landmark concept album marked a transition for the Beatles and everyone who listened to the various stories told therein. This album won the Golden Hippy for best album in Hippyland's Hall of Fame!

Other essentials for the Beatle fans are: **Rubber Soul, Magical Mystery Tour, Abbey Road,** and **The White Album** (named for its white cover). For just the hits try the **1962-1966 (Red Album)** and for the later hits, **1967-1970 (Blue Album)**.

Blind Faith

This short lived group was most notable for the matching of Eric Clapton's virtuoso guitar work with the sensitive vocals of Steve Winwood. Their one album, with the controversial cover of a nude girl fondling a phallic airplane is a classic.

💿 **Blind Faith**. This 1969 release with Eric Clapton, Stevie Winwood, Ginger Baker and Rick Gretch was the only recording this "supergroup" made. "Can't Find My Way Home" is a great tune.

Buffalo Springfield

Buffalo Springfield with Neil Young, Stephen Stills and Richie Furay helped popularize folk rock. Their unique sound, superb harmonies, and socially relevant lyrics were a hit with the hippies. Unfortunately, or fortunately, depending how you look at it, they split up and started CS&N+Y and Poco, which continued to expand the folk/country rock tradition.

🎼 **For What it's Worth** - (1967) **Retrospective: The Best of Buffalo Springfield**. A cautionary tale for those who go up against the system. Retrospective: The Best of Buffalo Springfield Cuts like "Expecting to Fly," "Mr. Soul" and "For What it's Worth" highlight how great this band was.

The Byrds

David Crosby and Roger McGuinn powered this group to the top with "Eight Miles High" and "Turn! Turn! Turn!" Their cover of Dylan's "Mr. Tamborine Man" was also a big hit in 1965.

🎼 **Turn! Turn! Turn!** - (1966) **Turn! Turn! Turn!** Very old lyrics (biblical), with a very timely message written by Pete Seeger.

💿 **The Byrds Greatest Hits** - (1996) A great collection for Byrds fans,

🎵 **Turn! Turn! Turn!** was digitally remastered and includes seven bonus tracks.

Joe Cocker

Joe made his mark at Woodstock '69 with an incredibly soulful version of "A Little Help From My Friends" that blew everyone away. His deep, gravelly voice, and on stage spasms brought the music home to us.

🎵 **Classics** - Joe can really belt out a tune with all his being. He does it here in "A Little Help From My Friends," "She Came In Through The Bathroom Window" and "Midnight Rider." His **Mad Dogs and Englishmen** is one of the all time greats, a two disc set recorded live at the Fillmore East in 1970.

Cream

Ginger Baker, Jack Bruce and Eric Clapton played together for a short time, but their influence lingers today. Their dramatic brand of heavy rock has been imitated by many, but surpassed by none.

🎵 **The Very Best of Cream** This recording contains 20 of Cream's hard rock tunes including "Sunshine of Your Love," "White Room" and "Strange Brew." **Disraeli Gears** is another great recording by Cream.

Creedence Clearwater Revival (CCR)

CCR's fans are legion. Their bayou rock sound crossed over and produced one hit after another.

🎼 **Fortunate Son** - (1969) CCR has had so many hits, but this one hit a nerve, and was used appropriately in Forest Gump's soundtrack. An anti-war/anti-draft song it reflected the sentiment at the time.

🎵 **Cosmo's Factory** - This 1970 album is packed with some of CCR's best material including "Heard it Through the Grapevine," "Lookin' out my Back Door" and "Who'll Stop the Rain?"

🎵 **Chronicle: The 20 Greatest Hits** - This collection has most of their hits including "Proud Mary," "Green River," and "Bad Moon Rising."

Crosby, Stills, Nash & Young (CSNY)

David Crosby, Stephen Stills and Graham Nash teamed up three great singers and songwriters whose harmonies can transport us to another time and place. Their socially relevant lyrics echo within and have inspired many a hippie to take up a cause. They have weathered many a storm (drugs, jail, alcohol, serious illness). They are reuniting again so don't miss their tour!

🎼 **Suite Judy Blue Eyes** - (1969) This was the first song CSN played at Woodstock. It went over very well. Their tight harmonies and excellent song writing scored right from the start.

🎼 **Ohio** - (1971) 4 Way Street "They're cutting us down!" refers to the

1970 Kent State Massacre, wherein four students were murdered by the National Guard.

🎼 **Chicago** - from the same album, is a call to protest at the trial of the Chicago Seven, who were facing charges for conspiracy and inciting a riot at the Democratic Convention in 1968. It's a moving song reminding us we can still "change the world."

💿 **Crosby, Stills & Nash** - Their first album together. A classic! "Suite Judy Blue Eyes," "Marrakech Express," and "Guinnevere" are just the first three cuts from this remarkable debut recording!

💿 **Deja Vu** - The second CSN album, this time with Neil Young. This classic recording includes some of their best tunes like "Carry On," "Teach Your Children" - with Jerry Garcia, "Deja Vu" and "Woodstock."

💿 **4 Way Street** - Crosby, Stills, Nash & Young. This two album live set is a landmark in American music. An outstanding collection of songs about love, hate, war and protest, it is the voice of a generation seeking answers. The unsurpassed live vocal harmonies make this work stand out. Released in 1971, it was updated in 1992 with four more cuts added.

> **Down through all of eternity the crying of humanity,**
> **'tis then when the hurdy gurdy man**
> **comes singing songs of love.**
> Donovan (Hurdy Gurdy Man)

Donovan

Donovan Leitch inspired us with his great music, excellent arrangements, and timely messages about love. His playful, joyful lyrics made us scratch our heads, light the candles and incense, and get mellow. Although his latest work is lacking those elements above, Donovan is still an icon of the Hippy movement.

🎼 **Mellow Yellow** - (1966) Donovan's Greatest Hits This song had thousands of people doing some very weird things with bananas. Some people are still trying to figure it out. I think it was plot by Chiquita to improve sales. By the way, that's Paul McCartney doing the backup vocals.

🎼 **Hurdy Gurdy Man** - (1967) A big hit for Donovan, it's a powerfully haunting song about the man who's "singing songs of love" at a time when it's most needed. John Bonham, John Paul Jones and Jimmy Page (who plays an outrageous screaming guitar lead) appear just prior to the formation of Led Zeppelin.

💿 **Donovan's Greatest Hits** - This is definitely the best selection of Donovan's early hits. It includes "Wear Your Love Like Heaven", "The Hurdy Gurdy Man" and of course "Mellow Yellow."

The Doobie Brothers

Formed in 1970, The Doobies had a number of hits including 'Listen to the Music', 'China Grove', 'Long Train Running', 'Jesus is Just Alright', and 'Takin' it to the Streets' (with Michael McDonald in the group).

Best of the Doobies - A very good collection of their hits, including those mentioned above.

The Doors

Jim Morrison still lives on as a rock icon. His sensuous voice, defiant attitude and iconoclastic lyrics along with Ray Manzarek's great keyboard work propelled the Doors to the top of the charts. Jim defied the authorities, pushing the envelope especially during his live performances. A passionate poet, he touched those most sensitive areas of our collective psyche.

Light My Fire - (1967) **The Best of the Doors** One of the top hits of all time. Who didn't get turned on by Morrison's sexy lyrics? The arrangement of Light My Fire, especially Ray Manzarek's keyboards make this a psychedelic classic.

The Best of the Doors - This two disc set contains the Doors biggest hits including "Light My Fire," "Riders on the Storm" and "L.A. Woman."

Bob Dylan

In the early '60's Bob Dylan transformed folk music into protest music with tunes like "Blowin' in the Wind" and "The Times They Are A-Changin'." These songs influenced a whole generation and just about everyone who calls themself a musician. Bob the poet reminds us that words and music can be a potent force. No one can be unmoved by the urgency and power of his lyrics. Bob's continuing metamorphoses keep everyone guessing what he'll do next.

Blowin' in the Wind - (1963) Bob Dylan's Greatest Hits This early protest song opened people's minds to music with a message. Powerful, direct lyrics + simple folk music + Dylan = a new musical paradigm. This too, became an anthem for the Civil Rights movement. The Times They Are A-Changin' - (1964) Bob Dylan's Greatest Hits Again, Dylan's forceful uncompromising lyrics tell it like it is! This song was prophetic.

Bob Dylan's Greatest Hits. This recording has all his early hits. Another great selection from 1966 is "Blonde on Blonde."

The Eagles

The Eagles currently consist of Don Henley, Glenn Frey, Joe Walsh, Timothy B. Schmit, and Don Felder.

Hell Freezes Over - This recent live recording does justice to all the tunes from the exceptional "Hotel California" to "Take it Easy." If you get a chance, check out their live performance on video. It's exceptional and the band has never sounded better. Another great album is Hotel California.

Emerson, Lake & Palmer

The talented ELP hit it big with their excellent arrangements and style, somewhat similar to the Moody Blues. What set them apart was Keith Emerson's fantastic keyboards and Greg Lake's mood evoking voice.

💿 **Emerson Lake & Palmer** - This, their first album of "pomp" rock from 1970 defines their intense orchestral style with some very fine tunes including "Lucky Man" and "Take A Pebble." Keith Emerson's keyboards and Greg Lake's vocals are timeless. Another good album choice is Tarkus.

The Grateful Dead

The enduring legacy of the Grateful Dead lives on. Jerry Garcia and company are an ongoing phenomena despite Jerry's death and the breakup of the band. The Dead's legions of devoted fans followed them everywhere, incorporating their music into a Hippy lifestyle.

Since the Dead were such an experimental and experiential band (they were involved with the Acid Tests, after all), they managed to carve out their own genre of American music. This is one group where the performance was the message. Many find their music is best enjoyed on psychedelics. The group's hip, laid back attitude was a departure from the ego-centric rock stardom that many pursued.

🎵 **Truckin'** - (1970) **American Beauty** One of the legendary Dead's few commercial hits. Once you got this song in your head, you couldn't get it out, and before you knew it you were a "dead head." The Dead became the epitome of the trippy hippy band. And what a long strange trip they took....

💿 **American Beauty** - This 1970 release showcases the band's song writing and is a perfect introduction. For those who want a brief overview of this prolific band try **Skeletons from the Closet**. For a more in-depth live experience (some of their best live recordings ever), I recommend **Europe '72**. Two more excellent choices are **Workingman's Dead** and **Wake of the Flood**.

The Guess Who

This pop band scored a number of hits, thanks to memorable lyrics, and strong music that echoed in your head over and over. They are now playing the revival circuit.

💿 **The Best of The Guess Who**. Hits include "Laughing," "American Woman," "These Eyes" and "No Time."

Arlo Guthrie

His folk style echoes the music of his famous folk singer father, Woody Guthrie. Arlo made a name for himself with the song and album "Alice's

Restaurant." His appearance at Woodstock included some memorable quotes (included in this book).

The Best of Arlo Guthrie - This recording includes the hits, "Alice's Restaurant," "The City of New Orleans" and "Coming into Los Angeles."

George Harrison

George was responsible for bringing the eastern influence into the Beatles. He got them to meditate with the Marharishi, use sitar in their recordings, and gave the group a more spiritual focus. George has been active in many causes including the Concert for Bangladesh which tried to raise funds for the flood victims.

All Things Must Pass - George's first solo effort after the Beatles broke up is an excellent overview of his philosophy. The song My Sweet Lord caused George a lot of grief as the chord progression was similar to another old song (He's So Fine), and George had to go to court and lost in a precedent setting case for copyright law.

Richie Havens

Richie opened Woodstock with his songs "Handsome Johnny" (an antiwar song) and "Freedom" (a civil rights tune). His unique style of rhythm guitar complements his deep resonant voice resulting in a powerful sound. With his intensity, Richie Havens can ignite your soul with his original songs or famous covers. From Woodstock to the present Richie still delivers music with a passion.

Resume - The Best of Richie Havens. All his classic tunes are here to enjoy.

Jimi Hendrix

Jimi Hendrix was one of those rare talents that appears once in a lifetime. Like a saint he walked among us to remind us that there are greater things than we can possibly understand. Through his music he let us hear and see these wondrous things. Whether in the studio, at Woodstock, Monterey, the Isle of Wight or the Fillmore, Jimi fed his heart and soul into his music. The result was music that could lift you so high you could "Kiss the Sky" or plunge you into a "Manic Depression." His influence on rock music was profound. Jimi's legend lives on now that some new releases are out.

Purple Haze - (1967) **Are You Experienced?** You ran right out and bought the record, **Are You Experienced?** Then you rushed home, put it on the turntable, and this was the first song you heard. What went through your mind? All of a sudden music was REALLY GROOVY, man!

Are You Experienced? This 1967 recording captured Jimi's best known works. The legendary guitarist/composer exposes his raw psychedelic talent on everything from "Purple Haze" to "Foxey Lady." Another good recording is **Electric Ladyland**.

🎵 **Jimi Hendrix - Live At The Fillmore East** It's a new double album of two concerts recorded at the Fillmore, New Year's Eve, 1969 and New Year's Day, 1970. Jimi was in turmoil, and these performances were his catharsis.

🎵 **Experience Hendrix: The Best Of Jimi Hendrix.** Yet another new release captures his greatest hits. This may be the best collection yet on one CD.

🎵 **Live At Woodstock** [2 CD-BOX SET] - This latest release contains 16 tunes from Jimi's performance at Woodstock. Not his best since he was reforming his band and the other instruments aren't clear in the mix, but as usual, Jimi shines! A must for fans.

It's A Beautiful Day

The LaFlammes put out several albums and ended up in an interminable lawsuit with their original manager (it's still on). Thus they have never made anything from their albums. That said, their first release, It's a Beautiful Day is a classic from the '60s.

🎵 **It's A Beautiful Day** - This album has become very famous due to it's scarcity. At one time a good copy would fetch about $60. The best cut, "White Bird," really grooves thanks to the blazing violin. Other good tunes are "Hot Summer Day," "Bombay Calling" and "Wasted Union Blues."

Jefferson Airplane

Grace Slick, Marty Balin, Paul Kantner, Jorma Koukonen and Jack Cassady had a sound that typified the psychedelic music from San Francisco. Grace's soaring vocals, Marty's sensitive lyrics, and the rest of the bands' electric energy turned on Frisco and the rest of the world. The band has had numerous incarnations with various members such as Hot Tuna and Jefferson Starship, but the original is still the greatest. They played at Monterey Pop, Woodstock, Altamont (tried to, until Marty got punched out by a Hell's Angel) and many Fillmore and Winterland shows.

🎼 **Somebody to Love** - (1967) **Surrealistic Pillow** The first hit off their Surrealistic Pillow album. When Grace Slick belted this song out, we all knew just what she meant.

🎼 **White Rabbit** - (1967) **Surrealistic Pillow** This song, with references to Lewis Carroll's Alice in Wonderland and certain drugs, got us high just listening to it. Feed Your Head!

🎵 **Surrealistic Pillow** - The Airplane first landed on the San Francisco music scene in 1966, and with this 1967 album (their second) took the country by storm. "Somebody to Love" and "White Rabbit" became instant classics. Another great album from the Airplane is Volunteers. For all you fans there's a new release, Live at the Fillmore East (1998) which showcases their legendary onstage energy.

Jethro Tull

Propelled by Ian Anderson's dramatic flute and eccentric lyrics, Tull brought a fresh edge to rock and distinguishes this band from others of the period. Jethro Tull's powerful portrait of a social reject, "Aqualung," hit you in the gut! It was an early cross of heavy metal and grunge. The whole record was a great social statement.

Aqualung - (1971) **Aqualung** The big hit that made Jethro Tull famous. A biting comment on social misfits.

Aqualung - Released in 1971 this record went to the top. The subsequent album, "Living in the Past" (1972) showed a mellower side of Tull.

Janis Joplin

No one sang the blues like Janis. She could put more feeling into one song, than many people put into their whole lives. We feel your pain, Janis!

Piece of My Heart - (1968) **Cheap Thrills** with Brother & The Holding Company or **Janis Joplin's Greatest Hits** Janis rips through this one like a tortured feline.

Janis Joplin's Greatest Hits. This album has a good selection of hits. For a more complete selection there's a three-CD set, Cheap Thrills/ I Got Dem Ol' Kosmic Blues Again Mama!/Pearl. Big Brother & The Holding Company (with Janis Joplin of course!) This is their first major album with a classic cover from R. Crumb. "Piece of My Heart," "Summertime" and "Ball and Chain" are as gritty as Janis gets.

Carole King

Carole is one of the most prolific and successful songwriters in history. Her tunes were sung by many popular stars. Her music always has an emotional storytelling that captures you.

Tapestry - (1971) One of the best-selling records of all time, **Tapestry** showcases Carole's gift of songwriting. For something more complete try **Carole King Natural Woman-Ode Collection** including many songs written for artists like James Taylor and Aretha Franklin.

King Crimson

In The Court Of The Crimson King - Originally released in 1969, this famous album features Greg Lake singing and the guitar work of Robert Fripp. For a taste of the band's new work (minus Lake) check out their 1998 release, **Absent Lovers-Live In Montreal**.

Led Zeppelin

Led Zeppelin defined heavy metal music. The hard rockin' blues of Robert Plant and Jimmy Page and their live concerts are the stuff of legends. Plant's extraordinary vocal range and Jimmy's mastery of the guitar are a great combination. Exotic influences permeate their sound sending us back in time to distant lands. If you get a chance check out their movie "The Song Remains the Same" to see their remarkable live performance.

🎼 **Stairway to Heaven** - (1971) **Led Zeppelin IV** One of the biggest hits ever! This song by the heavy metal band took everyone by surprise by being so mellow, then building to one of the great climaxes in music. Plant and Page at their best!

💿 **Led Zeppelin IV** This album marks the pinnacle of Led Zeppelin's career. With "Stairway to Heaven" the band scored it's biggest hit. The **Remasters** collection has all their hits sounding better than ever.

John Lennon

John's legacy and his inspired songwriting lives on in some new releases. Lennon's influence goes far beyond his music, as we've all been touched by his magic and spirit.

🎼 **Imagine** - (1971) **Imagine** or **Lennon Legend - The Very Best of John Lennon**. This song sums up John's philosophy. Just imagine if John's dreams came true...

💿 **Lennon Legend - The Very Best of John Lennon**. This recording includes all his post-Beatles hits. An excellent collection. Perhaps a better choice than the **John Lennon Anthology**.

Loggins & Messina

Kenny Loggins and Jim Messina struck up a great friendship in the early '70s. Their excellent harmonies and songwriting highlight the few recordings they did together.

💿 **Sittin' In** - (1972). This upbeat album shines thanks to great songs and good vocal harmonies on tunes like "Vahevalla," "Back to Georgia" and "Nobody Like You."

The Lovin' Spoonful

Led by John Sebastian, this group had many hippie hits in the '60s.

💿 **Anthology** - The Lovin' Spoonful includes "Do You Believe in Magic?" "Daydream" and "Summer in the City."

The Mamas and the Papas

John Phillips led this band of trippy hippies to stardom. With Cass Elliot, Denny Doherty, and Michelle Phillips they cranked out hit after hit. Super songwriting (John) and tight harmonies were sometimes happy, sometimes sad. Their autobiographical music told of their ups and downs, lives and loves, and we loved them for it.

🎼 **California Dreamin'** - (1966) **If You Can Believe Your Eyes and**

Ears We'll probably never know how many people went to California after hearing this song. I know I did!

🎧 **If You Can Believe Your Eyes and Ears** This 1966 classic has "Monday, Monday" and "California Dreamin'." If you want even more check out their **Greatest Hits** for 20 great tunes.

Bob Marley & the Wailers

Bob Marley introduced the world to Reggae music and Rastafari. His heartfelt music spoke volumes about injustice, freedom, and love. One of the great heroes of the common man, Marley has influenced musicians and free thinkers around the world.

🎼 **I Shot the Sheriff** - (1973) **Burnin'** or **Legend** This hit song (Eric Clapton's version) opened up the world for Reggae music, and Bob Marley. Typically, the subject is injustice.

🎧 **Legend** - This album showcases the King of Reggae's biggest hits. Whether singing about Love or Protest, Bob's funky soulful sound is always spiritually satisfying.

Paul McCartney

Paul's pop musical style doesn't appeal to everyone, but his good natured upbeat tunes usually make us smile.

🎧 **Ram** - (1971) Paul's best solo album has some good cuts including "Too Many People" and "Uncle Albert/Admiral Halsey." **Band on the Run**, (1973) with Wings, is another good choice.

Joni Mitchell

One of the original folk singers, Canadian Joni has explored other musical styles with great success. Her vocal range, excellent guitar playing and sometimes cynical lyrics make her a outstanding performer.

🎼 **Woodstock** - This tune, popularized by CS&N, pretty well summed up the event and the feelings of a whole generation.

🎧 **Blue** - Released in 1971 this great album has Stephen Stills and James Taylor on some tracks. From the love ballads here to jazz and rock Mitchell explores various styles with her unique vocals. Her latest, **Taming the Tiger** focuses on her jazz guitar and synth playing and is reminiscent of some of her best work. Two other great albums by Joni are **Clouds** and **The Hissing of Summer Lawns**.

The Moody Blues

Ever since their second album, **Days of Future Past** (their first had different band members), the Moodies captured our imagination with lush orchestrations, magnificent moog synthesizer, deep inspirational lyrics, wonderful melodies, and moving vocals. Their extraordinarily loyal and devoted fans still regard them as psychedelic rock legends, and I'm definitely one!

🎵 **Nights in White Satin** - (1967) Days of Future Past. Justin Hayward's haunting vocals highlight this song.

💿 **Time Traveler** - The Moody Blues. This five CD set covers the Moodies' extraordinary journey through time and innerspace, from **Days of Future Past** (1967) to **Keys to the Kingdom** (1991). Fortunately, they managed to keep together some of the more dramatic segues from their early albums. A must for those who don't have all the albums yet.

💿 **Days of Future Past** was one of the first concept albums with smooth segues between tunes (like "Sgt. Pepper"). The Moodies succeeded big time by blending their form of introspective rock with classical music, thanks to the London Festival Orchestra.

The Moodies' early stuff is their best including: **On the Threshold of A Dream, In Search of the Lost Chord, Every Good Boy Deserves Favor, To Our Children's Children's Children**.

1967

Rock 'n Roll's greatest year!

1967 brought to our attention such phenomenal artists as Jimi Hendrix, Janis Joplin, The Jefferson Airplane, The Grateful Dead, The Doors and The Moody Blues. The psychedelic San Francisco sound and the spread of LSD opened minds everywhere to new possibilities. Concept albums like **Sgt. Pepper** had us leaving our turntables on 33 instead of 45. Concerts like Monterey Pop were huge happenings where the audience was part of the show. Then there was the Summer of Love.... To be alive and part of this scene was something very special. It forever changed the face of music, society and our lives.

Van Morrison

This soulful crooner real packs a wallop when he wants to. He's scoring big with his new album.

💿 **Moondance** - The master of R&B romance scores on this one with "Moondance," "Crazy Love" and "Into the Mystic." Van Morrison was the inspiration for the movie "The Commitments."

💿 **Back On Top** - Morrison does it again with this hit album that harkens back to his '70s magic. A must buy for fans and those who love good R&B music.

The New Riders of the Purple Sage

NRPS rode to stardom with their laid-back country rock style with echoes of the Grateful Dead.

New Riders of the Purple Sage. This 1971 release includes backup work by Jerry Garcia, Spencer Dryden, Mickey Hart and Commander Cody. Their brand of mellow country/rock is highlighted in "Glendale Train" and "Louisiana Lady." The **Adventures of Panama Red** is another good recording from NRPS.

Peter, Paul & Mary

These aging Beats, along with Pete Seeger and Woody Guthrie were responsible for popularizing folk music in middle America. Their beautiful harmonies made us listen to the subtle messages of peace and freedom in the lyrics.

Puff the Magic Dragon - (1963) A drug song or a fairy tale? Depends on who's listening. After all Jackie Paper needs his friend Puff to have fun, and don't forget the sealing wax Jackie! This is still a popular children's song.

Where Have All The Flowers Gone? - Pete Seeger/Peter, Paul & Mary (1962) Includes songs that we baby boomers sang in school like "This Land is Your Land" and "If I Had a Hammer." These tunes put subtle yet influential messages in our virgin brains, whose seeds would bear fruit in our teenage years.

Around the Campfire - Yup, they're still around and this new album has lots of their old hits and four new recordings. You can gather "round the fire" with your kids (grandkids?) and sing along to "Puff the Magic Dragon" and "Leavin' on a Jet Plane."

Pink Floyd

I remember my friend Floyd trying to get us to listen to an album by Pink Floyd. We looked at the Pink cover, then at him and laughed (he was a little weird after all). Well, Floyd had the last laugh as we all became addicted to the hallucinogenic band called Pink Floyd. Their psychedelic leanings were evident in the early albums, but really peaked with **Dark Side of the Moon** and **Wish You Were Here**. Despite the band's break up, both David Gilmour and Roger Waters are still touring (separately), and packing in the legions who love to fly comfortably numb.

Time - (1973) Alan Parsons produced the album **Dark Side of the Moon** and all it's sound effects. This record stayed on the charts for an amazing 14 years! "Time" is one of the more compelling pieces, lamenting it's passage and aging. The opening sequence of clocks chiming is classic.

Dark Side of the Moon - This incredible album still gets lots of play on the airwaves. Their mastery of the electronic milieu is at its finest here. Today, as in 1973 this recording has messages for us all. For a taste of the Floyd live, you must check out **Pulse** available on CD and Video (VHS and laserdisk). Some of the tunes here are better than the originals, and the video is outstanding.

Poco

This underrated group still has many fans. Their upbeat country rock was highlighted by Rusty Young's pedal steel guitar, along with Jim Messina, Richie Furay, and Timothy B. Schmit's great harmonies.

The Forgotten Trail 1969-74 - This 2 CD set contains 38 cuts both live and studio and a 36 page book. Poco is a great country rock band and this recording covers all their hits including "Kind Woman," "A Good Feeling to Know" and "Pickin' up the Pieces."

Procol Harum

This band had a couple of great hits, then faded. Fortunately they're back with a new recording, that makes it seem like they never left!

The Best of Procol Harum (1973). This album contains their hits "Whiter Shade of Pale" and "Conquistador." Their latest release, **Prodigal Stranger** (1991) is much like their old stuff.

The Rascals

This group was very popular, and had a number of classic hippie hits.

The Very Best of the Rascals. The Rascals had some big hits in the '60s and '70s including "Groovin'," "Good Lovin'" and "A Beautiful Morning," all of which are included here.

The Rolling Stones

Since 1964, The Stones always seemed to be the best music to play at a party. Their infectious tunes got everyone up and dancing. The lack of current hits hasn't hurt their popularity any. As long as Mick, Keith and Charlie can still stand I guess we'll have more to look forward to.

Satisfaction - (1965) **Hot Rocks 1964-1971** This song of social angst hit our collective button, and gave the Stones one of their greatest hits.

Flowers - (1967). Digitally remastered, this early work with Brian Jones contains the hits "Ruby Tuesday," "Lady Jane" and "Mother's Little Helpers." Another blast from the past is the 1970 **Get Yer Ya-Ya's Out!**, their best live album.

Hot Rocks 1964-1971 - This collection of hits from their early period has everything. "Satisfaction," "Jumpin' Jack Flash," "Ruby Tuesday," "Sympathy for the Devil" and lots more!

Santana

Carlos Santana and company managed to define a whole genre back in the early '70s. His great performance at Woodstock made him a legend. And today he's back on the charts with a new hit. Santana's pioneering funky, latin, soul, rock sound is unmistakable. Carlos' mesmerizing lead guitar playing is your ticket to nirvana. It's nearly impossible to sit through this music. Dance, sister dance!

🎼 **Black Magic Woman** - (1970) **The Best of Santana** This song was their greatest hit. We couldn't stop dancing while Carlos Santana's scorching riffs burned into our brains. There have been many imitators, but no band ever did it better.

🎵 **Abraxas** - (1970) "Black Magic Woman," "Oye Como Va" and "Hope You're Feeling Better" are just some of the great cuts on this album. Carlos Santana's guitar work is electric and the beat is sensual. This mix of rockin' salsa is outstanding.

🎵 **The Best of Santana**. This new release showcases the bands forays into Latin/Jazz/Rock fusion. The early hits like "Oye Como Va" and "Black Magic Woman" are highlighted making this a great introduction to the band's tight funky sound.

Simon & Garfunkel

Paul Simon and Art Garfunkel made some beautiful music together. Their sensitive harmonies made us feel sensitive too. Simon's great songwriting talent produced hit after hit. Excellent melodies and interesting arrangements highlight their music.

🎵 **Old Friends** - This 1997 release went back to the old masters and sounds great! All their hits are here in this three-CD set. If you don't already have their old albums, this is a good way to get caught up. **Bookends** and the soundtrack from **The Graduate** are two other good recordings.

Sly and the Family Stone

Sly Stone embodied the upbeat, funkadelic sound that was widely copied by many. His very lively performances made him a legend. Sly's soul funk and his personal style influenced many a disco performer. "I Want to Take You Higher" is one of his best long live songs.

🎼 **Dance to the Music** - (1968) **Greatest Hits** This funky tune was the precursor to Disco music.

🎵 **Greatest Hits** - Sly and the Family Stone. This collection of great music from 1970 makes you want to get up and "Dance to the Music!"

Steppenwolf

Steppenwolf coined the term "Heavy Metal" and their sound was intense psychedelic rock.

🎵 **Born to Be Wild** - (1968) **20th Century Masters: The Best Of Steppenwolf** As the lead song on the soundtrack to Easy Rider this was sure to be a hit. It captures the spirit of the open road, freedom, and bikers. This song also was responsible for the term "Heavy Metal" as in "heavy metal thunder..."

🎵 **20th Century Masters: The Best Of Steppenwolf** Hits include: "Born to Be Wild," "Magic Carpet Ride" and "It's Never Too Late."

Cat Stevens

Cat Stevens' voice resonated somewhere deep within us. He kept us hanging on every word he sang. Few artists have ever been able to convey their feelings so dynamically. I can't help but feel we have lost him just as we lost our other great hippie icons, suddenly, never to return. He was not the only sensitive artist to reject the call to superstardom, but he turned his back on all his fans. Since the '80s, he has devoted his life to Islam, and our loss is their gain.

🎵 **Tea for the Tillerman** - This group of songs represents his best effort. They include "Father and Son," "Where do the Children Play," and "Hard Headed Woman." His **Greatest Hits** album includes "Peacetrain" and "Moonshadow."

Three Dog Night

This pop band had many hits and is still touring, much to the delight of their aging fans.

🎵 **The Best of Three Dog Night**. The hits came easily to this band including "Joy to the World," "Shambala," "Eli's Coming" and "One."

The Who

Pete Townsend, Roger Daltry, Keith Moon and John Entwistle entered my consciousness with the song "I Can See for Miles and Miles." Just like the song, the Who faded, only to return again much more triumphantly. The Who's legendary presence onstage was nowhere better than at the ill fated Isle of Wight Festival where they performed the entire **Tommy** rock opera among other tunes.

🎵 **Won't Get Fooled Again** - (1971) **Who's Next** A great synth riff, Keith Moon's driving beat, Pete Townsend's politically inspired lyrics, and a thunderous finale make this a true rock anthem.

🎵 **Who's Next** - One of the greatest rock albums of all time, and the Who's only #1 record. It has some of their best work, like "Baba O'Reilly," "Behind Blue Eyes" and "Won't Get Fooled Again." Full of existential and political messages, this 1971 release was remastered in 1995 with added tracks. **Tommy**, their famous rock opera (and movie) has several versions.

Yes

Yes consists of Jon Anderson, Rick Wakeman, Chris Squire and Steve Howe. This is another group that's back on tour again, with a new album, **The Ladder**.

Fragile - This 1972 recording was remastered and highlights Yes' dramatic rock style. "Roundabout" and "Long Distance Runaround" are two hits from this album. Their recent release, **Open Your Eyes** (1997) brought together the original band members.

Neil Young

This Canadian musician got his big break writing and singing with Buffalo Springfield. His popularity soared when he teamed up with Crosby, Stills & Nash. Neil went on to produce his own great solo recordings including **After the Gold Rush** and **Harvest**. Neil's style ranges from hard rock, blues, folk ballads to country. His heavy rock is credited with inspiring grunge music.

After the Gold Rush - On this 1970 solo album Neil Young sings "Tell Me Why," "Don't Let It Bring You Down" and "Southern Man." For a great live recording check out his **Unplugged** album. Neil's **Zuma** with Crazy Horse is really spacey.

Frank Zappa

Zappa's original group The Mother's of Invention's first album, entitled "Freak Out" was very popular and way out, even for it's time. Zappa's music was a very wild, creative satire on society. Remarking on Zappa's creative genius, one of his band members once said that Zappa would first make beautiful music, then turn it ugly (dissonant). Zappa coined many expressions and became a icon of the lack of respect for the establishment. A popular college poster from the '60's showed Zappa with his long, wild and stringy hair sitting naked on a toilet. The title was "Frank Zappa Crappa."

Freak Out! - Frank Zappa and the Mothers of Invention. The band's first album released in 1966 is still a monument to Zappa's satirical anarchy. A good place to start with Zappa.

Hippie Havens

The following is a list of places where there exists a sizable hippy population, where there is tolerance towards hippies, where hippies are free to pursue their lifestyle with community support. Whether you're looking to visit or relocate, you can be sure there'll be places to stay, interesting things to see and do, and lots of other hippies in these places. Since most of these were posted on the site by visitors to Hippyland, I cannot guarantee the accuracy of each report. You should check into these places more before visiting and certainly before moving here! If you know of any other places to add to this list please write to us - havens@hippy.com.

USA - Alabama

"We've got lots of forests in North Alabama and sometimes a group called the Rainbow People come to Mount Cheaha and harmonize with nature. There are a great number of hippies living in the Calhoun County area; mainly in Anniston, Oxford and Jacksonville, Alabama. If any hippies need somewhere to move to, come on to Alabama. We have plenty of room and the people of our land don't care what you look like."

Alaska

"After spending the past few summers in the wonderful state of Alaska, I must let you know that the entire state is a great place to be. All summer long there are bluegrass shows, festivals and trips to be taken. Whether you are into the Matanuska Thunderfuck, fruity pebbles, or any of the other delectables of the state, or just hitching around to see the land, you surely are welcome no matter what you are. I've had more amazing experiences in Alaska than I could ever imagine. My boyfriend and I hitched over a thousand miles to Homer. We had no problems getting a ride. Jerry's twin (right down to the nubby fingers) picked us up and let us camp in his front yard, fed us strawberry daiquiris and smoked all night. Let everyone know that Alaska is only part of the US because of it's government and monetary units. Go and visit, you may never come back :)"

Delta Junction, Alaska - according to a contributor is the "highest per capita weed smokin' community - about 85% of the town here does!"

Homer, Alaska - Located on the southern tip of the Kenai Peninsula it's FULL of people living as they wish. Some in schoolbuses, some in cabins, many w/o running water, electricity or with all the amenities, but their hearts are full. There are people living off the grid and the entire town is geared toward spirituality. The town of Homer has been called for many years, "the cosmic hamlet by the sea." Check out available web sites...although most of those are geared toward tourists. Do the bay...you will find many interesting people living a conscious, purposeful life.

Matanuska Valley, Alaska - Here grows the wonderful Matanuska Thunder Fuck, people all over the country who have tried Alaskan weed beg for more of this! Many laid back hippies moved to Alaska because marijuana was legal until 1990.

Arizona

Bisbee, Arizona - This small community really flourished when the mining-company which owned the town bailed out in the mid-seventies and hippies from all over moved in. There is a great community here, with a co-op and lots of hippy artists living out in the desert. Check it out for yourself! Have a brew and a few games of nine ball at the Bisbee Grand, or play hacky sack in the grassy park in front of the mining museum right in downtown.

Flagstaff, Arizona - A large community or family of hippies came here for the diversity of "the kind" and other "party favors." With the San Francisco Peaks and Sedona only twenty minutes away the opportunities for adventure are endless.

Prescott, Arizona - The home of Prescott University. You will find a large number of artists, mountain bikers, hikers, and outdoorsmen in this town, along with communes galore. Dancing circles of hippies beating drums and enjoying life in the middle of the wilderness are seen on mountain tops near here. People tell me that the university here is one of the most open-minded in the world, and it offers a variety of alternative majors (mountain climbing, kayaking, etc.) and the majority of students are studying from abroad.

Sedona, Arizona - A hippie haven since before the Harmonic Convergence, this little town grew way too big and unfortunately allowed McDonald's and other chains to destroy the charm. They say the vortexes are still there, humming in the mountains and sacred secret places.

Tempe, Arizona - A visitor wrote us that "Every Sunday there is a gathering of kind brothers and sisters in Tempe at the Sail Inn. We have been getting together for about two years for an afternoon of kind vibes with the incredible Grateful Dead cover band Noodles. They play from 4:20 till? If you're ever in town, we would love to have you join us. Hope to see ya sometime."

Tucson, Arizona - Home to the University of Arizona and a large hippy population, Tucson is happening! 4th Avenue and Congress St. are groovy hangouts with lots of cool shops, cafes and clubs. 4th Avenue occasionally gets transformed into a huge Art Festival. There's usually some good music around town, plus the nice climate and cheap smoke keeps everybody groovin'! That's why some call it "TooStoned."

California

Arcata, California - "This is the best place to go if you're a hippie.. well, besides the Haight-Ashbury. It's located in Humboldt County, which is pretty well-known for it's marijuana growing. The community is great, there are always festivals going on about the earth, such as the Mushroom Fair, the Hemp Festival, North Country Fair, everything you can imagine. I love it here! The people are so supportive of you.. they've even made a law which states that women can indeed go topless around the plaza in the centre of town. ;)

Arcata is a totally unreal place to check out and LIVE too! The rents are cheap and it seems everyone is way laid back, with Humboldt next door and being amongst the greatest redwoods in the world, how can you go wrong!"

Humboldt, California - "I Personally Don't Think You Emphasized how Many Hippies And How Much Ganja There really Is Out in Humboldt, Humboldt Is Like One Of The Main Places. We are the center of the "emerald triangle.".. need I say more?"

Mt. Shasta, California - "One of the most sacred places on earth. Everyone is so totally kind. The mountain pours out its love and watches over all its inhabitants. It snows for days in the winter, but in the summer I go live in the woods and draw off the healing energies. Another kind thing is that the cops realize that hippies are really laid back and we do a lot for the community and keep it beautiful, therefore we all do well living in harmony."

San Diego, California - San Diego has the perfect climate, and hippies congregate around Ocean Beach and Encinitas. Laid back mixture of surfers and hippies make for a cool scene. Check out The Black a famous headshop in O.B. O.B. also has a fabulous food co-op, a crystal store, a metaphysical/wiccan shop and an excellent herbstore (In Harmony Herbs & Spices). Don't forget "Blacks Beach every full moon at 8:00 p.m."

San Francisco, California - Some people say the Haight-Asbury and Berkeley areas are still happening, others say no. The Haight is the place where it all began in the Summer of Love, 1967 and now it's a great stop for a nostalgia rush.

Santa Cruz, California - "I'm not sure there is really a large population of hippies IN Santa Cruz—it's kind of a melting pot of all types of people—but if you're looking for some really beautiful scenery, kind people, and totally peaceful chillin', head to one of the towns a little bit north of Santa Cruz. Felton, Boulder Creek, Bonny Doon...it's way mellow there, and everyone's basically into mother nature and their brothers and sisters. It's also real close to the ocean. It's one of the prettiest areas you can imagine...head there on your travels. You won't be sorry!"

Venice Beach, California - every Sunday people get together and form a drum circle. "It's a hippie haven and it lasts until sunset. Come visit us!"

Colorado

Boulder, Colorado - "As one who has lived in and visited Boulder, CO over the years, I must warn everybody not to judge a book by it's cover. Sure, Boulder is a very hip & fun town, but times are changing. Due to an ever-increasing influx of hippies, Deadheads, Phishheads, etc., the local law enforcement has been cracking down on the free-spirited mentality of our lifestyle. I have personally witnessed numerous human rights violations & unnecessary arrests all stemming from pressure by the local government & Boulder residents to "clean up the town."

Nederland, Colorado - 17 miles west, up the canyon from Boulder. This town has old to young hippies from all over the country. Very awesome music scene for a little mountain town (Leftover Salmon, etc...). "Majical place." "Very kind in many ways."

Connecticut

Ellington, Connecticut. "Because, like there's a lot of hippies here - it's a real trip man."

Delaware

Newark, Delaware - this place is the home of the University of Delaware "Tons of hippies here. Most live on Madison which consists of apartment, townhouses and this friendly group is very intelligent and KIND."

Florida

Orlando, Florida - "Gainesville is not all the bomb that you say it is. it is not the "hippy capital" of phlorida. there are kydz there cause there is a college that's it. just a college. if there were no college, the town would be non-existent. there are some nice kydz there, but no family. they have some good shows maybe once a month. i live in Orlando. it is mofuckin awesome! i have lived in many places and for about 6 mos. in different places in phlorida. The "hippy capital" is definitely St. Augustine. SUCH A fabulous family!! there's a beach, there's plenty of places to sell crafts on the street all year round. there's tons of cool shit like an old fort that you can trip around in and plenty of kynd folks. not much of a nightlife unfortunately. They never have big name bands. Orlando on the other hand is a mecca. we get awesome shows here pretty regularly. we've got the house of blues, we've got a university, we're an hour from the beach, an hour from Daytona Beach, not much further from Gainesville, a little less from St Augustine. we've got the big ekon river. two drum circles every week. we've got the Orlando family. we've got the hippy hole."

Key West, Florida - "Despite the commercialism, the boat people and street performers, still living the good life. The town is tolerant of long hairs and pot is available from Jamaica. Love the town but there are some drawbacks."

Georgia

Atlanta, Georgia - "There is a certain area in Atlanta that is known as Mid-town which houses an area known as Little Five Points. This is truly the hippie haven of the south - or at least Georgia. In this little portion of town there are many body art and vintage shops, including a favorite of the locals called Groovy Girls. Other odds and ends are sold around here such as African drums, futons, and crystals. Just like the goods that are sold here, the people are an assorted mixture as well. New age Flower Children, aging Flower Children, skateboard-ers, and Rastafarians line the streets daily. Drum circles are common practices here. Little Five Points and the nearby Piedmont Park also host the Pot Festival every year."

Hawaii

Big Island and Kauai - "Lots of growers here. Scene is low key and laid back. Communes around. On Big Island, the hippies are all in the Puna District mainly in the Pahoa area from Kalapana to Pahoa and from Pahoa over to Volcano."

Maui, Hawaii - Maui is Paradise! It's still full of hippies living on the slopes of Haleakela, the dormant volcano, in places like Kipahulu, Kula, Hana, Paia. Little McKenna Beach is THE place for nude sunbathing and drum circles. You'll need a few gold cards to visit here, this scene is expensive. Don't forget to try the Maui Wowie!

Idaho

Moscow, Idaho - "You will find some of the most absolutely wonderful people there! Besides the people, Moscow is the Mecca of outdoor activities and being one with nature and life."

Indiana

Bloomington, Indiana - "This town has a modest, but decent, hippie community. At 4:20 (p.m.) at a park on 9th Street, there is a drum circle. Also a cafe/ restaurant called the Runcible Spoon is visited by many hippies and other interesting people. A few hippies (roughly 6) work there as well. The restaurant is located on 6th Street downtown. Across the back parking lot of this restaurant is a little natural foods Co-op store called Bloomingfoods, where many hippies are employed, and where most hippies buy all their essentials. On Kirkwood Avenue, the most active part of the downtown, there is a little shop called the Dharma Emporium, owned and frequented by lots of groovy people. On Walnut Street, there lies a shop called the Magic Bus, owned and operated by a bunch of hippies that live in the back; kind and gentle folk. Also, the town of Bloomington is mostly liberal, and there are a lot of interesting people. Just stay away from the west side of town: this is a "thriving" commercial part of town with no trees and a lot of new subdivisions. Bad, bad, bad."

Needmore, Indiana - "This is a tiny, tiny place way, way out in the boonies, but an ideal location for a commune, wouldn't you say? Yes, Lothlorien is the name of the place and is just south of Bloomington a ways. Lothlorien is the beautiful location of many festivals throughout the year, and they have an open season during which space can be reserved for celebrations. Lovely, lovely place. Their website is: http://www.kiva.net/~elf "

Iowa

Quad Cities, Iowa - "We have started a small hippie community. Our Rainbow Family has potlucks every other Sunday campouts every month or so."

Kansas

Lawrence - "The place is very chill and down to earth. As much as marijuana seems to be a symbol of hippydom, I would have to say that Lawrence grows some of the finer buds in the states, of course next to Oregon and Boulder."

Kentucky

Louisville, Kentucky - "Bardstown Road is a large street where you can not only find hippies, but every kind of person there is. The best parts of Bardstown Road stretch for about 3 miles. It's lined with eclectic shops, head and hemp and beads and vintage clothing...as well as vegetarian cuisine. It's a great place to just take a walk. It really does look like it's straight out of 1968. There are great coffee shops with outdoor cafes, "gently used" book stores, instrument and record shops, head shops, vintage clothing stores, specialty stores and everything in between. It's absolutely the best place in Louisville to visit!!!"

"There is a happy thriving hippie community here. **Cherokee Park** is home to many drummers and smokers. This city also has a solid gay community, and a well-known affinity for birthing original bands. There are very many opportunities for budding musicians to meet like-minded folks...Also many poets and artists claim **Louisville** for their home. It is groovy."

Maine

Industry, Maine - "Plenty of old hippies, die hard hippies, new hippies and a bunch of drunk ones too you. Ever hear of Hempstock? That's in the town right next to us. Then Harvestfest isn't too far away either."

Starks, Maine - "Home of the annual HEMPSTOCK. More than 30 bands will play through-out the weekend of August 14th...many local bands.......There were no reported arrests last year !!!! And everyone is Hippie like up there in Maine anyway..."

Maryland

Mount Rainier, Maryland - "A funky little town near DC that literally hasn't changed since the 60's. Or if it has, the resemblance has gotten even closer. Since there's a major African American presence it has a somewhat Rastafarian ambiance. Check out the Glut Food Co-op (started by Marxists in 1969), the Eye Opener coffee shop (owned by a Deadhead) and the used furniture/alternative health stores. Possibly the cheapest place you can live between the mountains and the Chesapeake, if you're a hippie."

Takoma Park, DC/Maryland - "Takoma Park is known as the Berkeley of the East. Competitors, we're more modest than that, please challenge us to greatness. DC is famous for being the most politically liberal big city, but then it's also famous for being the nexus of the Counter-Counter-Culture (it's actually hip to be drug free here, though you can do just about anything in public and still get elected to high office), so you may be wondering, where do hippies fit in? As it happens, Takoma Park is not the sad, commercialized, isolated enclave of hipness that you find in most big cities. It is at the geographic heart of a wreath of easygoing, progressive, really racially integrated, communities. Which is why we've escaped gentrification and "hip"-ization & remain a low-key, 70's style small town. White-bread hipsters with racial jones beware.

Hippiedom here is not about commercial lifestyle. It's part of the culture. Nobody moves here for the shopping or arts, but very large percentages of the populations are vegetarians, recyclers, renters, non-car owners, members of the two co-ops. We cheer on the annual Reel mower Brigade in their efforts to ban gas lawnmowers. To benefit our large illegal alien population, who can vote, we have a tradition of hiring police chiefs committed to not cooperating with the IMF. Bizarrely, we're also a mecca for evangelicals and libertarians who share a similar political zeal and fondness for natural food - one of the organic co-ops is the world's largest Christian book store, and the other is staffed by ex-Maoists. There aren't many tensions in the community, though. Our favorite mayor was a ninety yr. old Socialist. Anyhow, we used to have two wild roosters, but one got run over. You can hear the other one crowing behind the boarding houses downtown, between the House of Musical Traditions and the Metaphysical Chapel, on the spring solstice when the Foggy Bottom Morris Men gather to dance the sun up. Definitely a community for longtime residents & hippies-at-heart; fair-weather hippies will get bored and move to some overrated part of DC. We've already got too many yuppies, most of whom were still hippies before they moved here and got a job teaching at the Jane Goodall Institute or Nuclear Environmental Research group or something similar in town, so I guess they're okay."

Massachusetts

Amherst, Massachusetts - "Home to the annual "Extravaganja" festival, Amherst residents are about to vote on a decriminalization of marijuana referendum. Amherst boasts a huge student population from Amherst College, Hampshire College, and UMass and is less than 10 minutes from Northampton, another hippy haven. Great concerts and shows, wonderful cheap restaurants, and an extremely liberal community."

Northampton, Massachuesetts - "Great place for hippies and hippie-types. Tolerant largely gay community welcomes "alternative people." Love the place! Lots of hippie shops and restaurants too!!"

West Newbury and Newburyport, Massachuesetts - "are filled with tons of young hippies. In Newburyport there are a lot of cool little coffee houses located on an old 1800 waterfront. Many places to toke up and everything is always readily available. People such as Toots and the Maytalls, Livingston Taylor (James' bro) and David Grisman have performed in this small town."

Michigan

Ann Arbor, Michigan - "There is a Hash Bash every year there and so many hippies come. Ann Arbor is a great place."

Saugatuck, Michigan - "This is truly a hip community, located along the shores of beautiful Lake Michigan, surrounded by picturesque sand dunes. Saugatuck is the epicenter of many western Michigan coastal communities offering a very laid-back chilled atmosphere, and amongst the population you will find an immense multitude of artists and a majority of open-minded people. The downtown is very eclectic, with many far-out shops, including the popular Shakedown Street, offering a variety of Grateful Dead and hippy-related merchandise. Coffee shops are also quite abundant here. There's also a lot of very cool natural attractions, such as Mt. Baldhead and Oval Beach. The entire scene here reeks of peace. I must say that this town is the ultimate chill-spot."

Missouri

St. Louis, Missouri - "There is a substantial hippie community that exists on St. Louis' South Side around the area of South Grand Avenue. There is also another older, but growing hippie enclave in a close-in suburb of St. Louis. Known as the University City Loop along 10 blocks of Delmar Boulevard, the area is hopping with hippie-run shops and vendor stands."

Columbia, Missouri - Downtown Peace Park and Peace Nook.

Westport, Missouri - "Missouri has more then two hippy hangouts (gasp!). Westport's a very cool place. It has head shops, VW buses, and lots of drugs."

Montana

Missoula, Montana - "Missoula is a hip place with many hippies. Its population is small so everything is laid back. It's very similar to Eugene Oregon, but without the rain. There are a lot of hippy stores and vegetarian restaurants. The town lies over a pretty river and is next to a large mountain so many people hike, bike, hunt shrooms and river raft. Missoula is also the home of Plunker, one of the founders of the Rainbow Nation."

Nebraska

Omaha, Nebraska "Omaha is a pretty phun li'l town. Pretty good family. There are NO CLUBS there, so those annoying clubkids are not even present (woo-hoo!). They'll introduce you to a real rave, which everyone should experience. Omaha also has the oldmarket which is downtown and a fun place to hang out day and night with a park to the east, the Big Slides (extreme amounts of child-like fun) on the north, the abandoned warehouses are also right near where the parties rage at night. Lots of grassroots organizations are sprouting up. Definitely worth checking out if you're traveling through to Boulder or somewhere."

New Mexico

Taos, New Mexico - "I went to Taos, New Mexico last summer and found the place swarming with beautiful people. There are a few communes right outside of town... where Easy Rider was filmed. Lots of freaks around and so much to learn from each other... ecstacy. A bit touristy, but not yet too corrupt with society."

Silver City, New Mexico - It's a hippy mecca on the edge of the largest wilderness in the lower 48. Good year 'round climate. They have several herbal stores in the city with "classes" on locating and identifying local herbs. The co-op bulletin board is loaded with new age info. They have drum circles and a number of communes within 25 miles of the city, some better than others. Don't forget to ask about the hot springs.

New York

Ithaca, New York - "Ithaca has one of the largest hippie populations in New York State. It has natural beauty and is crawling with old and new hippies. It's home to many communes, head shops, natural groceries, drum circles, and kind bud. Ithaca has a sizeable college population."

New Paltz, New York - Home to State University of NY at New Paltz, this small town has a sizable hippy community as well as students. The young feeling is a refreshing change from upstate NY's older crowd. "There are just as many real hippies there as there are in Woodstock, N.Y. I know this because I am a long hair dreded hippy that lives near by both of these locations. The good thing about New Paltz is that it isn't nearly as hyped up as Woodstock. This provides for a nice relaxing atmosphere."

Tonawanda, New York - "There are a lot of hippies in Tonawanda NY. We have protested so many times and when we used to be the Lumber Capital of the world, we made them stop cutting the trees down, and we saved a lot of trees."

Woodstock, New York - Not the actual location of the famous festival (that is Bethel, N.Y.), and a bit of a tourist trap, but yes, lots of hippies live here.

North Carolina

Asheville, North Carolina "...is undoubtedly one of the kindest places on the East Coast. Nice nuggets, a lively and experimental music scene, and the overall friendly atmosphere make this town a must for nomadic freaky friends! I'll see you when I roll through town."

Ohio

Yellow Springs, Ohio- (east of Dayton) pop. 10,000 "Home of the Ivy League Antioch College, head shops, hemp and Earth Friendly clothing and jewelry stores, several music stores (one specializing in hand made drums) and several specialty gift stores. One of Dayton's biggest hippie hangouts."

Columbus, Ohio - High Street @ Ohio State University (Largest University in the US, 70,000 students) dozens of head shops, 100's of specialty stores including 50 record and tape stores (tons of used) dozens of hemp clothing stores.

Waynesville, Ohio - "Near Fairborn. The Renaissance Festival. Hippies everywhere you look and lots of stuff about medieval times.... you can buy clothes and different things. It's a great place to meet people and everyone shares everything."

Oregon

Just about any city in Oregon west of the Cascade Mountains is a Hippy Haven. Oregon is the only state where hippies enjoy a majority at the voting booths come election time. There's a saying going around "Hippies don't die. They just move to Oregon." During the past few years hippies have been moving to Oregon in droves because there's employment for hippies here, and we hippies can go full out in our glad rags in public view with out being accosted, laughed at or put down. Oregon is a true hippy Haven. Under an oz. of pot isn't illegal here. It's only a civil fine that would cost you $500.

Corvallis, Oregon - Corvallis, Oregon has a lot of hippies. "There are so many coffee shops and bookstores to see them at. The waterfront is a wonderful place to sit and enjoy if you are a hippy."

Eugene, Oregon - Near the site of the Oregon Country Faire (each July) where each year hippies gather to celebrate their hippiness. Home to the University of Oregon, many cooperatives, communes galore, a real cool Saturday Market, and eco-consciousness.

Portland, Oregon - is a wonderful place that is very tolerant of hippie-types. Plenty of great people, and home to some great places, such as the nationally famous Saturday Market, a great place to meet people and just chill on the waterfront.

Pennsylvania

"There's a place in PA. called **New Hope**. There are a whole lot of hippies there and lots of shops. It's on a river and there's a smaller one within it. Many, many shops a lot of artwork, nice places to eat (Places you can eat lunch outside by the river and exotic flavor ice creams)."

The Rainbow Gathering

This movable community of **Rainbow Family** members gathers for a few weeks each year in some remote location. Check out their web page for more info. http://welcomehome.org

South Carolina

Hilton Head, South Carolina - "Everybody on this li'l tourist island is flowing. There's a small, but vivid hippie population, who tend to gather at Looce Lucy's or Black Market Minerals in Coligny Plaza, and The Hemp Seed off Sea Pines Circle. Unless you're at the high school, nobody is a hassler. It's good as far as South Carolina goes, I'd say haul your asses down here for a little peace on the beach."

Spartanburg, South Carolina - "It's a medium size city in Upstate SC. I grew up on the east side with tons of hippies. Our parents were the original flower children and for the most part raised us in true hippie fashion. There isn't a lot for teenagers to do in Spartanburg, but we make do. One of our favorite places to hang out is Pill Hill, a park near the high school. Anyway Spartanburg is a nice city, kind of boring, but definitely full of hippies."

Tennessee

The Farm, Summertown, Tennessee - This commune founded by hippies including Stephen Gaskin, has pioneered the hippie communal lifestyle. Check out their website for more info! For a good history of The Farm see the Vegetarian Times story http://www.thefarm.org/general/vt95.html

Texas

Austin, Texas - "Austin has the second largest vegetarian population in the nation....along with some great scenery here in the hill country. People should check it out. My older brother lives there, and works as a chef. Almost every night we get 2 or 3 bucks from each of his roommates, head up to Central Market and get tons of fresh fruit, vegetables, etc. - and have a giant veggie-kabob for dinner. It feeds everyone and also provides for a great way to get together at night in the backyard and just hang out. Barton Creek Park is another great hangout - it's a linear park that follows Barton Creek - along the cliff walls there are several caves for exploring... just a totally surreal environment. Everyone in Austin just seems so mellow and content, i wish i could live there - but for now I'll just be happy with visiting...."

Utah

"Hey, there are more than Mormons in Utah! Check out **Moab** sometime, ou'll find plenty of hippies there!"

Vermont

"There aren't that many hippies but there is weed everywhere!!! And a lot of other drugs. What else is there to do up here?"

Burlington, Vermont - "Church Street is the coolest place to be. There's arieties of people including hippies, mostly new hippies. There's also a estaurant type place off Church Street called Necters, which is where all the ands eat when they come to play down the street at Club Toast. Necters serves he most addicting gravy fries you will ever eat. Bands such as Phish, Belizbeha, nd tons of others eat there. There's also really cool places to shop, and there's a green which is the hippies grassy knoll."

Virginia

Floyd, Virginia - "Having grown up in the Blue Ridge, I am fortunate enough o have been thoroughly familiarized with the hippie pilgrimage that has taken place since the early 70's.....and they're all still heading to Floyd county. I believe there must be upwards of 10 intentional communities up on the beautiful plateau where Floyd County is situated and the numbers are ever growing. The nice thing, too, is that the population is fairly consistent, that is to say that it's not really too transient. People go there and they tend to stay. It's amazingly beautiful, and I'm so glad that it's just right outside my back door."

Washington

"There is a large hippie community in Northeast Washington especially around he small town of **Republic** and **Northern Stevens county**."

Bellingham, Washington - "This beautiful place is an island of hip folk in the Northwest."

Olympia, Washington - "Old and young hippies hanging out among the earth nd animal friendly paradise in the Northwest. Veggie restaurants abound."

Orcas Island, Washington - "In the San Juan Islands. It's an old hippy commune where many hippies still go. It's a campsite so if you're looking for vacation, it's definitely the place."

Seattle, Washington - "I moved here two years ago from LA and find this own to be the most hip place on the west coast. From Fremont to Belltown, from Pike Place to Capital Hill, Seattle is what's happening."

West Virginia

Morgantown, West Virginia - "Downtown on High Street and surrounding areas are two REALLY good head shops...The Den and Cool Ridge, several coffee shops, including The Blue Moose (the best bohemian coffee shop}. There's also a really good bead shop, comic shops, bike shops, and bunches of restaurants. In West Va. anywhere long hair is the norm, (I even worked at Monkey Wards w/shoulder-length hair) and there are lots of long-haired self-sufficient

types living in the woods with sweat lodges, drumming parties, outhouses, lo
homes, herb gardens, and co-ops."

Wisconsin

Madison, Wisconsin - "A beautiful downtown, with a beautiful universit
right on the lake, lots of housing co-ops, and really friendly and nice people
People from Wisconsin tend to be slightly dingy, and Madison is considered t
be the craziest town in the state (it's also the state capital) - but it's the right kin
of crazy, in my opinion. The only drawback is that it gets a little cold there i
winter."

"**Madison** is a VERY groovy place, and state street is chock full of head shops
coffee shops/every shop that deviates from the norm that you can think of......ther
is even a Nepali restaurant that I loved....also loads of interesting people through
out the town. I couldn't believe how many street performers I saw, there wer
devil-sticks flying everywhere and lone saxophonists filling up the empty alley
ways, soothing your mind like a mental Halls cough drop."

Canada

Vancouver, Victoria and Nelson, Canada - "(A.K.A. hippytown in th
boonies)? Vancouver is the founding city of Greenpeace, and our mainstrean
neighbours to the south (of course not including you marvelous and open-minde
brothers + sisters) call us Columbia of the north! AND WE'VE LEGALIZE
HEMP TOO!"

Tofino, British Columbia, Canada - "It's right on the ocean, and I hav
never seen so many free spirited, beautiful people in my life. Everyone was s
kind to everyone. Lots of free flowing clothes and flowers. You're always near
beach for a picnic, or just lounging. My guitar was quite welcome there. Tofin
is not particularly friendly since the locals are inundated with the mass influx c
tourists every year, so they have become somewhat immune to outsiders."

Kitchener Ontario Canada - "Hippies roam the streets of Kitchener an
especially Cambridge. We are up there along with the freaks and jocks, geek
and the boring ones. Hippies are the best, with our butterfly shirts and bel
bottoms, we have our own twists to the 60's fashions."

In response another visitor wrote:

"Thought I'd add a note to what our obviously young friend above has said
the scene here is extremely diversified, there is much to do see and experience.
have jokingly referred to Kitchener for years as the Berkley of Canada. For som
strange reason this little city is a drawing card for hippies. But don't show u
expecting chaos and revolution in the air, because for the ten years I've live
here, most of what I've seen is behind the scenes, although the older hippie an
deadhead community here threw some of the biggest bashes going."

The Gulf Islands B.C. Canada - "particularly Gabriola, Hornby and Cortes
Enchanted, laid-back, new-age. Hornby Island does in fact have hippies
However, the island has become overcrowded and increasingly slick an
commercial. Not so "groovy" now.

Joussard, Alberta, Canada, Location of the NORTH COUNTRY FAIR. "Eac ummer on June 20-23 (sometimes on the 19th, depending which one falls on riday) there is a Summer Solstice Celebration held in this little northern Alberta own. Hippies and free spirits alike come from all over to enjoy this wonderful nlightening experience of live music, new age work-shops, dancing and of course ne artisan market. Situated beside the Lesser Slave Lake, there are many great laces to camp on and off the fair site. It's like taking a step back in time, if only or one memorable weekend a year, to see beautiful people join together and elebrate the longest day of the year. This year is the 20th celebration of the orth Country Fair and it will surely be a huge gathering of the free."

Sherbrooke and Lennoxville, Quebec, Canada - "the townships are also the nost English place in Quebec. Many old and younger hippies live out in the ountry here. There's also been a few sizeable communes, one of them nysteriously gone leaving all their stuff behind."

Montreal and Quebec, Canada - "also have huge countercultural activity. If ou're looking for cheap drugs you've come to the right place. Rent is super heap, but jobs may not be available."

"Just want to add a note about **Montreal**. This is a city with a lot of Spirit. It's place where freedom and individuality are cherished. Where people can still et by doing their art & music. Where hundreds of drummers and dancers meet n the mountain to celebrate regularly. Where you can always find a good veggie neal, and share a spliff on the street with a friend. Many Rainbow Family folks nere too."

Central America

Mexico - Long an escape for the gringos, still an interesting country to visit rom Baha to the Yucatan, lots of places to explore and hang out.

Maruata, Mexico - "On the coast of Michoacan, Maruata has been a mecca or some time now. The big Parties are Christmas and Easter. No hotels, only amping. Lots of drums and other music. The locals are Nahuatl Indians, and extremely friendly. Best beach on the West Coast of Mexico. Good herb for around ive dollars an ounce, plus the occasional peyote surprise. Please bring sheets of lotter acid, there's always a terrible shortage. Things are a bit weird since the gathering of '95-'96 but there's always room for a few more freaks."

Zipolite, Mexico - "I was there maybe 3 years ago and it was the best most beautiful hippy place ever. Hammocks on the beach $1 a night. Grass can be ordered and delivered from ones hammock. Food is great too. Strong waves - watch it! Nice sunsets."

Costa Rica - "is a way cool place. There are many kind nature spirits there. Hey, every time someone greets you they say "Pura Vida" (pure life). Just that ine shows you that the country is totally at peace."

"What can I say except for that this is the ultimate haven for anyone who has grasped peace and knows how to live life to the fullest.....Pura Vida (pure life) is not only the universal greeting, but it's a great substitute for "cool." (My bus driver Rodrigo used it that way). The people are very hip here. Incredible atmosphere......and the food is the best I've ever had!"

Guatemala - Lots of hippies live in communities here. Mayans are very cool people, but check with the State Department for warnings, as occasionally ther is political violence in certain areas.

Tikal, Guatemala - A very important hippy ancient Maya site. Stay on the island when in Flores. The town is a bit rough. Tikal is beautiful, make sure you go out into the jungles where you can see so many monkeys! The grass is top quality there too. But sometimes climbing those pyramids can be a bit of a scary experience, especially when remembering that they were built extra steep just so when you were thrown down the steps you weren't going to stop till you hit the bottom!

Europe

Amsterdam, Holland - THE hippy center of Europe. Marijuana sold legally in more than 400 coffeeshops, a long history of tolerance, beautiful old city great vibes everywhere, and yes the friendly Dutch speak English. Hippie Heaven Lots of headshops, smartshops, rave venues, hip fashions, museums and concerts. The Vondelpark has been a gathering place for hippies since the '60s. Please see our Hip Guide to Amsterdam at:

http://hipplanet.com/amsterdam/amsterdam.htm for lots more info.

Belgium - "I moved from Brussels to the little town of **Mesnil Eglise** (yes Belgium) and see from the 75 habitants half of them are old and new tekno hippies. From the solar energy professor to artists and bio food producers al invite friends to spend the summer in the woods of the Ardennes. This makes a lot of people smokin' and roamin' the 3 streets of the village... The melting po with the original farmers worked well out during the last 25 years."

Prague, Czech Republic - "The capital of Czech republic is also a capital o hippie life-forms here in Czech and also for a quite a lot of them from other countries. Mary Jane is not legal, but there are a lot of small clubs, organizing the festivals, concerts, theatre and a lot of other actions, where the MJ smoke is tolerated. It has a kind of legality as by our law you can smoke it, but can not grow it, trade it etc."

The Greek Islands - European hippies flock to dozens of islands in the summer. Hot spots are Ios, Santorini, and Crete. "Other really hot places in the Greek Islands are Paros and AntiParos. The two islands are half an hour from one another. I live in Greece so I know the really cool places. There you can find a lot of Hippies, (French, English and Greek usually...)."

Christiania, Copenhagen, Denmark - "is a free-city and the ultimate hippie haven in Europe, after Amsterdam, of course. In Kristiania you can smoke dope as much as you please and the city is very beautiful with many attractions and a lot of young people... among the hippies most popular rock band Gasolin. For more info, check out www.christiania.org."

Helsinki, Finland - "There is a small hippie-community here too... Not a big one, but a GREAT one... As said here before, there's a lot going on in Kaisaniemi Park, but also in Koff Park, where at night you can hear the congas and really get (high) into the spirit of Helsinki. Just in the neighbourhood where I live, Kallio, there are loads of hippie parties, smoky living rooms and little peaceful parks.

Of course, because of the cold winters, there's really no life after summer... but I highly recommend Finland from May to September…"

"If you want to have really psychedelic vibrations in Finland, please visit in **Kaisaniemi´s Park in Helsinki**. Lots of nice people, well, only in summertime, sadly. Bring your own shaman drum and enjoy... But be careful, the cops are not very friendly here."

"There is a huge hippy movement here started about 2 years ago. There are only 5 million people in Finland and 18% of the youth are on drugs, mostly ganja. I am very proud of the hippy movement here. You can spot the hippies here. If you dress like them they more than likely will offer you a joint!!"

Geneva, Switzerland - "It's a real hip city... Pot is almost legal here now, the town's full of somehow-illegal-but-tolerated places where you can sit, listen to some really cool music while rolling a nice one and have a beer for a couple of coins... Hey, it's a great place! And it ain't THAT expensive. Less than Paris! The best is in summer, at the end of July. There's a huge open air festival which really looks like a small Woodstock...Same spirit (almost) and lots and lots of friendly people who are just there for the music, the spirit and the party... It lasts for a week. It's the PALEO festival and I think you guys should get to know it!"

Spain - Spain is the European country that is closest to Morocco, with more than 1500 years of cannabis and hash smoking history. "Here are a couple of places in Spain that you NEED to visit: Altea (in the province of Alicante)- Paradise! A beautiful little Mediterranean town where everyone's as free as he wants to get.... Don't miss "Franky`s Place", in Benidorm (just 5 miles away), a little 20 year old semi-underground bar where you can find the "relax" and good music, and have a peaceful smoke.

Ibiza (Mediterranean Island, 75 N. miles out of Spanish Coast) This is THE place. Ibiza is the big party scene. Lots of young beautiful people, music, beaches, etc."

Asia

Thailand - A beautiful, friendly, tolerant country (it is full of Buddhists after all). Unfortunately economic development and unbridled tourism has deformed this country. Check out Ko Samui or Ko Phanghan for a real getaway. Stay away from Bangkok, Pattaya and Phuket. Chaing Mai too has changed for the worse. The hill tribes of the north are worth a visit though this is getting touristy too.

Bali, Indonesia - The beauty of this island is surpassed only by the beauty of the people and their Hindu/animistic culture. A mecca for hippies! Ubud is a great place to base. Give Kuta Beach a wide berth unless you like surfing, shopping and getting hounded.

India - A hundred lifetimes is not enough to absorb the culture, the land and the people of this amazing country. Many a seeker has found nirvana here. Goa is one of many places where hippies congregate. Other groovy places are Kerala State in the south, full of canals, Rajastan, deserts and forts, Benares if you want to get holy, the foothills of the Himalayas to get high on the mountains and charas.

The Himalayas - "There are hippies everywhere, man! Well, in India anywa
I was there from January to June and they seem to be most concentrated in th
Himalayas. You can find people high on all sorts of drugs, including the aw(
some sight of the mountains covered in snow (it was my first time in the snov
by the way and my somewhat awkward attempts at walking up and down th
slopes generated a few laughs from the stoned ones). I was told that being i
India is like being stoned without having to smoke anything. It is true! If you'r
a real hippy you won't want to go to Goa, find your own piece of hippy heave
like I did, (unless you really MUST go to Goa!). My advice for hippies is G(
NOW!"

Japan - Shimo-Kitazawa, Tokyo - "This is a great little hippy part of Tokyo
no cars, lots of nice shops and restaurants, home of Tokyo's first hemp shop an
hemp restaurant, also did you know that it is legal to sell mushrooms in Japan
Just look outside the station here! Hokkaido is Japans North Island and is
nature paradise. It also has lots of wild hemp growing, some of which is quit
smokable apparently. Japan Alps - during the summer it hosts lots of outdoc
festivals and rave parties. These are real hippy congregations - people you don'
see too often in Japan suddenly appear. Where do they live?!"

Down Under

Australia - Many communes in the bush, some small hippie communities
Australians now spend more money on marijuana than on wine, and almost a
much as BEER! How things have changed down under!

Byron Bay, Australia - The "Hippie Capital" of Australia is a place calle(
Byron Bay (look it up!) which is situated at the top of New South Wales, nea
Brisbane. Byron Bay and surrounding towns like Nimbin, Mullumbimby, an(
Lismore are absolute havens for the alternative, new-age folk.

New Zealand - Reports of hippies here and there. Kiwis are known for thei
friendliness and hospitality. Hippies can be found in the Coromandel, which is ¡
peninsula just kind of across from Auckland. In Nelson at the top of the soutl
island there are little communities of hippies scattered about.

Waiheke Island, New Zealand - a 35 minute ferry ride from the nation';
largest city of Auckland. (1.1 million people). With a population of about 5000
Waiheke Island is very popular with those who want to live closer to nature.

Elsewhere

The Caribbean - The laidback island lifestyle attracts many hippies. Warn
weather, beaches and life in the slow lane finds hippies in the Virgin Islands
Puerto Rico, St. Martin, the Grenadines, Jamaica and other tropical ports.

Bulls Bay, Jamaica..... "love—guavajelly "

Dahab, Egypt - "Dahab is a small Bedouin village located at the East Coast o
the Sinai desert. Since the 70's, it's full of hippie and vagabond types. The
atmosphere of the place is really nice and laidback with great music like ambien
techno, reggae, 60s rock playing every where. There are several campground;
where you can stay at rates around 1$ per night. In most restaurants you lay o
sit on the floor on carpets and pillows, outdoors or indoors just by the Red Sea

There are great coral reefs a couple of meters from the shore, so many people come here for the diving. Other activities are desert excursions to oases or Mt. Sinai, wind surfing, cheap grass, desert parties, backgammon etc. Definitely a place to visit. Dahab is a very, very special place. Those who like Amsterdam should go to Dahab in winter (Christmas, New Year). Many Divers, Surfers, Trampers. Most of them smoke, even the policeman, Bedouin people and taxi drivers are stoned. The desert is great. Imagine riding on a camel and smoking good stuff. Then go in the water and enjoy the fish!"

Nile River, Egypt - "Felucca (type of boat) on the river Nile can be a most pleasant experience. They fit up to 8, so make sure you are in with the right sort. The captain rolls the joints as its tough with Egyptian papers having no gum. He cooks good chow too. And you have never EVER seen a sunset like the one from a small little boat peacefully going up the Nile. We ordered our boat from the Bob Marley Hotel run by Mohammed Bob, he's a bit of a schemer but he's got plenty of ganja."

Israel - "Many hippies live here in the Holy Land. The only westernized country where communes are part of the system."

Morocco - Once part of the hippy trail from Marrakech to the Rif Mountains, Morocco is still an interesting place to visit. Hip, laid back places are Chefchaouen and Essaouira. Morocco is cheap and the hashish is excellent. Be aware of the local customs and act appropriately. See the Hip Guide to Morocco;
http://hipplanet.com/morocco/hipmorocco.htm for some first hand experiences and great photos!

Turkey - Perhaps the hottest destination for Europeans these days (it's cheap!). This friendly country has much to offer, including great beaches, culture, and shopping. Again, toe the line - remember the movie "Midnight Express!"

South Africa - "If you're looking for hippies South Africa has got them. Cape Town especially hosts a large hippy community, here we have the famous Green Market Square where hippies sell their creation from clothes to paintings. Every year from late June into early July thousands of people make their way to Grahmstown, a small town in the middle of nowhere, for the Grahmstown festival. Every hippy in the country winds up there sometime time during the 2-week festival. The festival is actually an arts festival where plays of all kinds (from miming to Shakespeare) can be seen, but along with the abundant actors come the hippies, hoping to make a profit off the large crowds of tourists and catch a few laughs at one of the many comedy plays. The entire town consists of two main streets and several theatre houses, what space is not being used for makeshift stages is a hippy market the size of a football field. As more and more people come and the hordes of hippies become uncountable the atmosphere seems to grow in a unique feeling of appreciation for the newfound peace in this unstable country. It's an experience of a lifetime not to be missed."

Rustlers Valley, South Africa - "This is a place where people come together in peace and celebrate life, arts and music. There is also a permanent community there. They have recently had a disaster. A fire destroyed most of their infrastructure, but they are rebuilding. Visit their website www.rustlers.co.za."

Hippie Names

We started the Hippy Names page on Hippyland because someone wanted a hipp name for their baby. We put up a Question of the Week asking for names. The respons was overwhelming. The following list was compiled in a short period and is typical, b no way a complete list of hippy names.

If you're looking for a name for your baby or you just want one for your new identi there's hundreds here from **Ashley** to **Ziggy**. There's a **Rainbow** of names stretchin from **Chelsea** to **China**. From **Dawn** to **Dusk** in **Winter** or **Summer** these hippy name are fun!

Many parents name their children after great people. Certainly a child named **Jerry** c **Janis**, **Marley** or **Lennon** will carry proudly the name of someone who left behind unique legacy.

Many popular hippy names derive from nature, like **Sky**, **Sunshine** or **Rain**. Som names with heavy meaning come from India like **Chakra**, **Dharma** or **Om**. Other name **Echo** the hippy philosophy of **Peace**, **Love** and **Freedom**.

We don't separate the names by sex, as many are obvious, and those that are not ca be either.

Hippy Names - Alphabetically

Aïsha	Breezeann	Cloey	Dusk	Haley
Alice	Breezy	Cloud	Dylan	Hanna
Alishia	Brianna	Clover	**Earth**	Hannah
Allegra	Briget	Coral	Echo	Harmony
Alma	Brisa	Coriander	Eclipse	Heady
Amanda	Bud	Cosmic	Ember	Heart
Andromeda	Burgundy	Coyote	Emerald	Heather
Angel	Butterfly	Crimson	Emmanuel	Holly
Angelica	Buzz	Crystal	Ethan	Honesty
Ariel	**Cady**	Cyress	Evaan	Honey
Ashley	Canuma	**Daisie**	**Faith**	Hope
Athena	Capucine	Daisy	Feather	**Indica**
Augie	Carmel	Dakota	Feelfree	Iris
August	Carmen	Dancer	Felicity	**Jaco**
Aurora	Casey	Danna	Fern Fillmore	Jade
Autumn	Cassidy	Dawn	Flight	Jan
Avery	Cassiopia	Daydream	Flow	Janis
Azura	Celeste	Dazy	Flower	Jasmine
Basil	Chakra	Deja	Floyd	Jay
Begonia	Chana	Delia	Free	Jaya
Belou	Charity	Delilah	Freedom	Jazzerus
Blaze	Chelsea	DeLorean	**Garcia**	Jerry
Blossom	Cherish	Desert	Georgia	Jewel
Blu	China	Destiny	Gia	John
Blue	Chloe	Dezra	Grace	Joplin
Brandon	Christian	Dharma	Gretta	Jorma
Breanna	Clayton	Doobie	**Hail**	Journey
Breeze	Cloe	Dude	Hailey	Journey

oy	Magnolia	Pink	Seed	Sunshine
ulia	Mandy	Promise	Serena	Sunstar
une	Manu	Prosperity	Serenity	**Talia**
ustice	Marigold	Prudence	Shadow	Terra
Kami	Marley	**Quentin**	Shalom	Thyme
Karma	Matthew	Quinn	Shannon	Timothy
Kassia	May	**Rain**	Shanti	Topaz
Laya	Maya	Raina	Sky	Tranquilla
Keenak	Meadow	Rainbow	Skye	Trent
Kelsey	Melody	Raine	Skylar	Trey
Korin	Micha	Rainey	Skyler	Trinity
Kukka	Mirakel	Rana	Smiles	Tuesday
Kyle	Mist	Rayne	Snowphish	Tyler
Kyley	Moon	Rayon	Soul	**Understanding**
Land	Moonjava	Renee	Spirit	**Violet**
Lavender	Moonshine	Revelation	Star	Vishnu
Layna	Morning	Revolution	Starbright	**Welcome**
Leary	Moss	Rex	Stardust	Wildwind
Lennon	**Natura**	Rhiannon	Starla	Willow
Lenzee	Nico	River	Starlight	Wind
Liberty	Nug	Rose	Starr	Windsong
Lief	**Ocean**	Rufus	Starshine	Winter
Light	Om	Ryvre (River)	Stone	**Xavier**
Lilly	Opal	**Sadie**	Storm	**Yuna**
Logan	Orian Paisley	Saffron	Sugar	**Zachary**
Lolita	**Papers**	Sage	Sugree	Zen
Love	Patches	Sapphire	Summer	Zennia
Lucy	Patchouli	Sativa	Sun	Zeyla
Luna	Peace	Scarlett	Sunburst	Ziggy
Lylee	Peaceful	Seashawna	Sunflower	Zoe
Lyric	Petal	Sebastian	Sunny	Zoey
Madrah	Phoebe	Secret	Sunray	Zora

Combination Names	Crystal Rain	Moon Beam	Sara Aria
Astral Plane	Dakota Rain	Moon Dance	Seagull Dream
Aurora Ashton	Dylan Alexander	Moon Love	Sahara Sunshine
Autumn Flowers	Ember Rose	Mountain Girl	Shamica Sativa
Balbo Shrooms	Georgia Rain	New Sage	Shelby Magnolia
Biebo Suncloud	Griffen Liberty	Nico Blue	Singing Hawk
Brian Joseph Lane	Holidais Peace	Nite Smile	Sky Larrisa
Burgundy Skye	Ilia Raye	Ocean Blue	Stormy Carl
Chasidy Rainbow Marie	Jacob Elton Michael	Ocean Breezes	Sunshine Daydream
Chelsea Morning	Lennon Karma	Ocean Lilly	Tangerine Dream
China Rose	Little Flower	Peaceful Willow	Trickle Rain
Cloud Flower	Marie Juana	Rain Dancer	Ty Kurt
Clover Deva	Mary Juanita	Rainbow Rose	Violet Skye
Cosmic River	Maryjane	Rainbow Sky	Wendy Crystal Sky
Crimson Rainbow	Miccah Sunrise Michael Rainbow	Rainbow Star	Wolf Song
Crystal Dove		Rainy Daylee	Zoe Renee
		River Stone	
		Sandy Moon	

Hippie Books (Bibliography)

There's no way I could possibly include all the information about hippies in this one book. So here's a long list of books of interest to hippies. Many of these are essential reading, and were an influential part of the hippie movement.

All the books mentioned in this chapter are available at the Hip Planet Bookstore. Go to **http://hipplanet.com/bookstore/bookstore.htm** to view the bookcover or to purchase.

Hippies & Hippy Philosophy

Be Here Now by Ram Dass. The classic guidebook for those on the inner spiritual journey. This inspired work blends Eastern Philosophy with the western mindset. Everything is connected and you can achieve nirvana if you can just Be Here Now! Good graphics and unusual format make this book a real trip.

Das Energi by Paul Williams. Paul wrote this book while living on a remote commune in Canada (his book about that experience is called "Apple Bay"). Das Energi contains illuminating revelations that cast light upon life's great mysteries. A manual for the Taoist within, full of hippie wisdom.

Chaos and Cyberculture by Timothy Leary. The LSD guru has a lot to say about society, culture, technology and the human mind. This book offers up thirty years of Leary's experience and knowledge. A good retrospective and introduction to his work.

The Politics of Ecstasy by Timothy Leary. In this book, Timothy Leary, the high priest of LSD, promotes the right to expand one's mind as he exhorts us to turn on, tune in and drop out! He questions the government's growing power to prevent individual experimentation with psychedelics. Includes the famous 1966 Playboy interview where he discusses LSD and sex.

Flashbacks: A Personal and Cultural History of an Era by Timothy Leary, William S. Burroughs. This is Leary's autobiography and includes fascinating tidbits from his days at Harvard to turning on celebrities to his escape from imprisonment. Leary is always delightful, entertaining and mind expanding.

Coming of Age in Babylon: Finding Your Own Reality by Doug De Bias. Candid talk about sex, sexuality, drugs, race and ethnicity, feminine facial hair, male and female masturbation, the myopia of upward mobility, parents, partners, politics, religion, the rat race and more. Comes with a CD with 20 songs! (New edition)

The Electric Kool Aid Acid Test by Tom Wolfe. This is Wolfe's book about Ken Kesey and the Merry Pranksters and how LSD invaded America's consciousness, peaking during the Summer of Love. A tribute to Kesey, the Pranksters (including Neal Cassady, Ken Babbs, Mountain Girl and Wavy Gravy), and the whole psychedelic generation. Good insight into how the torch was passed from the Beats to the hippies. It also contrasts Kesey's "up front," experiential

novement versus Timothy Leary's experimental, insightful approach to the LSD
rip.

On the Road by Jack Kerouac. One of the original "beats" writes about the
freedom of life On the Road from his sensitive Buddhist perspective. Kerouac
influenced a whole generation who went searching for another way to live.

Dharma Bums by Jack Kerouac. About the beat philosophy's roots in Zen
Buddhism. He chronicles his adventures in California and a trip across the country,
ending in a reflective stint up on a mountain as a fire lookout. This "rucksack
wanderer" sure met some interesting people on his journeys including poet Allen
Ginsberg and Buddhist Gary Snyder. The descriptions of Beat parties are not to
be missed. This book and "On The Road" inspired many a hippy to take to the
road in search of one's self.

Memory Babe, A Critical Biography of Jack Kerouac. Considered to be the
best book about Jack.

Seth Speaks by Jane Roberts. Seth speaks through Jane Roberts and has lots
to say. How you create your own reality, why we reincarnate. The Seth books
help you learn to integrate your experiences and put a good perspective on life.

**The Nature of Personal Reality: Specific, Practical Techniques for Solving
Everyday Problems and Enriching the Life You Know (A Seth Book)** by Jane
Roberts. Another in depth look at ways to improve your life by discovering and
understanding your true nature.

A Separate Reality by Carlos Castaneda. Don Juan is Carlos' guide into the
world of the brujo, the sorcerer. With Don Juan's careful tutoring, Carlos is
given mind-altering drugs to enable him to perceive the Separate Reality. Naive
Carlos is forever making a fool of himself, but Don Juan is patient and has much
to teach about the world beyond the veil. **Tales of Power, The Fire From Within**
and **The Power of Silence** are all good Castaneda books.

The Perennial Philosophy by Aldous Huxley. Huxley examines Eastern and
Western religions and finds their recurring themes. These themes form the basis
of a universal philosophy that is very close to that of the hippies which this book
predates. A must read for those seeking the spiritual path.

Looking for the Summer by Robert W. Norris. A Vietnam War conscientious
objector's adventures and search for identity on the road from Paris to Calcutta
in 1977.

Ishmael by Daniel Quinn. Unusual Socratic dialogue between human and ape
discussing the place of man in the nature of things. A cult book.

A New Model of the Universe by P. D. Ouspensky. Ouspensky makes use of
the "hidden knowledge" mystics have passed down through the generations
resulting in a mind expanding exploration of the universe beyond our senses.

Autobiography of a Yogi by Pramahansa Yogananda. This is a tale of devotion
of an incredibly loving person for his guru and all life. His life story and the
teachings within will touch your soul.

The Bhagavad Gita. The classic Indian gospel of Lord Krishna and his
devotees. Great inspiration for peace-loving, mantra-chanting, vegetarian-eating
hippies.

Tao Te Ching by Lao Tzu, Gia-Fu Feng translator. This has been hailed as the best English translation of Lao Tzu ever. And that's so important to convey the subtle meanings inherent in the Tao. The nature photography accompanying the text compliments and enhances reflection upon the words.

The Drifters by James Mitchener. Follow six hippie travelers on their outer and inner journeys to exotic places like Marrakech and Mozambique. This book will ignite your spirit of adventure.

Zen & The Art of Motorcycle Maintenance: An Inquiry into Values by Robert M. Pirsig. Now here's a book that really makes you think about how you approach life. This easy reading tale is packed with meaning.

Awakening the Buddha Within by Lama Surya Das. A westerner who has studied Tibetan Buddhism for twenty years relates how Buddhism can improve our modern lives.

The Tibetan Book of the Dead. Don't leave life without it! How to exit this world gracefully and assure your return in another body. If it's good enough for the Dalai Lama...

Cannabis & Psychedelic Books

Food of the Gods: The Search for the Original Tree of Knowledge : A Radical History of Plants, Drugs, and Human Evolution by Terence McKenna. Terence McKenna is the guru of botanical psychoactives. His shamanic approach to plants and human consciousness enhances our connection to the world beyond the five senses. If you're into expanding your awareness via plants this will help put it all in context.

True Hallucinations: Being an Account of the Author's Extraordinary Adventures in the Devil's Paradise by Terence McKenna. Another great book by McKenna about his psychedelic experiences.

Indoor Marijuana Horticulture by Jorge Cervantes. This is THE book for indoor growing. Jorge's thorough research and detail make the guesswork and problem solving easy.

Marijuana Indoors: Five Easy Gardens by Jorge Cervantes. Another great book looks at five indoor gardens, the techniques used, and the results. Lots of advice, detailed charts, illustrations and excellent photos.

Marijuana Outdoors: Guerrilla Growing by Jorge Cervantes. Jorge does it again, this time with stories from outdoor gardens in both hemispheres. He covers different climatic zones, remote growing techniques and concealment methods.

Hashish! by Robert Connell Clarke. This is the most definitive guide to hashish ever published. Well researched with lots of historical and practical information on the subject. Excellent detail, including the various techniques for making hashish. Indispensable for anyone fascinated by the subject.

Doors of Perception by Aldous Huxley. The classic of psychedelic literature. Based on Huxley's experiences with mescaline and how it "opened the doors" for him. Yes, the Doors named their group after this book.

Acid Dreams: The Complete Social History of LSD : The CIA, the Sixties, and Beyond by Martin A. Lee, Bruce Shlain. This book details the development

f LSD from a clinical psychologist's tool to a CIA mind control plot to the fuel
f a countercultural revolution. Essential reading for conspiracy theorists and
mind travelers.

The Little Book of Acid by Cam Cloud. This small book covers the history of
LSD from Albert Hoffman and the Sandoz Laboratories to Owsley and Timothy
Leary, and delves into the psychedelic and cultural impact. Includes information
about natural alternatives including Hawaiian Woodrose and Morning Glory
eeds.

Pihkal: A Chemical Love Story by Alexander Shulgin. Pihkal stands for
Phenethylamines I Have Known and Loved. Indeed, the Shulgins know of what
hey speak and they tell the story of psychedelics and designer drugs including
heir child, Ecstasy. If you're a talented chemist you might appreciate the 179
ecipes included. Tihkal is his other huge book about Tryptamines.

Steven Cerio's ABC Book: A Drug Primer by Steven Cerio. This is an
alphabet book of drugs, from Angel Dust to Heroin and from Nicotine to Zoloft.
Each letter is a different substance of abuse, with delightfully sweet and disturbing
full-color illustrations and a page of rhyming couplets suitable for banned rock
and roll lyrics. Children 18 and up will have hours of goofy fun looking for all of
the weird details in these deeply psychedelic drawings.

Primo Plant: Growing Marijuana Outdoors by Carolyn Garcia (Mountain
Girl). Jerry's wife shows you how to do it outdoors.

The Sixties

**On the Bus: The Complete Guide to the Legendary Trip of Ken Kesey and
the Merry Pranksters and the Birth of the Counterculture** by Paul Perry.
This book follows Kesey, Neal Cassady, and the Pranksters as they made
psychedelic history "on the bus."

Sleeping Where I Fall: A Chronicle by Peter Coyote. Peter tells all about
his life as a mime, actor, and former Digger! Lots to read about the 60's in San
Francisco.

Groovy, Man: A Trip Through the Psychedelic Years (Rhino Collectible
Music Series) by Alan Bisbort, Parke Puterbaugh. This is a new book about the
music of a generation that promises to take us back through time with jaded
eyes?

Summer of Love by Lisa Mason. Science Fiction book about a time traveler
from 2467 who returns to San Francisco in 1967 to find a girl named Starbright.
He encounters an assortment of characters and LSD during the Summer of Love.

1968 by Joe Haldeman. The story of one year in a soldier's life in Vietnam and
the 60's counterculture.

**Aquarius Revisited: Seven Who Created the Sixties Counterculture That
Changed America** (Citadel Underground Series) by Peter O. Whitmer, Bruce
Van Wyngarden. The seven are William S. Burroughs; Allen Ginsberg; Key
Kesey; Timothy Leary; Norman Mailer; Tom Robbins; Hunter S. Thompson.
These are some of the most influential thinkers of the 60s. Find out how they
influenced the hippie movement.

The Way the Wind Blew: A History of the Weather Underground by Ron Jacobs. This book chronicles the genesis and growth of the Weatherman/Weather Underground, a radical antiwar and anti-imperialist group of the late 1960s and early 1970s.

Assault on the Left: The FBI and the Sixties Antiwar Movement by James Kirkpatrick Davis.

The Sixties: Years of Hope Days of Rage by Todd Gitlin. Gitlin was elected president of the SDS, Students for a Democratic Society in 1963 and helped organize the first national demonstration against the Vietnam War. This is his story and that of the protest movement of the 60's.

Hippies by Peter Jedick. Jedick was enrolled at Kent State in the early '70s so he experienced firsthand the student protests leading up to that fateful day in 1970 when four students were shot. This fictional tale relives that era.

Ecology & the Environment

The Ages of Gaia: A Biography of Our Living Earth by J. E. Lovelock. The story of the Earth as an organism. This book details the planet's evolution over a billion years, emphasizing how life forms are interdependent. It also covers man's abuse of his host planet.

A Sand County Almanac and Sketches Here and There by Aldo Leopold. Leopold is a famous naturalist who helped found the Wilderness Society and worked for the Forest Service. This book is one the most famous works on Ecology. His view is that the 'balance of nature' must be preserved and as much land as possible should be set aside to allow species to continue to thrive.

Diet for a Small Planet by Frances Moore Lappe. You are not only what you eat, but you affect our planet by your food choices. We can indeed change the world just by changing our diet. Learn all the reasons to become a vegetarian, and in doing so you'll live healthier and so will the planet.

Silent Spring by Rachel Carson. This book did much to raise awareness about how we are poisoning our planet and ourselves, almost 40 years ago. The message is clear, as she presents the facts that will make you think and act to save our ecosystems.

The Biosphere by V. I. Vernadskii, David B. Langmuir (translator). This classic work from 1927 by Russian scientist Vernadskii founded the Gaian theory. Recently translated into English, it views life as the evolutionary force on the planet.

Hippie Travel Guides

By far the best series of travel books for the independent traveler is **Lonely Planet**. They focus on budget travel to out of the way places. Their frequently updated books contain a wealth of information including stuff that other guides leave out, like hassles and drug culture. I used "Southeast Asia on a Shoestring" on my trip through that region and I had a great time. Their website is awesome and has up-to-date info and traveler reports. Their popular TV show on the Travel Channel is one of the best shows about travel, period. Don't miss **Ian Wright**'s shows, he's funny.

Other series are the **Rough Guides** (available in several languages) and the
nsight series with wonderful photos. A new series, the **Eyewitness Travel Guides**
ire a visually stunning, graphically intense overview of specific cities and
ountries.

Don't forget our own guides to **Amsterdam** and **Morocco** at **Hip Planet!** Go
o **http://hipplanet.com** to get our inside view of these two amazing places.

How-To Books

The Complete Illustrated Book of Yoga by Vishnudevananda. Yoga relaxes,
stretches, revitalizes, balances, and tunes you into the life force. Anyone can do
it, you don't have to be in perfect shape, and it is one of the most healthy things
you can do with your body. This classic book shows you how to perform the
Hatha Yoga asanas to help you unify your mind, body and spirit.

Kundalini Yoga: A Simple Guide to the Yoga of Awareness by Shakti Pawha
Kaur Khalsa. This book shows you how to increase your awareness and strengthen
the nervous system, balance the glandular system, and harness the energy of the
mind and emotion as well as the body. Breathing and chanting your way to a
healthier life.

Batik and Tie Dye Techniques by Nancy Belfer. Learn the secrets to great
tie-dye and batiks.

The New Sensual Massage by Gordon Inkeles. A great guide to the art of
loving massage. Full of beautiful photos and instructions. Possibly the best book
on the subject.

Steal This Book: Twenty-Fifth Anniversary Facsimile Edition by Abbie
Hoffman. Yippie, media hound, author, anarchist, Abbie was many things to
many people. In this book he gives loads of tips on how to get by with no money,
how to take advantage of the "system," and how to undermine it. A classic!

**The Illustrated Kama Sutra: Ananga-Ranga : Perfumed Garden : Classic
Eastern Love Texts** by Charles Fowkes, Richard F. Burton, F. F. Arbuthnot. The
Kama Sutra is the Tantric guide to spiritual union through sexual and yogic
techniques. This beautifully illustrated book will inspire and guide you.

Anne Hooper's Kama Sutra by Anne Hooper. A more contemporary guide to
this ancient text emphasizes the finer points of intimacy rather than gymnastic
ability.

**Anne Hooper's Ultimate Sexual Touch : The Lovers' Guide to Sensual
Massage** by Anne Hooper. Another excellent guide book to sensuality.

**Alternative Weddings: An Essential Guide for Creating Your Own
Ceremonies** by Jane Ross-MacDonald. This book has lots of ideas for creating a
unique ceremony reflecting your personal values. It includes legal requirements,
sample vows, poetry/music ideas, and info on the humanist association and
Unitarian churches who can officiate at your ceremony.

Poetry

If you like poetry, at Hippyland we have a large number of poems from hippies
posted that you can view. Just go to **http://hipplanet.com/poetry/poetry.htm**.
You can also post your own poetry there!

Here are some selected works of poetry by some of the great poets. These ar filled with emotion, love, spirituality, angst and awareness. Good poetry ca bring joy, enlightenment and wonder into our lives.

Howl and Other Poems by Allan Ginsberg. Ginsberg's controversial book c poetry that was declared obscene and banned. Ginsberg won the court case, landmark for free speech. Ginsberg pioneered a new style of writing and artfull expressed his innermost rage at society's shortcomings. Ginsberg's dramati reading of this work at coffeehouses in the '50s and '60s enthralled thos "angelheaded hipsters" and established his reputation in literary circles.

Wilderness: The Lost Writings of Jim Morrison by Jim Morrison. Too ofte we consider Jim Morrison just as a handsome face with a good voice, but thi work really proves that there is much more. It is filled with amazing poetr written throughout his life. Don't expect this book just to be another collectio of beautiful flowing words. It gives vision in each poem to places never see before.

The Prophet by Kahlil Gibran, Aubrey Beardsley (Illustrator). Gibran' inspirational masterpiece. Divinely inspired philosophy without dogma. A poeti guide to life and peace of mind.

Leaves of Grass by Walt Whitman. This classic book of poetry by one c America's greatest poets is full of spiritual wisdom.

101 Classic Love Poems. This book contains a great selection of love poem from the likes of Edgar Allen Poe, The Brownings, Shakespeare, Shelley, an Yeats.

Seeds from a Birch Tree: Writing Haiku and the Spiritual Journey b Clark Strand. A lot of Zen philosophy and haiku exercises, help you learn t write this simple expressive form of poetry while discovering your inner nature

The Complete Tales and Poems of Edgar Allan Poe by Edgar Allan Poe Poe was one great storyteller. His poems and stories are full of horror, myster and the macabre. A must for any fan as it includes much more than most Po books (over 1000 pages).

Music and Musicians

Garcia by Rolling Stone Magazine. This book contains over 150 photos an many articles from Rolling Stone about Jerry and the Grateful Dead.

Living with the Dead: Twenty Years on the Bus With Garcia and th Grateful Dead by Rock Scully, David Dalton. Scully the former manager of th Grateful Dead details the ups and downs of the group from an insiders viewpoin

Bob Marley: Songs of Freedom by Adrian Boot, Chris Salewicz, Rita Marley 400 photos, illustrations and graphics highlight this book about the life of reggae' superstar from the slums of Trenchtown, Jamaica to legend.

Catch a Fire: The Life of Bob Marley by Timothy White. This book looks a Marley's legend and life including the Rastafarian culture and reggae's roots.

The Hendrix Experience by Mitch Mitchell, John A. Platt. Mitchell, th drummer for the Experience offers a lot of insights about Hendrix, as well a some great photos and posters.

Pearl: The Obsessions and Passions of Janis Joplin by Ellis Amburn. This account of the most powerful blues singer's troubled life and rise to stardom includes 16 pages of rare photos.

John Lennon in His Own Write by John Lennon. Enjoyable and funny stories, poems and drawings by Lennon.

Lennon : The Definitive Biography by Ray Coleman. At 784 pages this book covers his life with details galore. Book was updated in 1992 with more sources including his family.

Break on Through: The Life and Death of Jim Morrison by James Riordan, Jerry Prochnicky. This in depth look at Morrison the rock god and shaman touches all the bases. With more than 50 photos.

Science Fiction

Here are some essential classic works of science fiction for everyone, not just hippies. Most of these are dark visions of a future that may still come to pass. It's fascinating to see how well some of these older works have withstood the test of time. A few have been eerily prophetic. Much of yesterday's sci-fi is today's technology.

Science fiction allows us to ponder "what if" scenarios. These selections focus on the social impact of technology and too much governmental control. Sometimes it's a fine line between utopia and nightmare.

1984 by George Orwell. A dark scenario of a world where the government controls every facet of your life. Totalitarian Big Brother is watching you! Winston Smith works at the Ministry of Truth "correcting" little snippets of fact here and there, so the government truth is always correct. Pick up a whole new vocabulary with terms such as "newspeak" and "doublethink" to confuse your mind. Read **Animal Farm** for another horrifying Orwellian nightmare vision of society gone mad.

2001 A Space Odyssey by Arthur C. Clarke. A fabulous movie that introduced some new psychedelic special effects. The book was great reading as well, leaving our brains to supply the imaginings realized so well by Stanley Kubrick on film. Arthur C. Clarke expanded this from a short story he wrote back in the 1940's. The story continues in **2010, 2061** and **3001, the Final Odyssey**.

The Andromeda Strain by Michael Crichton was scary stuff indeed (the book and the movie). The military develops a method of capturing alien microbes floating through space. One gets loose on earth and time is running out for scientists in a top secret facility to discover a cure.

A Clockwork Orange by Anthony Burgess was published in 1962 and later made into a 1970's movie classic by Stanley Kubrick. Alex, our young protagonist is on violent binge when he gets busted, and the powers that be try brainwashing him into a model citizen. Of course it doesn't work, and he reverts to terror even more enthusiastically.

Brave New World by Aldous Huxley. Test tube babies, cloning, Soma holidays, so what's new? Perhaps the fact that Huxley wrote about these things in the 1930's when they seemed as unlikely as time travel is today. This classic SF book deals with a scientifically ordered society where everyone has their place and the populace is groomed to consume. More frightening than it was in the 30's, as it becomes today's reality.

Childhood's End by Arthur C. Clarke. Another classic by the inventor of the satellite. Utopian society is achieved on earth when aliens arrive and straighten out our affairs, but after fifty years things get weird.

Dune by Frank Herbert. A book about Melange, the addictive spice (drug) that permits space travel, hehe. Paul Atreides moves with his family to the spice planet of Dune. His father gets killed, his mother gives birth to a psychic witch and Paul becomes the savior of the planet. The first in a series of books later made into an intense sci-fi film by David Lynch.

Fahrenheit 451 by Ray Bradbury. A chilling tale of government mind control. The title refers to the temperature at which books will ignite and burn. In the future books are banned. Your only source of information is the government. You can't have your own ideas. But a group of people are determined to save the great works from the past.

Foundation by Isaac Asimov. This is a series of books about the future, and the science of Psychohistory, or pre-history of the future as predicted mathematically. Spanning millennia; the underlying theme is a utopian society on a hidden planet, secretly observing the passing of history, constantly updating and comparing the pre-written psychohistory written ages ago.

The Left Hand of Darkness by Ursula K. LeGuin is for thinkers, philosophers and everyone who likes sci-fi and fantasy. A classic from 1969 the theme is about the differences between civilizations and how to bring them together. A primer for utopia? Heavy reading but well worth it.

Lord of the Rings and **The Hobbit** by J.R.R. Tolkien. Is it sci-fi or is it fantasy. Who cares, we all read this tale of Middle Earth and the evils lurking under mountains. These books inspired a generation of dungeon and dragon tales and games, as well as many an acid trip. The incredible characters ranging from Frodo to Gollum will amaze and entertain you for days.

Naked Lunch by William S. Burroughs was a breakthrough Science Fiction book about controlling the masses of the Interzone. It is a world dominated by drugs, sex, and power. Allen Ginsberg and helped Burroughs piece together the stream of consciousness fragments of prose. Considered a landmark work of fiction, it was banned in Boston as obscene until the courts ruled otherwise creating a legal precedent for free speech. Made into an excellent movie by David Cronenburg.

The Postman by David Brin. This book is an interesting essay on what could happen in a New World where civilization has completely broken down, and hippie communal ideals come to the fore and everyone strives to achieve lasting peace. The movie totally trashed the plot of the book - skip it.

Stranger in a Strange Land by Robert Heinlein. It's "a brilliant mind bender" according to Kurt Vonnegut. The story is of a Mars-born human who is transported back to earth as an adult. Naive at first, he ends up transforming society by way of his shocking perceptions of earth society. This book should be read by all who are interested in the dangers of trying to create a new society without destroying the old.

To Your Scattered Bodies Go by Philip Jose Farmer was the first in a vast series about the fabled Riverworld. Imagine a planet covered by land with one long incredibly sinuous river snaking across it's surface. The place isn't real, but every soul that has ever lived on Earth has suddenly awakened along the banks of this mighty stream. Historical characters band together and attempt to figure out why they are there and what is the purpose of this place. Four other books followed in the series.

Vegetarian Cookbooks

Greens Cookbook: Extraordinary Vegetarian Cuisine from the Celebrated Restaurant. This fabulous cookbook let's you sample the famous cuisine of the legendary Green's restaurant in San Francisco. Unusual, creative dishes are a welcome relief from ordinary vegetarian cooking. If you ever get to San Francisco visit the Green's. Until then you let these tempting recipes whet your appetite!

Moosewood Cookbook - by Mollie Katzen. Gourmet vegetarian recipes from the Moosewood Restaurant that started a culinary trend. Revised edition with healthier (less fat) recipes.

The Enchanted Broccoli Forest by Mollie Katzen. Another classic vegetarian cookbook from Katzen!

Still Life With Menu Cookbook by Mollie Katzen. Mollie does it again this time with whole menus emphasizing freshness and variety.

Book of Tofu by Willam Shurtleff. This is the bible of making tofu at home or in a small shop. Shurtleff has thoroughly researched tofu making in Japan and walks you through the process. This healthy, tasty food along with it's wonderful by products, okara and whey, should be on every vegetarian's menu. By making it fresh at home you achieve the finest quality and taste.

Tassajara Bread Book by Edward Espe Brown. This book from the famous Zen Monastery in California is full of great recipes for whole grain breads. Find out just how good bread can be!

The Laurel's Kitchen Bread Book: A Guide to Whole-Grain Breadmaking by Laurel Robertson, Carol Fliners, Bronwen Godfrey, Lavyrl Roberston. Another great baking book.

Vegetarian Times Complete Cookbook by Editors of Vegetarian Times (Editor), Lucy Moll (Contributor) Over 600 recipes make this a new standard for vegetarian cooking.

Vegetarian Cooking for Everyone by Deborah Madison Over 800 excellent recipes covering every style of vegetarian cooking. A new classic.

The Complete Italian Vegetarian Cookbook: 350 Essential Recipes for Inspired Everyday Eating by Jack Bishop.

30-Minute Vegetarian Thai Cookbook by Sarah Beattie. If you love Thai food, here's how to make it quick, easy, and vegetarian at home.

Videos

The '60s - The complete miniseries. (1999) This fictional story traces a family's experiences through the turbulent '60s. Excellent combination of documentary archival footage and great music of the period brings home the messages of the decade. A relatively accurate portrayal of the times, though rather melodramatic. VHS, also available: DVD, VHS-Spanish subtitles.

Woodstock: Three Days of Peace & Music (The Director's Cut - Widescreen) (1970) This is the movie that captures the spirit of a generation. With legendary performances by Jimi Hendrix, Crosby, Stills & Nash, Janis Joplin and Santana you get as close as you can to being there. Lots of footage of the crowds and interviews with the stars and audience. This won the Academy Award for best documentary. The director's cut has 40 more minutes and improved audio. But the way to go with this one is DVD.

Monterey Pop-The Film (1967) This was the first rock 'n' roll festival, two years before Woodstock. An event which brought out the hippies from L.A. to S.F. and Europe. Landmark performances by Janis Joplin and the U.S. debut of Jimi Hendrix are not to be missed! Other great sets by The Who, Otis Redding and Ravi Shankar make this classic movie a must.

Gimme Shelter (1970) This excellent documentary of the Rolling Stones and their concert at Altamont is a grippingly real portrait of the dark side of rock and roll. The Stones and their promoters had to jump through hoops just to give a free concert outside of San Francisco. The ensuing drug fueled debacle climaxed as Mick sang 'Sympathy for the Devil' with the murder of one man who drew a gun. Charges against the Hell's Angels (who provided security) were dismissed. It's a harrowing vision of the flower people out of control.

Message to Love, The Isle of Wight Festival (1970) This documentary captures the highlights and low points of this controversial event. Outstanding performances by The Who, Jimi Hendrix, Joni Mitchell, Miles Davis and the Doors contrast with the hassles involved and the corporate greed surrounding the event. Many say this (and Altamont) were the closing chapter of the hippy decade. Also on DVD.

Jimi Hendrix (1973) This excellent documentary on the life, loves and music of Jimi is a must for fans. Lots of tidbits including an interview with Dick Cavett show the sweet gentle man as he is. Lots of great concert footage from Woodstock, Monterey and Isle of Wight. Dig it!

Easy Rider (1969) This famous cult movie starring Peter Fonda, Dennis Hopper and Jack Nicholson has many fans. It's about a couple of guys "on the road" looking for the "real" America. This is a movie about hippies and freedom. Highlighted by a great soundtrack with tunes by The Byrds, The Band, Steppenwolf and Jimi Hendrix. Also available in Widescreen.

Hair! (1979) Directed by Milos Forman, the movie has more of a plot than the play. Choreography by Twyla Tharp. The excellent music is the standout, bringing it together. Also available: DVD, The Broadway Cast on Audio CD.

Jesus Christ Superstar (1973) Andrew Lloyd Webber's broadway rock opera smash stars Ted Neely in the title role. You've read The Book, now see the movie! No, really it's a great telling of the tale in true hippy style. The classic songs are full of emotion. Also available in widescreen and DVD and Audio CD.

The Fabulous 60's, An Overview. Peter Jennings reviews the 1960s with tons of archival footage and commentary. This is part of a series that covers each year one video at a time.

Webguide to the Best Hippie Links

I wanted to give you a list of the best hippy links, but when we checked the ones we had so many sites were gone, and many new ones have appeared. So the best thing to do is go to Hippyland where the sites are all categorized according to subject, and updated regularly. We list only those quality sites with the most content of interest to hippies. All can be accessed from our Homepage at

http://hippy.com

Our categories include:

The '60s, Hippiedom, Drugs, Music, Mind Expansion, Travel, Peace, Mother Earth, The Arts, Love, Munchies, Connections (to other hippie sites). If you're looking to buy something check out the Hip Market page:

(http://hipplanet.com/hipmarket.htm)

That's located on our sister site, Hip Planet: **(http://hipplanet.com)** where you can also get Free-Email, Fashion & Travel tips, leave free personal or classified ads and much more.

Famous Hippies, Friends & Enemies

The following list of people includes those who influenced or were part of the hippy movement as well as those who sought to repress it. Some of these outstanding individuals have devoted much of their lives to causes that benefit everyone. Many have suffered as a result of their beliefs and actions. We list some musicians here, but for more music go to the Hippy Music with a Message chapter!

Agnew, Spiro: Vice President during Nixon's reign, he antagonized almost everyone, but especially liberals with his pompous verbal ranting. He claimed the antiwar movement was the work of "an effete corps of impudent snobs." He survived a bribery scandal but was convicted of income tax evasion. He was forced to resign much to everyone's delight. Recently declassified FBI files show Agnew did receive hundreds of thousands of dollars in kickbacks as Governor and Vice President.

Baez, Joan: Singer, songwriter, antiwar activist, called the "Queen of Folk." Joan was arrested for her participation in antiwar rallies, and her ex-husband David Harris spent several years in jail for draft resistance.

Bhagwan Shree Rajneesh: Also know as OSHO. Controversial Indian guru who had a large American following. In his ashrams (communes) in Poona, India and Oregon he taught liberation through the release of personal inhibitions. His methods included gestalt therapy and sexual freedom. Cult members showered wealth upon Rajneesh and he had dozens of Rolls Royces.

Brand, Stewart: A hard working, future looking hippie who blends philosophy with activism. Brand produced the Whole Earth Catalog, The Trips Festival, founded The WELL, the Point Foundation, Global Business Network, the Long Now Foundation and the Co-Evolution Quarterly. He's on the board of directors of the Electronic Frontier Foundation.

Browne, Jackson: Songwriter, singer, record producer, activist. Browne is a prolific songwriter and has written tunes for The Eagles, The Nitty Gritty Dirt Band as well as several very successful solo albums like "The Pretender", "Running on Empty", and "Lives in the Balance." He also was involved in organizing rock concert fundraisers for the anti-nuclear movement.

Bruce, Lenny: As a standup comedian in the '50s, Lenny felt nothing was sacred. So he joked about racism, drugs, homophobia, nuclear testing, and abortion. What made him famous was his unmitigated use of profanity. He was arrested many times, for obscenity and narcotics. He paved the way for others to exercise free speech, and inspired just about every comic since.

Bukowski, Charles: Author and poet, "honorary Beat," Bukowski wrote about life on the streets. His humourous, free-form style made him popular with the

Beat Genration.

Burroughs, William S. : Beat author wrote autobiographical books like "Junky" and "Queer" about his life as a drug addict, murderer and homosexual. His controversial, cut-up style "Naked Lunch" is his most famous work. Burroughs' thing was personal freedom. To him this meant breaking all the rules, which he did whenever he could. Burroughs' talent is undeniable. Despite (or because of?) being a junkie, he was able to convey what it's like to be living on the dark edge of reality. His intake of all sorts of drugs obviously inspired some people to experiment. Many beats and hippies can relate to Burroughs' life situation as a social outcast from mainstream American society (remember much of this happened in the '50's). Burroughs wrote about those things that no other writer of his time (except Allen Ginsberg) would consider suitable subjects. Indeed the publishing and subsequent banning of Naked Lunch turned into a landmark case for free speech in America. Burroughs influenced many around him including other authors and musicians.

Captain Beefheart: Singer, songwriter, sculptor and painter. Beefheart (Don Van Vliet), has had an unusual musical career making very strange music. His extraordinary vocal range includes a deep raspy voice as shown on Frank Zappa's "Hot Rats."

Carlin, George: Comedian. George Carlin turned us on with his "Let's Get Small" routine. He pushed the envelope with his "Seven Dirty Words" and ended up in court on obscenity charges. He's still doing his shtick, and stirring up controversy.

Cassady, Neal: The inspiration for Dean Moriarty in Jack Kerouac's On The Road and The Dharma Bums, Neal linked the beat generation with the hippies by joining Ken Kesey and the Merry Pranksters on their Bus trip across the U.S. (as the driver!) in 1964. He was part of the famous "Acid Tests." Neal sought the freedom of the open road and could rap endlessly in stream of consciousness style about everything.

Castaneda, Carlos: An Anthropologist at UCLA, Castaneda wrote a series of books about the shamanic tradition of the indigenous people of Mexico. His apparently first hand accounts of life as a sorcerer's apprentice ignited decades of controversy as to their reality. His portrayal of himself as a bumbling student of Don Juan, the powerful brujo, are now literary classics. The journeys he took on the path of the warrior through the world of spirits inspired many to seek out what lies beyond our perceptions. His books include: A Separate Reality, Tales of Power and The Eagle's Gift.

Chavez, Caesar: Chavez was the charismatic leader and founder of the United Farmworkers Union. He championed the underpaid, underrepresented migrant farm worker. Chavez organized the five-year grape boycott. Chavez helped to inspire Chicano activism of the 1960s and 1970s, combining the lessons of the civil rights movement and nonviolent protest with Mexican-American traditions and values.

Cheech & Chong: Cheech Marin & Tommy Chong hit it big with their comedy act on several recordings and movies. Their stoner humor made us laugh hysterically, particularly when we too, were stoned. By laughing at them, we laughed at ourselves and for awhile life seemed less serious.

Cleaver, Eldridge: Author of "Soul on Ice," written during his nine years in prison. After his release he joined the Black Panthers and became their Minister of Information. Involvement in a gun battle forced him into a seven-year exile.

Coyote, Peter: Actor, author, member of the San Francisco Mime Troupe, one of the original Diggers. His new book Sleeping Where I Fall, tells of his days in S.F.

Cronkite, Walter: Uncle Walt was considered the most believable broadcaster in U.S. history. In 1968, he broke the code of neutrality among major newscasters, by opposing the Vietnam War in a national television broadcast. His integrity is still unquestioned.

Crumb, Robert: Famous cartoonist of the '60s and '70s, Crumb introduced the world to his somewhat depraved, yet humorous visions via Zap Comics, Mr. Natural, and Fritz the Cat. His inspired and unique style captured the essence of the times. Always the social critic, Crumb used his art to convey the anti-establishment sentiment that swept the country.

Dass, Ram: also known as Dr. Richard Alpert. Author of Be Here Now and Grist for the Mill. He worked with Timothy Leary at Harvard on LSD studies. Alpert was so changed by the ingestion of LSD, he left his post and wandered through India, where he met his Guru and changed his name. Finding enlightenment he returned to write several books and do the lecture circuit.

Davis, Angela: Radical black teacher at UCLA. She was dismissed from UCLA in 1969 due to her radical politics. She was a Black Panther and made the FBI's most wanted list in 1970 on false charges. She became an icon as an intelligent, outspoken radical young black woman.

Donovan: aka Donovan Leitch. With his song "Mellow Yellow," Donovan made the music scene in the '60s. His sensitive voice, spacey lyrics, and unusual arrangements evoke a very hippie feeling. Other hits include "Sunshine Superman," "Hurdy Gurdy Man" and "Wear Your Love Like Heaven."

Dylan, Bob: Dylan exploded on the music scene in Greenwich Village in the early '60s. His blend of rock and folk ballads took everyone by storm, and in turn inspired just about every rock musician who was to follow in his footsteps. His early hits "Blowin' in the Wind" and "The Times They are A-Changin'" took the protest song and gave it an edge.

Ferlinghetti, Lawrence: Poet, publisher and owner of the City Lights Bookstore in North Beach, San Francisco. Part of the beat scene in San Francisco, Ferlinghetti published Allen Ginsberg's controversial poem "Howl" in 1957, which landed him in jail, but led to a landmark decision upholding free speech.

Fonda, Jane: Actress daughter of Henry Fonda, Jane made a name for herself as a political activist when she married Tom Hayden, one of the Chicago Seven. Jane was also outspoken and made a controversial trip to Hanoi, North Vietnam during the war. She's now married to CNN creator Ted Turner.

Gandhi, Mahatma: Once a lawyer in South Africa, Gandhi came to India and fought British oppression through the pioneering use of non-violent protest. His methods were adopted in the '60s by the civil rights and antiwar movements. The confrontative, yet passive techniques are now the standard for peaceful protest.

Garcia, Jerry: Musician, songwriter, artist. Jerry was a founding member of the Warlocks and Grateful Dead. His varied musical influences including Blue Grass, Rock, and Jazz enabled him to establish his own genre of music. With the Dead, the ultimate hippie band from San Francisco, he became a cult figure and was worshipped by fans. His laid back attitude and lifestyle was a sharp contrast to the lives of many egotistical rock stars. For thirty years Jerry Garcia and his faithful band brought hallucinatory music to their legions of fans.

Gaskin, Stephen: Stephen gained famed for his Monday night classes at San Francisco State where he talked about hippy values. When he took to the road his students followed and soon there was a caravan of wandering gypsies, 400 people in 60 vehicles. He eventually settled down with them and started The Farm, an ongoing Tennessee commune which pioneered organic and alternative methods of agriculture, education and social interaction.

Ginsberg, Allen: Controversial Beat poet from the '50s who wrote about following your instincts and free love. "Howl" (1956), is one of Ginsberg's most famous poems. Along with his friends Jack Kerouac and William S. Burroughs, he helped define and document the activities of the Beat Generation. Ginsberg was active in the anti-war movement appearing at rallies and also the Human Be-In. Ginsberg is credited with coining the term "Flower Power."

Graham, Bill: Rock impresario whose Fillmore Auditorium in San Francisco, and Fillmore East in New York highlighted the best rock acts of the sixties including the Grateful Dead, Jimi Hendrix, the Jefferson Airplane and more.

Gregory, Dick: Comedian, author, black activist survived more than 100 hunger strikes to protest discrimination, the Vietnam War, and drug addiction. His autobiography "Nigger" sold a million copies. Lately he is involved in promoting nutritional solutions to world hunger.

Griffin, Rick: Graphic artist noted for his famous psychedelic posters for rock concerts in San Francisco in the '60s. His unique trippy style has made him a legend and his posters are now very valuable.

Grimshaw, Gary: Another prominent graphic artist well known for his posters and flyers of rock bands that passed thru Michigan in the late 60's-early 70's. His body of work reads like a who's who in the 60's music/counter-culture scene.

Guthrie, Arlo: Son of legendary folk singer Woody Guthrie, Arlo made a name for himself with his record Alice's Restaurant. Arlo's folk rock style combines protest and storytelling.

Harrison, George: Beatle, musician, activist. George was responsible for bringing the eastern influence into the Beatles. He got them to meditate with the Marharishi, use sitar in their recordings, and gave the group a more spiritual focus. George has been active in many causes including the Concert for Bangladesh which tried to raise funds for the flood victims.

Hayden, Tom: Political activist, one of the Chicago Seven, ex-husband of Jane Fonda. Now he's a congressman from California.

Havens, Richie: A unique style of rhythm guitar combined with his passionate

ocals makes for an unforgettable experience. At Woodstock he sang 'Handsome
Johnny' and 'Freedom' to open the event.

Hendrix, Jimi: The greatest guitar player ever. Jimi could coax sounds from
his axe that no one had ever heard before. His guitar mastery has impressed
every great musician since. His on stage persona and charisma is unmatched.
Jimi gave legendary performances at Monterey Pop, Woodstock, and the Fillmore.
He died at the peak of his career. Jimi was a great soul who soared so high he was
able to take us along for the ride of our lives.

Hoffman, Abbie: Co-founder of the Yippies. Author of "Steal This Book."
One of the Chicago Seven. Outspoken advocate of anarchy, Abbie challenged
authority every chance he could. By his outrageous actions he tried to highlight
the hypocrisies inherent in the system.

Hoffman, Albert: Sandoz company scientist who inadvertently discovered
the mind transporting properties of LSD.

Hoover, J. Edgar: Infamous Director of the FBI who kept an enemies list in
the '60s. Included just about everyone active in the counterculture, even politicians
and musicians. If your name was on that list, the FBI was spying on your activities.
Hoover ordered many illegal acts to fight the antiwar, black power, and other
movements that sought change and a redistribution of power.

Huxley, Aldous: Author of the famous science fiction novel, "Brave New
World," and the ground breaking "Doors of Perception," Huxley explored the
inner realms of the mind. His thirst for the insightful psychedelic experience led
him to LSD, which he ingested as he lay on his deathbed.

Joplin, Janis: Blues singer extraordinaire. Janis could belt out the blues like
no one else. Her performances at The Monterey Pop Festival and Woodstock
were legendary. With Big Brother and the Holding Company they blew everyone
away with their psychedelic blues. "Cheap Thrills", their debut album featured a
classic cover by Robert Crumb and the hits "Summertime" and "Ball and Chain."
Janis' melancholy life came to an end with a drug overdose in 1970.

Kerouac, Jack: Beat author wrote "On the Road" and 'The Dharma Bums',
about the freedom of living each day as it comes. He inspired a whole generation
to get backpacks and take to the road. His beat friends Allen Ginsberg and Neal
Cassady appear in his works. Kerouac coined the term "Beat Generation" to
describe his friends and the phenomenon.

Kesey, Ken: Famous author, Merry Prankster, Ken wrote: "Sometimes a Great
Notion" and "One Flew Over the Cuckoo's Nest." His famous Acid Tests were
the first LSD parties with music and light shows. His legendary 1964 psychedelic
cross-country trip in a brightly painted bus inspired many hippies to do the same.

King, Martin Luther: Leader of the Civil Rights movement, Dr. King was a
firm believer in non-violent protest to achieve the goals of integration and
economic, political and social equality for all people.

Krassner, Paul: Humorist and publisher of the Realist newspaper, he's been
called the founder of the underground press.

LBJ - Lyndon Baines Johnson - He became President of the United States
upon the death of John F. Kennedy. Was elected in 1964 and served another four

years. This Texas democrat was responsible for the buildup of forces in Vietnam and was in office during the bloodiest fighting. Along with the next president, republican Richard Nixon were considered the epitome of the government run by the military-industrial complex that prospered during the Vietnam war. These two presidents highlighted the generation gap as they found it impossible to see the world from a youthful perspective.

Leary, Timothy: The psychedelic guru, acid impresario, prolific author, unchallenged hero of the "free your mind" movement. "Turn-on, tune-in, and drop-out." Those words inspired a generation to experience the mind-expanding capabilities of LSD. Leary's determination to experiment and turn people on got him kicked out of Harvard. Richard Nixon called him "The most dangerous man in America."

Lennon, John: Beatle, poet, artist, activist, singer, musician. One of the great figures of the 60s. Controversial, he once said the Beatles were more popular than Jesus (he was right at the time). He sang about love and peace and his music inspired millions. He was murdered outside his apartment building in 1980.

Leopold, Aldo: Naturalist, conservationist, author of "The Sand County Almanac," a classic in ecology. He helped found the Wilderness society and wrote about preserving the "balance of nature."

Maharaj-ji: Also known as Neem Karoli Baba. Famous Indian guru who established over 100 temples in India. Thanks to Ram Dass, his disciple, many westerners made the pilgrimage to visit this holy man.

Maharishi Mahesh Yogi: Famous guru to the Beatles, Beach Boys, and other famous personalities. First everyone went to visit him in India, then he brought his teachings to the U.S. Emphasizing the power of meditation, he drew a huge following among the hippie generation.

Manson, Charles: Convicted along with his followers of the 1969 murders of Sharon Tate and the La Biancas. Manson had created his own cult out in the California desert. In his warped mind, he believed that John Lennon's song "Helter Skelter" was a call to war and mayhem. He used mind control to get his followers to do whatever he wanted. He is still serving his life sentence.

Marley, Bob: Rastaman supreme. The charismatic Bob Marley and his band the Wailers burst onto the music scene in the early 70's bringing Reggae into the world. His music about love, Jah (God), freedom and equality touched so many people and inspired many hippies to become rastas.

Max, Peter: Hippie artist famous for album covers, movies, paintings, advertising. His colorful, flowing style graphics had a great influence on art in the 60s.

McGovern, George: Democratic candidate for president in the 1972 elections. He lost out to Richard Nixon. McGovern was supported by liberals and hippies. We can only wonder, what might have been...

McKenna, Terence: Ethnobotanist and author of the book "Food of the Gods," about organic psychedelics. Terence is a popular speaker and visionary who likes to focus on discovering our place in the universe, our reason for being here, and the future of mankind.

Mitchell, Joni: Famous Canadian singer, composer and songwriter. Joni's excellent vocal range is evident in music that varies from folk to blues to rock to jazz. One of the great songwriters, her constantly evolving style has resulted in varied success on such albums as "Blue", "The Hissing of Summer Lawns," and "Mingus." Most famous for writing the song "Woodstock" which CS&N made into a hit.

Morrison, Jim: Poet, anarchist and debaucher, Morrison was a passionate, if somewhat disturbed visionary. See the psychedelic shaman section for more about Jim.

Mountain Girl: Aka Carolyn Adams. One of the Merry Pranksters. She lived with Ken Kesey, and had his child, then married Jerry Garcia.

Nixon, Richard M.: Republican President of the United States from 1968 until his resignation in 1973, after the Watergate scandal led to an impeachment vote. Nixon provoked the anger of hippies with his dirty tricks, refusal to deal with protesters peacefully, ordering the spying upon leaders of the antiwar, black power and other counter cultural movements, as well as the deeds of his cronies.

Owsley: Augustus Owsley Stanley III was the first man to manufacture LSD in large quantities for the market in San Francisco in the 60's. Colorful Owsley acid is legendary for its purity.

Pryor, Richard: Considered the black Lenny Bruce, Pryor was famous for his standup comedy and movies replete with four-letter words. His humor attacked racial stereotypes. His crack cocaine addiction nearly killed him.

Rubin, Jerry: Co-founder of the Yippies, one of the Chicago Seven. He and Abbie Hoffman pulled outrageous stunts to poke fun and make serious statements about our society. One such stunt was throwing dollar bills onto the floor of the NY Stock Exchange, disrupting trading as brokers got down on the floor to pick up the money.

Russell, Bertrand: British philosopher, anti-nuclear and antiwar activist, logician, essayist, and social critic. In 1954 he condemned the Bikini H-bomb tests. A year later, he and Albert Einstein, published the Russell-Einstein Manifesto demanding the curtailment of nuclear weapons. He was the founding president of the Campaign for Nuclear Disarmament in 1958 and designed the Nuclear Disarmament Symbol, now called the "peace symbol."

Shankar, Ravi: Famous sitar player from India. He wooed the crowd with his mastery at the 1967 Monterey Pop festival and got a very long standing ovation and thus became a legend. He taught George Harrison how to play the sitar in 1966.

Simon, Carly: Singer and songwriter once married to James Taylor. Carly had hits with "You're So Vain," "Anticipation" and 'That's The Way I've Always Heard It Should Be."

Smothers Brothers: Famous comedians and musicians of the 60s, Tom and Dick Smothers had a top rated TV variety show until it became too controversial and was canceled by CBS. Seems they spoke their minds too often, usually protesting the Vietnam War, police brutality and racism.

Sinclair, John: A dude from Michigan who got put in prison for ten years for selling two joints to an undercover cop. His conviction was overturned thanks mainly in part to John Lennon and seven others who organized a movement to set him free. Lennon even wrote about him in a song: "It ain't fair, John Sinclair..."

Snyder, Gary: Beat Poet, Buddhist, professor. Snyder is perhaps most famous for influencing Jack Kerouac and the Beats and turning them on to Buddhism.

Spock, Dr. Benjamin: His baby book was The Bible to mothers of the hippy generation. He was against spanking children, and his non-violent stance carried over when those same children were sent to war. He spoke and marched at many peace rallies and counseled draft evaders. For this he was sentenced to two years in jail.

Steinhem, Gloria: Feminist author, founder of Ms. Magazine.

St. Marie, Buffy: Singer, songwriter, activist. Since the early '60s, Buffy has been writing protest songs about war ("Universal Soldier"), Indian Rights and the Environment. Her song "Up Where We Belong," sung by Joe Cocker, won an Academy Award.

Taylor, James: Singer, songwriter. Taylor's mellow "Sweet Baby James" album was a big hit. He was married to Carly Simon.

Tiny Tim: Famous for his one hit record, "Tiptoe Through the Tulips." With his shrill falsetto he became a cultural icon of the hippy movement. Popular but unattractive, the mini-ukelele playing Tim eventually found love, Miss Vicki, and got married.

Twiggy: English model who made being skinny popular in the '60s. Twiggy modeled the latest colorful, psychedelic fashions on her extremely thin boy like frame. Her slender build, big sad eyes and short haircut set her apart from other models of the day. Today she is an actress and has filled out a bit.

Warhol, Andy: Pop artist supreme, Andy was a scene himself. He took the icons of popular culture and turned it into art. Some of his most famous works feature Campbell's Soup Cans and Marilyn Monroe. Andy filmed several low budget films of questionable quality including: "Trash" and "Frankenstein" (in 3D).

Wavy Gravy: aka Hugh Romney, Merry Prankster, Hog Farm leader, clown, Acid Test Graduate, and so much more. A person who embodies the hippy spirit especially by helping his fellow man. Now a flavor of Ben and Jerry's ice cream. At Woodstock '69, the Hog Farm helped feed the assembled multitude. Wavy Gravy announced from the stage, "What we have in mind is breakfast in bed for 400,000."

Winwood, Steve: Talented songwriter, singer, keyboardist, Steve played with Spencer Davis Group, Traffic and Blind Faith before going on to a successful solo career. Steve was also a session man and sat in with Jimi Hendrix and B.B. King

Yogananda, Pramahansa: Founder of Self-Realization Fellowship, guru author. Yogananda taught Bhakti (devotional) Yoga and has quite a following His book "Autobiography of a Yogi" is very inspirational.

Young, Neil: Canadian musician got his big break writing and singing with uffalo Springfield. His popularity soared when he teamed up with Crosby, Stills Nash. Neil went on to produce his own great solo recordings including "After e Gold Rush" and "Harvest." Neil's style ranges from hard rock, blues, folk allads to country. His heavy rock is credited with inspiring grunge music. Some ll him the grandfather of grunge. His slightly off key vocals don't appeal to veryone, but when he's singing with CS&N, he fits right in!

Zappa, Frank: Famous musician from the 60's and 70's. His group The 1other's of Invention's first album, entitled "Freak Out" was very popular and ay out, even for it's time. Zappa's music was a very wild, creative, but dissonant atire on society. Zappa coined many expressions and became a icon of the lack f respect for the establishment. A popular college poster from the 60's showed appa with his long, wild and stringy hair sitting naked on a toilet. The title was rank Zappa Crappa. Frank's children Dweezil (son) and Moon Unit (daughter) ave dabbled with music too. Despite Zappa's outward persona, his real ersonality was far different and at one point he became a vocal opponent against rugs.

Hippi

Hippie Glossary

Hippies had to develop a whole new language to communicate their daily
experiences for which there were no precedents. The counter-culture was so
intimately involved with the psychedelic revolution and drugs that many new
words found their way into the language. The drugs themselves with such
laboratory names as LSD25, begged for more colorful, descriptive terms. Thus
catchy names like Acid, Purple Haze, and Orange Sunshine made the drug sound
more appealing. Many of the words passed around among hippies were from
other cultures, particularly India. Karma, yoga, ashram, mantra were typical of
the exotic words introduced into everyday speech in the '60s. If you're looking
for a name, please go to the section on famous hippies.

1-A: Status determined by draft board that you are currently fit and available
to serve in the military.

1-O: See Conscientious Objector.

4-F: Exemption from military service due to mental or physical disability.

45: A vinyl recording that was played at 45 RPM, with one song on each side.

Acapulco Gold: Legendary Mexican marijuana from the '60s. Today it wouldn't
be considered so special, but back then it was great!

Acid: see LSD.

Acid Tests: Ken Kesey and the Merry Pranksters did the first Acid Tests.
These were events were everyone dropped acid together for an extraordinary
group experience. Tom Wolfe wrote The Electric Kool-Aid Acid Test about the
adventures of Kesey the Pranksters.

Activist: A person who participates in protest actions. Anyone involved in a
cause, usually political.

Afterglow: A state of peace that can follow after a psychedelic experience
when your mind is still detached from worldly concerns. "He's bathing in the
afterglow of his last LSD trip."

Altamont: Controversial, ill fated rock concert headlined by the Rolling Stones
and Jefferson Airplane at Altamont Speedway on Dec.24, 1969. Hell's Angels,
acting as security, had their hands full as people kept rushing the stage. One
man pulled a gun, and the Angels killed him. The film "Gimme Shelter"
documenting the concert was used in evidence to clear the Angels.

Amnesty International: Organization for global human rights founded in
Amsterdam in 1961. They monitor the treatment of prisoners around the world,
especially "prisoners of conscience." They seek the abolition of the death penalty,
torture, and other cruel, inhumane, or degrading treatment of those in custody.

Animal Liberation Front: ALF is an organization that rescues animals (like
minks) from industrialized farms where they are raised only to provide luxury

garments to the rich. ALF has been declared illegal and its participants are bein hunted down like terrorists by the FBI and ATF.

Antiwar Movement: The organized resistance by students, veterans and oth activists against the draft and Vietnam War in the 1960s and early '70s. Rallie marches, speeches, teach-ins, sit-ins, slogans, banners, and songs were some the non-violent tactics used to get the message out.

Asanas: Sanskrit word. A series of body postures that stretch and tone muscle increase endurance, and improve flexibility. Along with breathing and meditatic they make up the practice of Hatha Yoga.

Ashram: A monastery where monks practice yoga.

Astral Plane: A dimension of existence beyond the physical world. A plac where disembodied spirits dwell. Many people attempt to contact the astral plan through meditation or by focusing their psychic energy.

Babe: Affectionate term for female, now with slightly different meaning.

Baby: Similar to Babe.

Bad Acid: Poorly made LSD, probably cut with speed which can cause a ba trip. Some people at Woodstock downed bad acid and the crowd was warne about it, making the term instantly popular.

Bad Trip: An LSD trip that goes awry. Usually indicated by paranoia, intense, uncontrollable feelings or rarely suicidal urges. Also used to descri any bad experience.

Bag: What you're into. Your profession/obsession. What you enjoy. "I he your bag's nude meditation on acid!"

Ball: To have sex. "I hear Mountain's been balling your old girlfrien Harmony."

Ban the Bomb: Slogan calling for the end of nuclear weapons. The hippie were a generation raised in fear of THE BOMB. Trained as children to hid under school desks in air raid drills, they grew up to understand there was n hiding from nuclear war.

Ban the Bra: Slogan symbolizing the Feminist Movement, women's righ and the sexual liberation of the 60s.

Bangles: Hippie jewelry. Large, solid bracelets, several are often worn togeth on arms or legs.

Bandanna: Bandannas are headbands that keep your long hair out of you face. They also mop up the sweat on warm days. And since men don't usuall wear berets or other feminine hair restraints, the bandanna does the job.

Basmati Rice: A delicious aromatic rice from India.

Batik: The 'lost wax' process used to create colorful patterns on fabric Indonesian origin.

Beat Generation: See Beatniks Term coined by Jack Kerouac.

Beatlemania: Used to describe the virtual hysteria that accompanied the Beatle on their tours. Also refers to the successful marketing of the Beatles, their record and other products.

Beatniks: Derived from the term "beat," beatniks were the precursors of th hippies. This tribe included authors Allen Ginsberg, Jack Kerouac, William S

Burroughs and others who believed the essence in life is to follow your desires and experience all life has to offer. The beat music scene included jazz, folk and the emerging rock music. Beatniks had hangouts like Greenwich Village in New York when they weren't "On the Road." Beatniks experimented with unusual living arrangements, drugs, and innovative art. Word attributed to Herb Caen, a San Francisco columnist describing the Beat Generation in 1958.

Beautiful People: Used to describe hippies or cool people.

Bean bag chair: A big amorphous chair covered with Naugahyde vinyl (or leather or other material)...usually filled with little styrofoam balls. You could sit in it and it would shape itself to you. They were very comfortable and relaxing.

Be-In: One of the first gatherings of hippies, January 14, 1967 was at the Polo field in Golden Gate Park. It was called "A Gathering of the Tribes." In attendance were the Grateful Dead, the Jefferson Airplane, Timothy Leary, Allen Ginsberg, and thousands of stoned, tripping hippies with painted faces, beads, bells, robes, etc. The Diggers were there giving out free food. There was no big reason to be there, other than to be there, hence a Be-In. An event where you groove on everyone else.

Bellbottoms: Pants with wide bell shaped legs worn by hippies. Originally bought as cheap clothing at Army/Navy surplus stores, these were navy issued denim pants for sailors, once they caught on they were popularized to the point that major manufacturers started making them.

Benzedrine: 'Bennies'..'Pep Pills' 'Uppers'. Prescribed originally as diet pills, these became abused as mood elevators, and by college students studying all night.

Berkeley: City on San Francisco Bay where the primary campus of the University of California is located. Berkeley was the origin of the Free Speech movement where the students confronted the University's policies regarding the right to be vocal and politically active on campus property. Berkeley was one of the centers of the protest movement in the 60's. Sproul Plaza was a gathering place for the protests.

Biodiversity: Ecological concept that a healthy planet requires a diverse range of life forms. Threats to biodiversity are the destruction of rainforests, pollution, overfishing the seas, ozone depletion, etc.

Biomass: The sum total of life within a given ecosystem.

Birkenstocks - These sandals were all the rage in the early 70's. They are shaped to your foot and toes with a fair amount of support. Unfortunately they're not for everyone, as I could never get a pair that felt right for my feet.

Black Muslim Movement: Black separatist movement advocating racial division and separation from White society. Two of these developed. One was under Elijah Muhammed. Malcolm X was part of this movement and chose to splinter off into a separate movement when he found himself in disagreement with Elijah Muhammed over the approach to separatism, Islam, and religious philosophy.

Black Panthers: Armed, radical black political action group. Panthers were a response to the victimization of Black people by the white majority. Its leaders were imprisoned on various charges. See Black Power

Black Power: Attributed to Stokely Carmichael who used it to encourage blacks to attain more political clout. For a time this was a uniting theme among black people in the U.S. It became a rallying cry for action against the racial injustice of the 50s and 60s. Black activists were ready to fight the system. Huey Newton, Bobby Seal, Eldridge Cleaver of the Black Panthers, Stokely Carmichael, Dick Gregory and Angela Davis were leaders in this radical movement. Some advocated revolution and the overthrow of the U.S. government. The Black Power movement struck fear into the heart of America's bigots and all the leaders were soon in jail, sometimes on trumped up charges, sometimes on real crimes. In any case the movement fractured, but the legacy of radical black activism had left its mark on America's psyche.

Black is Beautiful!: Slogan used to instill pride among black Americans.

Blacklight: A special purple light that causes certain colored paint to glow brightly in the dark. Found in head shops, they are used to add a psychedelic effect to posters and body paints.

Blast: A really great party or time. British origin. "We had a blast at the Stones concert!"

Blotter: A type of LSD on assorted colorful paper, often with funny or unusual designs, cut into small doses.

Blow: Cocaine. To waste something. "Don't blow your dough on that schwag."

Blow Your Mind: Surprise you in a mind expanding way by something unbelievable. "She really blew my mind with that head trip."

Bong: A long cylindrical tube with a bowl, used to smoke marijuana, tobacco or other substances. The smoke is filtered through cold water in the bottom of the bong.

Body Paint: To paint designs, words or slogans on one's body parts. Usually in wild patterns and often in paints that would glow under Blacklight. Body painting wasn't invented in the 60's, it's a very old form of decoration going back to the dawn of man.

Bogart: To hog a joint while others are waiting. Term refers to Humphrey Bogart, who usually had a cigarette dangling from his mouth.

Bread: Money. "Hey man, gotta any bread for the groceries?"

Bring Down: Something or someone that ruins your day, and makes you lose your high. "My ol' man's bringin' me down."

Bro: Used to describe any male friend. Usually someone you can trust. A spiritual brother.

Buds: Not beer, but cannabis flowers.

Bug: To bother someone. "Quit buggin' me!"

Bummer: A bad thing.

Bum Trip: See Bad Trip.

Bunk: Bad drugs (fake not real like bunk doses).

Bunker: Someone who sells fake drugs, rips people off.

Burn: To get ripped off. "I got burned on that dope deal." Also to get mad. "I'm all burned up about that dope deal!

Burn Baby Burn!: Slogan used to describe rioting during Black uprisings in U.S. cities during the civil strife of the late 60s. Detroit, Watts, Chicago, Cleveland and other cities experienced days of rioting and arson. See the The Hippy Timeline for what happened when.

Burn-out: The tired feeling you get when you do too much drugs. Exhaustion. Inability to handle a situation that has gotten too familiar. Wasted. Feeling of never ending repetition. Inability to function.

Busted: To get arrested. "Did you hear? Joe got busted for loitering."

Buzz: Feeling of being high. "Did you catch a buzz from that joint?"

Caftan: A long, loose, brightly colored garment with long or elbow length sleeves from the eastern Mediterranean, similar to a dashiki.

Came Down: When the drug wears off you come down.

Cannabis: Formal Latin name for marijuana. Two main subspecies are Cannabis Sativa and Cannabis Indica. Indica has wide leaves and is short, while Sativa has narrow leaves and grows taller. Hybrids from both subspecies, blending the best traits, are often grown for commercial purposes.

Capitalist Pig: Insult. Someone who represents the Business Establishment and all its greed.

Cat: A male person who's hip. Beatnik term adopted by hippies.

Centering: Figuratively, to find one's balance. To center one's awareness.

Chakras: Yogic concept. The seven chakras are physical and vibrational energy centers associated with the human body. The first begins at the base of the spine moving to the seventh at the top of the head. It is believed that by raising one's awareness through the practice of Yoga one can transmute the lower energies of the first three chakras into the higher, finer vibrations of the remaining four chakras.

Chapati: A flat round bread from India, similar to a Mexican Tortilla, used to scoop food, especially when eating with hands.

Charas: Hashish made by extended pressing of marijuana resin by hand, resulting in a black, cylindrical potent piece.

Chicago 1968: Refers to the protests at the Chicago Democratic Convention where thousands of protesters, reporters and bystanders were caught up in a battle with the police. Mayor Daly took credit for the bloodshed while millions watched on T.V.

Chicago Seven (Eight): The group of organizers of the protests at the Chicago Democratic Convention in 1968. The Chicago Seven included Abbie Hoffman, Jerry Rubin, Black Panther leader Bobby Seale and Tom Hayden. They were charged with conspiracy and defended by William Kunstler.

Chick: A girl.

Choice: Like the FDHA stamp, refers to something of quality. "I got some choice buds for the party."

City: Following certain words indicating profoundness or a lot of the previous word. "John Coltrane and Miles Davis were at the concert, man it was Jazz City!"

Civil Rights Movement: Started in the 50's the civil rights movement gathered steam in the early '60s with marches, passive resistance and speeches. Foremost among the leaders were Martin Luther King Jr., Medgar Evers, Jesse Jackson, and Malcolm X. These protests and the non-violent means used were inspiration for the student anti-war protests that were to follow a few years later.

Clean: After prolonged drug use, a period of abstinence which allows the body to remove all traces of drugs. A drug-free state. "I've been clean for six months now."

Commune: Word comes from Communist ideology. Used to describe a group of people living together, and the place they live. Communes practice self-sufficiency, often farming the land.

Conscientious Objector: A draftee could apply for 1-O status if they could prove that serving in the military went against their religious or moral beliefs. With 1-O status your were excused from military duty, but still required to do civilian service. During the Vietnam War, this status was rarely granted.

Contact High: An altered state of consciousness that people get just being around other people who are doing psychedelic drugs.

Cool: Groovy, OK, far out. "That's a real cool tie-dye!"

Cool it: Or Be Cool. Mellow Out. Calm down or stop what you're doing. "Hey can you cool it with the loud music, I'm trying to mellow out."

Co-op: Cooperative business, usually a health food store run by hippies. Members are part owners and many actively participate in the business. Based on Marxist principles.

Cop out: Escape from responsibility. "Don't cop out when your bro is in need."

Cosmic: An idea or person really out there on the edge of comprehension.

Counterculture: The encompassing word for the hippie movement. Not just a sub-culture, but an entire spectrum of individuals rejecting the values of the dominant society. This term was far more acceptable to everyone than the word "hippies."

Crash: To stay in someone else's place. To come down off Acid or another intense drug.

Crash Pad: A place where hippies could hang out, do drugs, sleep, have sex, etc. without having to pay rent. They would come and go, with different people staying there every night.

Crawdaddy: First magazine to cover the Rock Music scene. Published by Paul Williams, author of Das Energi. Crawdaddy is publishing again!

Credibility Gap: This phrase was used to describe the public's growing unease with the U.S. government's public statements about the war in Vietnam ("we're winning", "it'll be over soon", etc.) and the increasingly obvious truth (more troops going over, more body bags coming back).

Cuban Missile Crisis: - When U.S. satellite photos showed Soviet missile bases in Cuba, President Kennedy ordered a naval blockade of Cuba. The tense standoff nearly caused a nuclear war in 1962.

Da Kine: Term for top quality Hawaiian pakalolo.

Dahl: A very tasty, spicy Indian lentil stew, usually served with Basmati rice or chapatis.

Dashiki: A very colorful long sleeved African shirt. They pullover your head and have a v-cut below the neck. The dashiki is never tucked into your pants but worn as loose as possible. They are cool in summer. Hippies wore these because they have beautiful and colorful designs with African patterns. They are still very popular with African musicians.

Day-Glo: Colorful paint that glows in the dark. Popular with psychedelic art on objects and faces, especially during the Electric Kool Aid Acid Tests.

Deadheads: Fans of the Grateful Dead. Some dead heads formed a sort of cult that followed the band on tour.

Designer Drugs: Any of a vast number of custom made drugs that are designed to be chemically different from illegal drugs, but similar in effect to those drugs.

Dharma: Indian word for one's life purpose and work. The principle or law that orders the universe.

Dharma Bums: Jack Kerouac's book about the beat philosophy's roots in Zen Buddhism. He chronicles his adventures in California and a trip across the country, ending in a reflective stint up on a mountain as a fire lookout. This "rucksack wanderer" sure met some interesting people on his journeys including poet Allen Ginsberg and Buddhist Gary Snyder. This book and "On The Road" inspired many a hippy to take to the road in search of onself.

Dig: To understand. "Dig it?" To like something. "I really dig the Monkees."

Diggers: Group that gave away food and clothes in Haight-Ashbury. They followed the anti-materialist teachings of the English Diggers who fought against private ownership of land and property.

Dime Bag: $10 worth of dope.

Discotheques: Places to go hear rock music and see light shows and dance. Converted to Discos in the mid 70's.

DMT: Dimethyltryptamine. A very powerful hallucinogen that is smoked in a pipe. It gives short intense trips of a very specific nature.

Do your own thing!: Be yourself! Do what you want to do. "I got a few acres out in the country where I can do my own thing."

Don't trust anyone over 30! - Popular saying on buttons in the 60s highlighting the generation gap.

Doobie: A joint.

Dope: Drugs.

Dose: From the word dosage, a single hit of a drug, especially LSD. If you do too much you overdose.

Dovetail: A European styled and rolled joint, looks like a bird.

Downer: Someone or something that brings you down, makes you sad. Derogatory. "It's a downer having Nixon as president!"

Downers: Any drug used as a depressant-includes Seconal, Phenylbarbitol, and others.

Draft: The mandatory call to military service for young men. All 18-year-old males are required to register with the Selective Service, which maintains records of your availability to serve in the military. It takes an act of Congress to reinstate the draft.

Draft Card: Issued by the draft board, it was usually your ticket to Vietnam. Many antiwar protesters and draft dodgers burned their draft cards in public antiwar protests. This activity sent many of them to jail.

Draft Dodger: Anyone who avoided the Vietnam era compulsory draft either by getting the draft board to declare him undesirable or by fleeing to another country, usually Canada. To be declared undesirable or 4-F, you would have to fail the physical or mental qualifications. Draft dodgers used techniques that ranged from conscientious objector (which rarely worked), to acting gay or pretending to be a junkie.

Draft Lottery: The current system whereby your birthdate determines your draft eligibility. A number is drawn for every day of the year. If your birthday gets #15, then people born on your birthday will all be 15th in line to be called.

Drag: Bummer, something definitely unenjoyable. "It's a drag that we're outta dope!"

Drop Acid: To take a dose of LSD.

Drum Circle: A fun event where hippies get together to play drums or other percussion instruments and dance. These are reminiscent of pagan celebrations of special occasions like rites of passage or harvest. The rhythm of the beat tunes the participant into the group mind. The effect leads to a sense of community and transcendence. In other words it gets you high! Drum circles can be part of a larger event.

Dude: A cat.

Earth First!: Radical environmental group that uses direct confrontation to save the environment. They are the group that put nails in trees to prevent logging.

Earth Shoe: A shoe especially designed with a "negative heel" (heel lower than the rest) to mimic a footprint in the sand. It was popular fad in the 60s that was supposed make you healthier, but in reality really screwed up your feet. Needless to say the company went out of business.

Easy Rider: 1969 film starring Peter Fonda, Jack Nicholson and Dennis Hopper contrasting the freedom loving hippie lifestyle and more conservative American values with an unfortunate, but symbolic outcome. The song 'Born to Be Wild' by Steppenwolf added to the flavor.

Ego Trip: The whole world revolves around people who are "on an ego trip."

Electric Kool-Aid: Another term for LSD, coined when the Pranksters combined Kool-Aid and Acid during the Acid Tests of the 1960s. Used in the title of Tom Wolfe's book about Ken Kesey and the Merry Pranksters, "The Electric Kool Aid Acid Test."

The Electric Kool Aid Acid Test: Tom Wolfe's book about Ken Kesey and the Merry Pranksters. One of the great books about how LSD invaded America's consciousness, peaking during the Summer of Love. A tribute to Kesey, the Pranksters (including Neal Cassady, Ken Babbs, Mountain Girl and Wavy Gravy) and the whole psychedelic generation. Good insight into how the torch was passed from the Beats to the hippies. It also contrasts Kesey's "up front," experiential movement versus Timothy Leary's experimental, insightful approach to the LSD trip.

Endangered Species: Any animal, plant or other species that is on the verge f extinction. Since the 1960s hundreds of species have either been placed on the ndangered Species list or have been removed due to extinction.

Enlightenment: Attainment of a higher awareness of the reality beyond the lusion (Maya).

Environmental Defense Fund: Organization that seeks to prevent pollution rough education and coordinated efforts.

E.R.A.: The Equal Rights Amendment. Bans discrimination based upon sex. till not law. Written in 1921 by suffragist Alice Paul it passed Congress in 972, was ratified by 35 states, 3 short of the number needed to make it law.

Fabulous Furry Freak Brothers - Gilbert Shelton's popular comic about the dventures of three stoned out hippies.

Fad: A popular craze, a temporary fashion.

Far Out!: Something wonderful. An expression of glee or approval. Also a ay of saying thanks.

Feds and Heads: A classic dope dealing game.

Fillmore posters - The Fillmore East and West were concert venues in the 0's that had introduced some of the biggest rock acts to American audiences cluding The Grateful Dead, Jimi Hendrix, Jefferson Airplane, etc. The posters or those concerts are now collectors' items and some are very valuable since the rtwork was very psychedelic and symbolic of the times.

Finger Hash: Potent Black Nepalese hashish formed into finger shapes or haras.

Flaky: Someone or something unreliable, untrustworthy.

Flashback: A spontaneous psychedelic experience that reminds one of a revious trip, but without any drugs. "Every time I climb that mountain I get lashbacks from my acid trip there back in '69."

Flip Out: To lose it. To go crazy. "Mike flipped out after his chick Sunshine eft."

Floating: High on drugs.

Fly: To be high. "Two tokes of that stuff and you're flying!"

Flower Children: The hippies were called Flower Children because they wore lowers in their hair, on their clothes and painted flowers on everything.

Flower Power: Term coined in 1965 by Allen Ginsberg at an anti-war rally in 3erkeley. It was Ginsberg's way of encouraging a non-violent response to violence rotesters encountered. Since hippies were fond of wearing and sharing flowers, 'lower Power was the hippie equivalent of the Black Power movement. An xtension of the Peace and Love theme, Flower Power assumed that the power of ove would win out over violence and hate.

Flowers: Cannabis buds.

Four-Twenty, 4:20: New hippy term. Adopted by heads as the time to light p your joint! It's currently very popular for the name of websites, and it appears egularly in marijuana magazines. It's a myth that 4:20 is related to the California enal Code reference for the use of marijuana.

Freak: To be very excited about something. "He's a VW bus freak." Also to get upset or to be afraid of something - see Freak Out.

Freak Flag: Long Hair

Freaks: A descriptive term for hippies. Like the old Freak show in a carnival, hippies were so different and their behaviors so bizarre by ordinary standards they were considered freaks. But really it's an affectionate term used within the hippy community to describe someone really into being themselves, however outlandish that might be.

Freak Out: To go wild over something, or to have a really wild experience. "They all freaked out when he showed up in body paint alone." To get very upset about something or to be very afraid.

Freaky: Something really weird or frightening.

Freedom Fighter: Current Hippie term (late 80's-90's) for a person involved in the political movement to legalize marijuana.

Free Love: The idealistic concept embraced by the hippies that love and sex needn't be bound by convention. People are free to love whomever they please, whenever they please, wherever they please, without attachment or commitment. This was practiced by many hippies and helped spawn the Women's and Gay Liberation Movements.

Free Speech Movement: Arose in 1964, on the Berkeley campus of the University of California as a result of the administration prohibiting student political activities on campus. Students held rallies on the steps of the Administration building (Sproul Hall) and sit-ins inside demanding freedom of speech. Many students were beaten, arrested, and some were suspended including Mario Savio, the founder of the movement and one of the more outspoken student protesters. Eventually the Berkeley faculty members came up with a proposal to restore free speech and the University Chancellor was replaced.

Fried: Burned out from doing too much dope.

Fritz the Cat: Cartoonist R. Crumb's fabled feline became famous for appearing in two feature films.

Fry: To be high, almost too high, usually on psychedelic drugs. "I did 300 mikes, I'm frying!"

Friends of the Earth: An affiliation of international environmental organizations in 63 countries. Friends of the Earth seeks to raise awareness of ecological issues affecting the planet, and provide coordinated solutions to the most pressing problems facing the planet.

Funky: This word was given a new meaning by the hippies. It described clothing that wasn't supposed to go together, but somehow managed to look good. Over time, the meaning of the word became more vague, but still meant something with an unusual campy style, like clothes, music, or attitude. Get Funky!

Fuzz: Another name for the police. Pigs, cops, and "the man" were other commonly used terms.

Gay Liberation Movement: An outgrowth of the Sexual Liberation movement that started when NYC police raided a Greenwich Village gay bar in 1968. In the resulting riot 2000 demonstrators battled 400 police with many injuries.

Generation Gap: Term highlighting the differences in perspective between ippies and their parents.

Get High: To turn on. To do a drug. To alter your consciousness in a pleasant way. "I got high just listening to Joni sing!"

Get into it!: Dig it! Go for it! Do it with your whole being.

Get it together!: Also: Get your shit together. Shape up!

Get Laid: Have sex.

Get Real!: Stop dreaming! "Get real man, nobody's gonna get high smokin' anana peels!"

Getting Off: When a drug takes effect and you start to get high. Also means to njoy something. "I get off on Jerry's licks."

Gig: A concert or a job. Something to do.

Gimme Shelter: Documentary movie about the ill fated Altamont concert. Also a Rolling Stones song about the event.

Give Peace a Chance: Saying on banners and John Lennon song sung by rotesters.

Go Down: Something happening. "What went down at the protest yesterday?" Also a blow job (oral sex). "She went down on me and I let loose!"

Going through Changes: To have a transforming experience. A negative xperience. "My parents are putting me through changes."

Go For It!: Do it!

Gone: Really out of it. Not aware. Asleep.

Go Straight: To stop using drugs. To get your "act" together.

Go with the Flow: Taoist philosophy of living in the moment, without struggle, etting things happen as they may.

Granny Glasses: Small wire framed glasses with round or square colored enses. Made popular by rock musicians including John Lennon and Jerry Garcia.

Grass: Marijuana

Great Society: LBJ's far-reaching economic and social plan begun in the oom years of the early 1960's. It achieved some worthwhile goals including Medicare and other workers benefits. It got sidetracked by the financial burden f the Vietnam War.

Green: Someone active in the Ecology Movement. A product that respects cology, using biodegradable substances for example.

Greenwich Village: Also referred to as "The Village." Home to the Beats in he late '50s, early '60s when the coffeehouse scene was hot. Artists, writers, oets, musicians all were attracted to the area. Later in the '60s, the hippies nvaded and the scene moved to the less expensive East Village where institutions ike the Fillmore East kept things lively.

Greenpeace: Activist organization founded to fight for the global environment. Greenpeace has the highest profile of environmental groups due to their daring actions especially on the high seas.

Grok: A deep understanding of a concept. From Robert Heinlein's novel "Strangers in a Strange Land."

Groove: A good habit or style. "I'm getting into the groove of doing gigs every week."

Groovy!: Very pleasing, wonderful.

Guitar Army: Book/Manifesto written by John Sinclair outlining the counterculture revolution of the Woodstock Nation

Guru: A teacher, often spiritual, especially in India.

Haight-Ashbury: The famous intersection in San Francisco near Golden Gate Park where the hippies came in the Summer of Love, and never left! This area was the focus for much of the hippie movement's beginnings and inspiration.

Hair!: Hit Broadway rock musical famous as much for its nudity as for its music. Famous tunes include "Aquarius," "Hair," and "Good Morning Starshine."

Hallucination: An altered state of awareness where one perceives a completely different objective reality. More than just visual distortions, the person believes the hallucination to be real.

Hang Up: A personality quirk resulting from something bothersome that makes your life miserable. "She ignored me! She must be all hung up about my new girlfriend."

Happening: An event where people get together just to be together, usually involving music and other hippie rituals.

Happy Trails!: Have a nice TRIP! Refers to the visual distortions perceived under the influence of LSD.

Hare Krishnas: Religious group which grew during the 60s by recruiting many hippies. Characterized by their chanting, colorful robes, shaven heads and pigtails they could be seen parading through city streets around the country. They worship the Hindu God, Krishna and abstain from meat, hoping to achieve higher consciousness through devotion.

Hash Bash: The first and longest running protest for the legalization of Marijuana. (Takes place at the University of Michigan every April 1st). Also a show/contest displaying various types of hashish and marijuana in Amsterdam.

Hashish: Compressed potent form of marijuana, produced in the Middle East, Himalayan region and Africa. Also known as hash. Process separates then presses resin containing THC from the marijuana plant usually using screens, or hands.

Hassle: A bother, something that you'd rather not deal with. "Don't hassle me about the rent, I'll get it later."

Head: Some one who enjoys and does a lot of certain drugs like "pot head" or "acid head."

Head Shops: Stores that catered to hippies or the young. Clothes, comics beads, candles, jewelry and drug paraphernalia were obtainable at these shops. They also made good hang outs.

Head Trip: To play games with someone's mind. A person or situation that messes with your mind.

Heavy Metal: Hard, loud rock music, characterized by a heavy beat and thunderous guitars. Term originated with Steppenwolf ("heavy metal thunder" in the song "Born to Be Wild."

Hell No We Won't Go!: Popular chant of draft resisters at demonstrations against the war in Vietnam.

High: Stoned. An altered state. Pleasantly turned on.

High Times Magazine: Monthly magazine focused on marijuana and other drugs. A leading proponent of decriminalization of marijuana, and the producer of the annual Cannabis Cup event in Amsterdam.

Hip: Aware of what's going on. Knowledgeable. "I'm hip to what's happening." Something cool or groovy. "Those are the hippest love beads I've ever seen!"

Hip Huggers: Jeans that rested low on the hips, exposing the navel, especially on a girl wearing a halter-top.

Hippie: A person who's hip. Hippies did not refer to themselves as such. The term became derogatory but is again fashionable if not entirely complementary. The whole anti-materialist, anti-war, pro-peace, pro-mind expansion counterculture has been termed the Hippie Movement. San Francisco writer Michael Fallon applied the term "hippie" to the SF counterculture in an article about the Blue Unicorn coffeehouse where LEMAR (Legalize Marijuana) & the Sexual Freedom League met, & hippie houses.

Hit: A dose of a drug, like a "hit of acid" or a "hit from the joint."

Hit and Run: To be at a demonstration or protest and be chased by police while stopping to take a toke, then running off to avoid arrest.

Hog Farm: This activist, mobile commune once was located on a mountain top near L.A. in the 60s. Later, the Hog Farm went on the road living in a fleet of converted school buses and traveled the country protesting the Vietnam War. At Woodstock '69, the Hog Farm helped feed the assembled multitude, and assisted those having bad trips. After Woodstock, the Hog Farm personnel traveled through Europe to Nepal, and distributed medical supplies to Pakistani flood victims. The Hog Farm's most famous personage, Wavy Gravy, a Merry Prankster, was a founding member.

Holding: In possession of something, usually dope. "I'm holding a special lid for you."

Howl!: Allen Ginsberg's controversial book of poetry that was declared obscene and banned. Ginsberg won the court case, a landmark for free speech. Ginsberg pioneered a new style of writing and artfully expressed his innermost rage at society's shortcomings. Ginsberg's dramatic reading of this work at coffeehouses in the 50s and 60s enthralled those "angelheaded hipsters" and established his reputation in literary circles.

Hype: To promote something excessively. "This book sure hypes hippies!"

I Love You Alice B. Toklas: 1968 Peter Sellers' movie where he is a lawyer who falls for a hippie girl who teaches him to mellow out with the help of some marijuana brownies.

If it feels good do it!: Don't be inhibited, explore what life has in store for you.

IFIF: International Foundation for Internal Freedom. Founded by Timothy Leary to promote LSD research & publish The Psychedelic Review.

Imperialist: Description of U.S. foreign policy where we sought to impose our system or dominate other countries economically and politically.

In: Whatever's trendy at the moment. "Beatle boots and granny glasses are really IN now!"

Incense: Incense has been used for millennia to provide a ritual cleansing of a room for religious services. Temples and churches are fond of it. Supposedly it drives out the "evil spirits." Most of the incense we use in the west comes from India. When the hippies got high they would buy incense to mask the smell of marijuana. Incense can also assist in meditation by giving your space an exotic feel. Since incense comes in a wonderful assortment of scents you can just use it to add a nice fragrance to your house.

Jackson State: Two student protesters at Jackson State University (Mississippi) were shot and killed by state police on May 15th, 1970.

Jay: A joint.

Jeanette Rankin Brigade: A coalition of women's peace groups, who demonstrated against the Vietnam war at the opening of Congress in 1968. 5000 women attended.

Jesus Freaks: A movement of people who just discovered Jesus and Christianity. They would get together with signs and banners to promote Jesus. Some hippies went this route. Often they were 'false' hippies, who used the hip image to proselytize Christianity. Hippies who were sincere Christians were also Jesus Freaks...and were cool.

Joint: A marijuana cigarette.

Jonesing: When you want something real bad, especially drugs.

Joneser: Someone who wants drugs so much that he'll rip you off if he has to.

Junkie: A heroin addict.

Kama Sutra: Tantric Indian guide to enlightenment though sexual union. Lots of sexual positions to help you get there!

Karma: Indian term for fate. You reap what you sow. Our condition in this life is a result of our actions in past lives. We reincarnate until we free ourselves from our Karmic indebtedness.

Kefir: A yummy yogurt like drink with live cultures, often mixed with fruit. A staple in Health Food stores.

Kent State: University where four students were shot and killed by National Guardsmen during an antiwar protest on May 4, 1970. There is a monument to the students on the Kent State Campus which is still incomplete. Student activists still have an annual memorial gathering on the day of the shootings.

Key: A kilo of marijuana or other drug.

Kicks: Something you do for fun. Something enjoyable.

Kif: The Moroccan term for marijuana that hasn't been processed into hashish. Often mixed with tobacco and smoked in a sipsi.

Kilim: Islamic rug, with colorful geometric patterns, usually made of wool and silk.

Killer: Something really great, powerful, or impressive. "That was sure some killer weed we smoked."

Kundalini: A form of energy that lies dormant at the base of the spine that is channeled upward through the chakras via yoga.

Laid Back: Someone relaxed, easygoing. A place that's cool. "I've been to the commune, it's real laid back."

Lassi: No, not a dog or young girl, but a refreshing, cooling drink from India made with yogurt. Sometimes served cold, sometimes with a touch of rosewater, often with mango or other fruit. A delicious precursor to the smoothie.

Later: Good bye. See you later.

Lay: To have sex, or someone with whom you have sex. "She was a great lay."

Lay it on me: Give it to me.

Laugh-In: A popular sixties comedy show with Dan Rowan and Dick Martin as the hosts. Stars included Flip Wilson, Goldie Hawn, Judy Carne and Arte Johnson. Famous for its humor, zaniness, social commentary and frenetic pace and editing. It captured the sixties style and attitude and added it's own set of expressions to the times, like "sock it to me!."

Lava Lamp - The original is a glass lamp lit from the bottom with an oily liquid inside that rises in colorful amorphous bubbles. These lamps are now enjoying a revival and can be purchased via the net.

Lemon Pipers: One or more person(s) who puts a hole through a lemon (other fruit can also be used) then inserts a joint at the other end and inhales thereby not only cooling the smoke but giving the smoke a scented flavor. (Rolling papers eventually caught up to this fad and offer a flavored paper commercially).

Licks: Chops. Groove. A musician's musicianship. The music they make.

Lid: A bag of grass, usually about an ounce (28 grams).

Light Shows: A visual performance accompanying music at clubs and concert venues using strobes, film, video, special effects and more recently lasers. First pioneered by Ken Kesey & the Merry Pranksters during the Acid Tests, The Trips Festival and the Fillmore during the 60s. Andy Warhol also put on some famous light shows in NYC.

Love beads: Love beads were originally made from small seeds and were worn as a necklace. They came in numerous patterns, and were given as gifts between friends or made by the wearer. They were a common sign of friendship.

Love-In: Like a Be-In it was a reason to get together with other hippies and have fun. Loving everyone and everything was the general theme of the event.

LSD or LSD25: Lysergic Acid Diethylamide. Acid. A rye ergot derivative. First synthesized and absorbed inadvertently by Albert Hoffman of Sandoz Labs, Switzerland in 1938. Extremely hallucinogenic in minute doses, measured in micrograms. Effects can last up to 24 hours depending upon dose. Used in psychotherapy in the '50s and '60s. Researched at Harvard by Timothy Leary and Richard Alpert. Both left Harvard and Leary continued as high priest of the LSD movement. In the '60s acid became the popular way to "trip." An LSD trip is not to be taken lightly. It is a profound soul shaking experience that expands one's perceptions and broadens one's mind. Reactions to LSD, which include physiological and behavioral changes, anxiety, and hallucinations, are influenced by the amount of the drug taken and the user's personality and expectations.

Lude: A Quaalude, a depressant drug.

Maintain: To keep one's shit together. "Ever since my baby left me I'm finding t hard to maintain."

Make Love Not War!: Slogan that sums up the hippie attitude. Appeared on signs and buttons during protests against Vietnam War.

Man: A dude. The Man is the police. Man! means damn! My Man! means a friend.

Mandala: A colorful Tibetan Buddhist geometric artwork used to assist meditation.

Mantra: A form of meditation that uses repeated phrase(s) that help to free the yogi from random thoughts by focusing on the phrase. Different mantras have different effects.

Marinol: Pharmaceutical extract of marijuana, allowed (by U.S. gov't) for those who have prescription for marijuana.

Mary Jane: Marijuana

Maui Wowie: The fabulously sweet, potent pot grown on the island of Maui in Hawaii.

Maya: The veil of materiality and self-delusion that screens us all from the true reality of oneness.

Meditation: An exercise where one focuses one's attention, relieving stress, allowing contemplation.

Mellow: Something pleasant and enjoyable. Often used to describe the marijuana high.

Mellow Yellow: Donovan song that had everyone thinking you could get high smoking banana peels. One of the greatest put-ons courtesy of the Berkeley Barb.

Mellow out!: Calm down! Equal to chill out!

Mescaline: A hallucinogenic alkaloid in the peyote cactus plant, still used for Native American ritual purposes. These cacti are eaten in raw form. Processed mescaline compound was ingested as a pill form. Synthetic mescaline made a brief appearance mixed with chocolate powder and was one of the best highs ever - it made you laugh uncontrollably for hours. Anyone know how to make more?

Microdot: A type of LSD in a colorful tiny pill.

Mikes: The number of micrograms as in a dose of LSD.

Military-Industrial Complex: The leading force in the American economy in the '60s. The combination of large American industries with huge defense contracts. Reaps profits from war. Blamed for lobbying Congress to increase military spending, to step up war in Vietnam. In 1960 President Eisenhower warned that the Military-Industrial complex was getting too big and powerful. Today this group of special interests is still determining US foreign policy and keeping the Defense budget ever growing.

Mind Game: When someone tries to control your mind, often by trying to bullshit you.

Mini-skirt: A very short skirt that usually reveals not only a lot of intimate feminine curves, but much about the personality of the woman wearing it! A controversial symbol of Sexual Liberation because on the one hand women wearing it were touting their sexual freedom, but on the other hand were perpetuating the stereotype of women as a sexual objects. Go figure!

Miso: A salty thick paste, the residue from making soy sauce, popular for naking Japanese soups. Supposedly it has healing properties. They say it can essen the effect of radiation poisoning (who better to know about this than the apanese?).

Moby Grape: San Francisco band that made great music, but failed commercially.

Monterey Pop Festival: This was the first rock festival ever. Held in 1967, it howcased a whole new genre of music. Produced by Paul Simon, Johnny Rivers and John Phillips (of the Mamas and Papas) it was an event that almost didn't happen. Disagreement between the producers (who wanted to charge for the concerts) and the musicians (who wanted it to be free) were resolved thanks to impresario Bill Graham. Acts included memorable performances by Jimi Hendrix and Janis Joplin. The event was filmed and is available on video.

More power to you!: Good for you.

Movie: The reality we create for ourselves based upon a script we are constantly writing. This concept allows us to take control of the circumstances of our lives by recognizing we are not victims but actors in a play who can change our role whenever we choose.

Mr. Natural: Cartoonist R. Crumb's popular philosophical character was a spoof of gurus and their followers.

Munchies: Also known as the raving munchies. The mad craving for food, often sweets that you get after smoking marijuana. It's so effective as an appetite stimulant, that's one of the main reasons it's prescribed by doctors for AIDS patients and those undergoing chemotherapy.

Naked Lunch: William S. Burroughs' breakthrough autobiographical/Science Fiction book about the Interzone, where drugs, murder, and homosexuality rule. Allen Ginsberg and Jack Kerouac helped Burroughs piece together the stream of consciousness fragments of prose (Kerouac is credited with the title). Considered a landmark work of fiction, it was banned in Boston as obscene until the courts ruled otherwise creating a legal precedent for free speech. Made into an excellent movie by David Cronenburg.

Napalm: Controversial inflammable defoliant used in Vietnam by U.S. military to clear ground cover and expose enemy. However many civilians including women and children were seriously burned or died when napalm fell from the skies upon their villages.

Nehru Jacket: Very dressy Indian made shirt/jacket with short collar turned up and rounded buttons. Usually made with very fine material, like silk or linen. Became popular around the time the Beatles went to India.

NEPA: National Environmental Policy Act. In effect since 1970, it mandates that the Federal Government monitor and regulate the quality of the environment. It was followed by the Clean Air and Water Acts.

Nepalese Temple Balls: Top quality Nepalese hashish shaped into balls. Supposedly used by monks in Buddhist rites.

Nickel Bag: $5 worth of dope.

No nukes is good nukes!: Popular bumper sticker and banner in the sixties protesting nuclear weapons.

N.O.W.: National Organization for Women. Started in 1966 this activis organization seeks economic equality, abortion, sexual and reproductive right for women. They also oppose racism and violence against women. One of it founders and first president was Betty Friedan, author of The Feminine Mystiqu (1963). NOW is the largest feminist organization in the world.

Nuggets: Buds. Also Nugs.

Number: A joint.

OD: See Overdose.

Off the Pigs: Radical slogan used by Black Panthers encouraging confrontatior with the police. Literally meant: Kill the Police.

OM: Also AUM. The cosmic vibration. A very powerful sound, especially when chanted by a group. Used as a mantra and in affirmations and blessings.

OP Art: Optical illusion style of art. Many artists tried this style in variou mediums. Geometric patterns that fool the eye with an illusion of three dimensions This style reached a peak during the hippie era.

Organic: Something grown and processed without the use of chemica fertilizers, insecticides, fungicides, etc. Organic farming methods includ mulching, composting, use of natural pest control, crop rotation, etc. Mor generally something from nature, not man-made.

Orange Sunshine: A type of LSD in the form of a tiny orange barrel, usuall containing other adulterants like speed. Also called Orange Barrels.

Out: Gone, no more left. "Bummer, I'm outta smoke!"

Out of it: Some one who's out there. Not with it. Asleep.

Outtasight!: Fantastic!

Overdose: Take too much of a drug. "Jimi overdosed on life." Also OD.

Paisleys - These fractal like patterns appeared on clothes in the sixties an were a popular psychedelic design.

Pakalolo: Hawaiian marijuana.

Paraquat: Chemical defoliant supposedly used by Mexico and U.S governments to eradicate marijuana. Paraquat is very toxic as it contains dioxin which poison the ground and water and is carcinogenic.

Patchouli: For some reason this is the fragrance most associated with hippies probably because it masks the smell of marijuana. You can still smell it in mos head shops. A very strong earthy, flowery smell, usually found on hippie girl wearing long peasant dresses. Origin - India.

Peace Now!: Rallying call to end the war in Vietnam.

Peak Experience: Refers to any intense personal experience, often drug induced. See Peaking.

Peaking: Term for reaching the highest high on an LSD trip or othe psychedelic experience.

Peace Symbol: The familiar circle with lines was originally the symbol fo nuclear disarmament. Bertrand Russell is credited with creating the symbol in 1958 from the semaphore flag signals for letters N(uclear) and D(isarmament) It first appeared in the anti-nuclear protest of the early sixties, and was use extensively during the anti-war movement as a more generic peace symbol.

People's Park: In 1969, hippies setup camp on some vacant land near UC erkeley and called it the People's Park. On Memorial Day, 20,000 appeared ith flowers at the park. By July the authorities forcibly removed all the squatters urting many) and the park was closed.

PETA: People for the Ethical Treatment of Animals. Activist organization for nimal rights. They have staged many dramatic actions to free animals from ersecution and experimentation. They've also had many court cases against dividuals and companies that abuse animals.

Pigs: Derogatory name for police.

Pissed-Off: Also Ticked-Off or Pissed. Upset or angry.

Plastic: Something or someone artificial, unreal. "I hate shopping malls, they're o plastic."

Plateau: The period of maximum effect of a drug, just after the peak, and efore coming down.

Platform Shoes: Raised shoes that were all the rage in the '60s. The first were)utch klogs, but they soon became higher, more colorful, very fashionable, and ven men started wearing them.

Pot: Marijuana.

Power to the People!: Used by Black Panthers and others to describe the need o change the existing power structure.

Primo: First quality stuff. "Those buds were primo!"

Psilocybin: A hallucinogen contained in certain mushrooms of the genus)silocybe. Fresh mushrooms can be found in many places around the world, isually popping up in cowpies. Can be eaten raw (after washing), or brewed as ea, or cooked in omelets. The mushrooms are sold over the counter in enlightened :ountries like Holland. Very popular with the rave set.

Psychedelic: Hallucinatory experience sometimes brought on by altered state)f awareness, via drugs like LSD or some other experience or art work. The vord originated in correspondence between Aldous Huxley and Humphrey)smond in the '50s. From Greek, it literally means a substance that reveals the iature of the soul.

Puna Butter: The smooth, sweet, and strong sinsemilla marijuana grown on :he Big Island of Hawaii.

Purple Haze: A type of LSD, also a famous song by Jimi Hendrix about the drug.

Purple Micro-Dot: Known for its color and considered the little sister of the legendary Purple Haze!

Pusher: Someone who sells drugs, usually in reference to hard drugs like heroin.

Put On: A joke on somebody. "Is that story real or are you just putting me on?"

Quadrophonic: Four channel surround sound first introduced in movie theaters then in home hi-fi systems. Now evolved into Dolby or DBX surround sound.

Question Authority!: Popular button in the sixties encouraging people to challenge the powers that be, particularly the government.

Rainbow Family: Group of hippy gypsies who meet up once a year for a Rainbow Gathering. During the Gathering they live together and cooperate in a communal setting. They incorporate many American Indian customs in their Gatherings. Local chapters also have events.

Rainbow Gathering: See Rainbow Family.

Rainbow People's Party: Movement and political party that grew out from the White Panther Party.

Rainforest Action Network: Founded in 1985, this activist organization focuses on the needs and problems of the Earth's rainforests. It has a good emphasis on educating children to the perils facing our planet.

Rap: To have a friendly discussion. Also a jail sentence or penalty.

Rasta: Rastafarian. Someone who follows the teachings of Marcus Garvey and Haille Sellassie, and worships Jah (God). Rastafarians wear their hair in dreadlocks, and smoke ganja as the sacred herb. Bob Marley was the most famous Rastafarian.

Redstockings: Radical feminist group who published "The Bitch Manifesto." They split from the National Organization of Women (NOW) and sought to raise the consciousness of women.

Reefer: Old term for marijuana from the '30s-'50s.

Reefer Madness: Term allegedly describing how crazy people get after smoking marijuana. This was typical of the propaganda promoted by the U.S. government following marijuana prohibition. This was also the title of a famous movie purporting to show the dangers of marijuana. Now more of a funny cult film. The poster from the film was very popular in the '60s-'70s.

Resin: The clear sticky liquid marijuana produces to capture pollen. It is very high in THC content. Heating this resin causes it to vaporize the THC, and when inhaled it gets you high. Resin is separated from marijuana to make hashish. Resin is also the term for the dark, coating formed inside pipes used for smoking marijuana and hashish.

Right On!: Strong agreement, affirmative, yes! Sometimes accompanied by a clenched fist.

Righteous: Something really great.

Rip Off: To steal, or have something stolen. "Someone ripped off my last lid!"

Ripped: Very stoned. "I got really ripped on that Colombian last night!"

Roach: What remains of joint of marijuana when you smoke it way down. Often saved and smoked later in desperation when you're tapped out.

Roach Clips Small devices that hold on to a roach so it can be smoked.

Rolling Stone Magazine: Music magazine with famous covers of just about everyone in the biz. Stories, reviews, and music calendar make this magazine a must.

RPM: Revolutions per minute. Not a measure of anarchy, but the speed of a turntable that plays vinyl records. 45 rpm was for singles, 33 rpm for albums, and 78 rpm if you're really old, or you're trying to find hidden meanings (don't forget to play it backwards too!).

Rush: What you experience as a drug takes effect. A quick change of consciousness that creates a dizzying sensation. "I love it when the Dead jam, what a rush!"

Samadhi: Derived from Yoga, this term refers to the transcendence of personal ego to attain a state of oneness with true reality. A state of bliss.

Sandoz: The Swiss drug company that discovered LSD25 and made it available for psychological therapy. A term for LSD.

Scam: A plot to defraud people.

Scene: The locale and the cool people who attend comprise the "scene." A party with an atmosphere you appreciate.

Schwag: Low quality weed, or just something that sucks in general.

Score: To finally get something highly desired. "Dude, I scored a gram of some killer Nepalese finger hash."

SCUM: The Society for Cutting Up Men. Founded by feminist Valerie Solanis, the woman who shot Andy Warhol. In 1967, she wrote the SCUM Manifesto, which declared war against men and the male dominated society.

Screw: To have sex. "We screwed all night." Insult. "Screw you!."

Screw Magazine - Pioneering Porno Magazine published by Al Goldstein.

SDS: Students for a Democratic Society. Leftist group that organized many student protests against ROTC on campus, against the draft and the war. Some of the more radical elements formed the Weathermen, who believed in using violent means to get their message across. They were responsible for bombing banks and businesses of the establishment. After an explosion at a Greenwich Village Brownstone killed several Weathermen, the remaining members went underground.

Self-Determination: The right of any people to determine for themselves who should govern them and how. The U.S. action in Vietnam denied the Vietnamese the right of self-determination.

Selling Out: To sacrifice one's counterculture ideals for acceptance by society or material gain.

Shag: To screw, have sex. (British)

Shake: Loose leafy (sometimes seedy) marijuana left at the bottom of the bag after the buds have been removed.

Shit: Dope of one kind or another. Could be called "good shit" or "bad shit," both meaning it's good.

Shotgun: To reverse the joint in ones mouth and blow the smoke into the mouth of another.

Sierra Club: Founded in 1892 by conservationists including John Muir, the Sierra Club tries to influence public environmental policy through legislation and lobbying rather than activism.

Silent Majority: President Richard Nixon used this term to describe the majority of Americans who he felt supported the government's policies in Vietnam but weren't as vocal as the minority of protesters.

Sipsi or Sebsi: A long narrow pipe with a small bowl, made from wood or metal. Used to smoke kif or hashish in Morocco.

Smashing!: (British) Something really cool!

Smoking Stone: A ceramic styled small stone with an opening at both ends to cool the heat off the weed before inhaling.

Smoothie: A delicious drink, popularized by hippies, usually made with yogurt, fresh fruit, fruit juice, ice cream or milk. Popular additions are bee pollen, protein powder, nutritional yeast, dates, nuts, you name it!

Skunk: Descriptive term for very strong smelling marijuana. Also a popular hybrid variety of marijuana.

Sock it to me!: A recurring segment on Laugh-In, a popular sixties comedy show. Richard Nixon appeared on the show turning it into a question, Sock it to me? And we did!

Soul on Ice: Book written by Eldridge Cleaver, minister of information for the Black Panthers, during his imprisonment, baring his soul.

Soybeans: One of the best sources of nutrition on the planet. Soy can be made into so many products, and is healthy for the planet because it puts nitrogen into the earth. Soybeans are made into tofu, tempeh, soymilk (great for dairy allergies), TVP (texturized vegetable protein - used in place of meat), soy sauce, miso, printer's ink (biodegradable!), ice "cream," soy oil (the most common type of oil!) even animal feed. The only plant that might have more uses than the soybean is marijuana - believe it or not (higher protein, better oil, great fiber, excellent medicine, etc.)!

Space Cadet: Someone really spaced out on a regular basis.

Spaced Out: Not all here, possibly stoned. Also Spacey.

Split: To leave the scene. "I gotta split now, or my ol' lady's gonna be pissed."

Sproul Plaza: Rallying point on the UC Berkeley campus where students gathered to hear music and speeches during the student uprisings of the '60s. In May 1969, Gov. Ronald Reagan ordered the gassing (by helicopter!) and disbursement of students at the plaza, wounding 60 people and setting off 17 days of street fighting where 130 were shot and wounded. Police cordoned off the plaza prior to the gassing, trapping all the students and causing panic. "If it's a blood bath they want, then let it be now." - Ronald Reagan.

Square: Someone who follows all the rules or is part of the establishment. Something uncool.

Stash: Your hidden dope supply. "I'll get my stash and meet you at the Be-In."

Sticks: Small stems from cannabis plant. "That bag was fulla sticks, but the smoke was choice!"

Stoked: Totally happy or psyched up about something.

Stoned: High, from having ingested a drug. Common description of getting high on marijuana. It refers to the mind numbing effects of a drug.

Stop the War!: The Vietnam War.

STP: An extremely long-lasting and potent psychedelic drug. Trips would last three days, and some would never come back. Fortunately, this drug is no longer available.

Straight: Some one who doesn't do drugs, or isn't into the "scene." A square. Also when you're drug free (see clean).

Strawberry Alarm Clock: No, not a fruity timepiece, but a band that recorded ne big hit, "Incense and Peppermints."

Strobe lights: Used at parties and rock concerts. These bright flashing lights added a groovy psychedelic effect like flash bulbs going off in sequence. It would freeze the action for a split second, allowing the camera in your mind to record the moment.

Strung out: Feeling really bad because you're out of dope or something else you really want. The mental stress resulting from a craving.

Student Deferment: Exemption from military service due to high school or college enrollment. This type of deferment was terminated when the draft lottery began. Now students can only get deferments until the end of their current term, or until they graduate high school.

Suck: Something distasteful or awful. "Nixon really sucks!"

Summer of Love: The summer of 1967 when thousands of young people converged on San Francisco to experience being free. Highlights of that summer included the Monterey Pop Festival which showcased the talents of Jimi Hendrix, Janis Joplin, the Jefferson Airplane and many more. The Grateful Dead exploded on the scene and Love-Ins and Be-Ins were excuses for everyone to get high together.

Synchronous/Synchronicity: When two separate events or thoughts manifest at the same time with a similar meaning. Carl Jung gave much significance to such events and the person(s) who recognize the synchronicity.

The System: The catchall phrase for the evil power structure that oppresses the masses, controls the economics, and creates war. Refers to Capitalism.

Tab: A hit of Acid.

Tamari: A high quality Japanese soy sauce.

Tantra: Yogic sexual practice that seeks to raise awareness by moving energy from the lower to higher chakras through the sexual act.

Tapped Out: Out of money. "I'd lend you the dough, but I'm all tapped out."

Tao: "The way." Oriental philosophy taught by Lao Tzu, and adopted by many hippies. "Going with the flow" is following the path of least resistance, indicating that you are in synch with the universe.

Teach-In: In the early days of the antiwar movement, college professors held teach-ins where they explained the situation in Vietnam to students who then got active in the movement. In October, 1965, Jerry Rubin and the Vietnam Day Committee staged a 24 hour teach-in at U.C. Berkeley about the escalating war.

Teeny Boppers: In the '60s, teenagers too young to be hippies, had their own social group. Teeny boppers presented a new market for the media to conquer. They had their own music like the Partridge Family, The Cowsills, The Jackson 5, and The Monkees. Since big business couldn't sell to the hippies, they targeted their commercialism at this new group. Older hippies used this term to describe this younger generation.

Tempeh: A cultured soy product from Indonesia. It comes in flat blocks and can be served numerous ways. Somewhat of an acquired taste.

Tetrahydrocannabinol: See THC.

THC: Tetrahydrocannabinol. The active ingredient in marijuana that gets you high. One of several cannabinoids found in marijuana. The percentage of TH in marijuana or hashish usually determines how strong it is.

Thing: Catch phrase for your obsession or something you enjoy. "Liberati the mind through LSD is Leary's thing."

Threads: Clothes.

Ticked Off: Also Teed-Off, Ticked. Pissed-off, upset, angry.

Tie Dye: Colorful abstract artwork usually done on clothing by dying fabric tying it together.

Together: All right. O.K. Once you sort out your problems, you're togeth "Get it together, man!"

Toke: A "hit" of marijuana. To smoke marijuana.

Tolerance: What results from prolonged recent use of drugs requiring one use more to get the same effect. "I've built up a tolerance to LSD, now I have take at least 500 mikes to get off." Also something we all need more of, and le intolerance!

Totaled: Completely destroyed. "Bummer! I totaled my car, and I got insurance!"

Trails: The visual effect usually seen while on a trip when something mov through your field a vision. It seems like multiple images of the moving object it passes by.

Travel Agent: Euphemism for an acid dealer.

Traveler: A person who takes psychedelic drugs.

Tricky Dick: Nickname for Richard Nixon. He certainly earned it after h dirty tricks in the Watergate scandal.

Trip: A profound experience. What you experience on LSD or oth hallucinogen. A dose of LSD. Can also mean an unusual experience, "That w a trip!" or when someone tries to blow your mind "He's laying a trip on you."

Trip Out: To get spaced out. To get really stoned. To trip on LSD or oth hallucinogen.

Tripping: What you do on acid. "I'm tripping my brains out."

Trippy: Something unusual or psychedelic.

Trips Festival: Stewart Brand produced this LSD party in San Francisco January, 1966. It was a three day festival of music at Longshoreman's Hall wit dancing and a light show that would simulate "an LSD experience without LSD Ken Kesey and the Merry Pranksters showed up as this was the most public the acid tests. The success of this event inspired Bill Graham to start holdin these parties on a regular basis at the Fillmore Auditorium.

Turn-On, Tune-In, Drop-Out: Timothy Leary's famous quote encouragin young people to discover their true nature through LSD and drop out of society program.

Turn On: Something that excites you. Also to get high.

Underground: Something anti-establishment, working undercover or hidde Term applied to newspapers and comic books or other media that was directe towards freaks. These were often small publications that covered the hippy scen including radical politics, sex, drugs and rock and roll. Berkeley Barb, Zap Comi

East Village Other. Also people hiding from the government went "underground."

Uptight: Stressed out, tense. "Hey don't get so uptight, it's no big deal!"

Unreal: Something unbelievable.

Vaporizer: Method of smoking cannabis by heating it until the THC vaporizes, without actually burning the marijuana. Most vaporizers consist of a heating element, a glass dome, and a hose to smoke from.

Velvet Underground: Lou Reed's dark pre-gothic urban band included John Cale and Nico. They explored the underbelly of rock (as opposed to the flower-power movement) with haunting drug songs like "Heroin," and sadomasochism "Venus in Furs."

Vibes: Short for vibrations. Used to describe the overall feeling or mood of a place, person or thing. "I kept puttin' out good vibes, but I still can't get a ride!"

Vietnam War: The catalyst for the Peace Movement in America. The compulsory draft took students to the killing fields of Southeast Asia who then returned to the U.S. in body bags by the tens of thousands. The insensitive administrations refused to listen to protests and refused to provide a satisfactory explanation for the war. This prolonged the war and eventually the U.S. pulled out leaving their Vietnamese allies to fend for themselves. Make no mistake, the U.S. lost this war, but the government and people are now much more aware of the implications of foreign military involvement and the repercussions of sending young men to their death.

Vinyl: The material used to make records back in the old days. A record.

Vision: A dreamlike inspirational experience or scenario viewed in one's mind. Sometimes happens under the influence of psychedelic drugs. "I had a vision of you flying over the desert."

Visuals: The hallucinations or visual distortions experienced on a psychedelic trip.

Wasted: Very stoned to the point where you can't even move. "We got so wasted on those buds we missed the Dead concert!"

Watergate: The scandal that brought down Nixon. Nixon authorized the burglary of the offices of the Democratic Election Committee at the Watergate complex in Washington. A series of blunders, cover-ups and tape recordings all led to Nixon. He finally resigned before his term was over.

Way Out: Something so far out there, it's almost unbelievable.

What's Happenin'?: What's going on? A greeting. "Hey man, what's happenin'?"

Weathermen: An extremely radical group that split off from the SDS. Responsible for several bombings including banks. Their enemy was the establishment, big business and the government. A bomb destroyed their hideout in Greenwich Village, killing several members. The others ran away and hid for decades.

Weather Underground: Less sexist term the Weathermen used to describe themselves.

Weed: Marijuana.

Where it's at!: The place with the happening "scene." "Hey, babe, you're where it's at!"

White Lightning: Last of the finest acid available.

White Panther Party: Founded by John Sinclair from Ann Arbor as a white middle class hippie movement to support the Black Panthers.

Wilderness Society: Founded in 1935, the Wilderness Society has been working to protect forests and endangered plant and wildlife species, conserve biodiversity, and restore ecosystems throughout the world.

Whole Earth Catalog: Huge catalog for hippies founded, edited and published by Stewart Brand. Contained information, products, business listings, illustrations. Focused on ecology, living off the land, do-it-yourself, alternative everything. A lot of ideas and contacts done with spirit.

Wicked: Something very good or very effective.

Window Pane: A potent form of pure LSD in a tiny clear square of gelatin that melts in your mouth!

Wiped Out: Totally wasted on drugs. Exhausted.

Wired: Over stimulated by drugs, like amphetamines or caffeine usually resulting in a hypersensitive, extremely alert state of mind.

Women's Liberation Movement: This movement united women seeking legalized abortion, subsidized childcare, equal pay for equal work, an end to job discrimination, an end to the war in Vietnam, an end to sexism, Lesbian rights, in general an end to the male dominated society. Leaders in the movement were writers Gloria Steinem (who founded Ms. magazine), Betty Friedan, Kate Millet and Anne Koedt.

Woodstock Music Festival: A three-day outdoor event in Bethel, NY in 1969 that marked the peak of the flower power/hippie movement. An unprecedented half a million people gathered on Yasgur's Farm to hear the likes of Richie Havens, Ravi Shankar, The Who, Crosby, Still & Nash (in their second public performance), Janis Joplin, Jimi Hendrix and many more. The festival was a paean of cooperation, harmony and peace. There was no violence, but lots of marijuana and LSD.

Wow!: An exclamation of excitement. "Wow! Did you see what Jimi did with his guitar?"

Yippies: Group founded by Abbie Hoffman, Jerry Rubin and others in 1968, the Youth International Party for pranksters and activists. They helped organize the protests at the Democratic Convention in Chicago in 1968, which turned into a police riot. The Yippies got arrested and it became the trial of the Chicago 7. The conspiracy charges were dismissed, but some were convicted of lesser offenses.

Yin-Yang: In Taoist philosophy, Yin represents the passive, female principle and Yang the active, male principle, each balancing the other.

Yo Yo: A weekend hippie.

Yoga: Union. 3000 year old Hindu discipline that unites the mind and body usually through a series of exercises that raise awareness, thus allowing spiritual insight and tranquility. Many different kinds including Hatha (postures), Kundalini (breath), Bhakti (devotion), and Ashtanga (combination).

Z: An ounce of marijuana (28 grams).

Zero-Zero: Very high quality Moroccan hashish.

Zippies: The Zippies were founded by Abbie Hoffman in early '72 as a evolutionary street army of Hippie Anarchist for the Miami Anti-Nixon epublican Convention. Abbie stated when asked about the name change from ippies to Zippies he stated, "We have gone from A to Z!" Also a new term for ippies with computers and ravers. Not to be confused with Zippy the Pinhead, popular underground comic.

Visit Our

Hippyland
http://hippy.com

This is our award winning website for the hippy community. It's the biggest site about hippies on the Internet, with thousands of pages of information, comments and links. It's highly interactive with great Chatrooms and fascinating Forums as well as features like Ask the Old Hippy, Hippy Postcards, Events, Hippy Calendar, an extensive Hippy Glossary, surveys and quizzes.

Hip Planet
http://hipplanet.com

Hip Planet is our other site for hip people to find out about Fashion, Travel, News, Events and Food. Hip Planet offers Free E-Mail, Free Classifieds, Personals and Chatrooms.

Hip Planet Bookstore
http://hipplanet.com/bookstore/bookstore.htm

We've carefully selected the best books for hippies. The subjects include Hippies & Hippy Philosophy, Cannabis & Psychedelic books, Hippie Travel Guides, Humor, The Sixties, Ecology & the Environment, Science Fiction, How to Books, Music and Musicians, Poetry, Vegetarian Cookbooks, Videos and Art & Photography.

Websites:

Hip Planet Music Store

http://hipplanet.com/music/musicstore.htm

Here you'll find our best selections of classic rock music from the 60s along with some great jazz, new age and techno music. You can purchase CDs right online.

Hip Market

http://hipmarket.com

This is the hippest shopping place. You can find whatever you need, herbs, t-shirts, tie-dyes, jewelry, hemp products, smoking accessories, incense, hammocks, you name it!

Hip Guide to Amsterdam

http://hipplanet.com/amsterdam/amsterdam.htm

A groovy guide to what's happening in this famous city. From the Red Light District to museums out in the country there's advice and lots of photos, tips, places to visit, links, etc. Includes a great Coffeeshop Guide to the best cannabis in the city.

Hip Guide to Morocco

http://hipplanet.com/morocco/hipmorocco.htm

Travel along with Primo & Red Bud through the Rif Mountains to Marrakech, the Sahara Desert and the Atlantic coast. Not an ordinary guide, they find the coolest places to hang, discuss the most interesting things to see and do. They even give you great tips about how to find the best hashish.